Python Data Science Essentials

Second Edition

Become an efficient data science practitioner by understanding Python's key concepts

Alberto Boschetti
Luca Massaron

BIRMINGHAM - MUMBAI

Python Data Science Essentials

Second Edition

First published: April 2015

Second edition: October 2016

Production reference: 1211016

Published by Packt Publishing Ltd.
Livery Place
35 Livery Street
Birmingham
B3 2PB, UK.
ISBN 978-1-78646-213-8

www.packtpub.com

Credits

Authors

Alberto Boschetti

Luca Massaron

Reviewer

Zacharias Voulgaris

Commissioning Editor

Veena Pagare

Acquisition Editor

Namrata Patil

Content Development Editor

Mayur Pawanikar

Technical Editor

Vivek Arora

Copy Editor

Vikrant Phadke

Project Coordinator

Nidhi Joshi

Proofreader

Safis Editing

Indexer

Aishwarya Gangawane

Graphics

Disha Haria

Production Coordinator

Arvindkumar Gupta

About the Authors

Alberto Boschetti is a data scientist with expertise in signal processing and statistics. He holds a PhD in telecommunication engineering and currently lives and works in London. In his work projects, he faces challenges ranging from natural language processing (NLP), behavioral analysis, and machine learning to distributed processing. He is very passionate about his job and always tries to stay updated about the latest developments in data science technologies, attending meet-ups, conferences, and other events.

I would like to thank my family, my friends, and my colleagues. Also, a big thanks to the open source community.

Luca Massaron is a data scientist and marketing research director specializing in multivariate statistical analysis, machine learning, and customer insight, with over a decade of experience of solving real-world problems and generating value for stakeholders by applying reasoning, statistics, data mining, and algorithms. From being a pioneer of web audience analysis in Italy to achieving the rank of a top ten Kaggler, he has always been very passionate about every aspect of data and its analysis, and also about demonstrating the potential of data-driven knowledge discovery to both experts and non-experts. Favoring simplicity over unnecessary sophistication, Luca believes that a lot can be achieved in data science just by doing the essentials.

To Yukiko and Amelia, for their loving patience. "Roads go ever ever on, under cloud and under star, yet feet that wandering have gone turn at last to home afar".

About the Reviewer

Zacharias Voulgaris is a data scientist and technical author specializing in data science books. He has an engineering and management background, with post-graduate studies in information systems and machine learning. Zacharias has worked as a research fellow at Georgia Tech, investigating and applying machine learning technologies to real-world problems, as an SEO manager in an e-marketing company in Europe, as a program manager in Microsoft, and as a data scientist at US Bank and at G2 Web Services.

Dr. Voulgaris has also authored technical books, the most notable of which is *Data Scientist - the definitive guide to becoming a data scientist* (Technics Publications), and his newest book, *Julia for Data Science* (Technics Publications), was released during the summer of 2016. He has also written a number of data-science-related articles on blogs and participates in various data science/machine learning meetup groups. Finally, he has provided technical editorial aid in the book *Python Data Science Essentials* (Packt), by the same authors as this book.

> *I would very much like to express my gratitude to the authors of the book for giving me the opportunity to contribute to this project. Also, I'd like to thank Bastiaan Sjardin for introducing me to them and to the world of technical editing. It's been a privilege working with all of you.*

www.PacktPub.com

For support files and downloads related to your book, please visit `www.PacktPub.com`.

Did you know that Packt offers eBook versions of every book published, with PDF and ePub files available? You can upgrade to the eBook version at `www.PacktPub.com` and as a print book customer, you are entitled to a discount on the eBook copy. Get in touch with us at `service@packtpub.com` for more details.

At `www.PacktPub.com`, you can also read a collection of free technical articles, sign up for a range of free newsletters and receive exclusive discounts and offers on Packt books and eBooks.

`https://www.packtpub.com/mapt`

Get the most in-demand software skills with Mapt. Mapt gives you full access to all Packt books and video courses, as well as industry-leading tools to help you plan your personal development and advance your career.

Why subscribe?

- Fully searchable across every book published by Packt
- Copy and paste, print, and bookmark content
- On demand and accessible via a web browser

Table of Contents

Preface

"A journey of a thousand miles begins with a single step."

–Laozi (604 BC - 531 BC)

Data science is a relatively new knowledge domain that requires the successful integration of linear algebra, statistical modeling, visualization, computational linguistics, graph analysis, machine learning, business intelligence, and data storage and retrieval.

The Python programming language, having conquered the scientific community during the last decade, is now an indispensable tool for the data science practitioner and a must-have tool for every aspiring data scientist. Python will offer you a fast, reliable, cross-platform, mature environment for data analysis, machine learning, and algorithmic problem solving. Whatever stopped you before from mastering Python for data science applications will be easily overcome by our easy, step-by-step, and example-oriented approach that will help you apply the most straightforward and effective Python tools to both demonstrative and real-world datasets. As the second edition of Python Data Science Essentials, this book offers updated and expanded content. Based on the recent Jupyter Notebooks (incorporating interchangeable kernels, a truly polyglot data science system), this book incorporates all the main recent improvements in Numpy, Pandas, and Scikit-learn. Additionally, it offers new content in the form of deep learning (by presenting Keras–based on both Theano and Tensorflow), beautiful visualizations (seaborn and ggplot), and web deployment (using bottle). This book starts by showing you how to set up your essential data science toolbox in Python's latest version (3.5), using a single-source approach (implying that the book's code will be easily reusable on Python 2.7 as well). Then, it will guide you across all the data munging and preprocessing phases in a manner that explains all the core data science activities related to loading data, transforming, and fixing it for analysis, and exploring/processing it. Finally, the book will complete its overview by presenting you with the principal machine learning algorithms, graph analysis techniques, and all the visualization and deployment instruments that make it easier to present your results to an audience of both data science experts and business users.

What this book covers

Chapter 1, *First Steps*, introduces Jupyter notebooks and demonstrates how you can have access to the data run in the tutorials.

Chapter 2, *Data Munging*, gives an overview of the data science pipeline and explores all the key tools for handling and preparing data before you apply any learning algorithm and set up your hypothesis experimentation schedule.

Chapter 3, *The Data Pipeline*, discusses all the operations that can potentially improve or even boost your results.

Chapter 4, *Machine Learning*, delves into the principal machine learning algorithms offered by the Scikit-learn package, such as, among others, linear models, support vector machines, ensembles of trees, and unsupervised techniques for clustering.

Chapter 5, *Social Network Analysis*, introduces graphs, which is an interesting deviation from the predic-tors/target flat matrices. It is quite a hot topic in data science now. Expect to delve into very complex and intricate networks!

Chapter 6, *Visualization, Insights, and Results,* the concluding chapter, introduces you to the basics of visualization with Matplotlib, how to operate EDA with pandas, how to achieve beautiful visualizations with Seaborn and Bokeh, and also how to set up a web server to provide information on demand.

Appendix, Strengthen Your Python Foundations, covers a few Python examples and tutorials focused on the key features of the language that are indispensable in order to work on data science projects.

What you need for this book

Python and all the data science tools mentioned in the book, from IPython to Scikit-learn, are free of charge and can be freely downloaded from the Internet. To run the code that accompanies the book, you need a computer that uses Windows, Linux, or Mac OS operating systems. The book will introduce you step-by-step to the process of installing the Python interpreter and all the tools and data that you need to run the examples.

Who this book is for

If you are an aspiring data scientist and you have at least a working knowledge of data analysis and Python, this book will get you started in data science. Data analysts with experience in R or MATLAB will also find the book to be a comprehensive reference to enhance their data manipulation and machine learning skills.

Conventions

In this book, you will find a number of text styles that distinguish between different kinds of information. Here are some examples of these styles and an explanation of their meaning.

Code words in text, database table names, folder names, filenames, file extensions, pathnames, dummy URLs, user input, and Twitter handles are shown as follows: "By using the to_bokeh method, any chart and plot from other packages can be easily ported into Bokeh."

A block of code is set as follows:

```
File: bottle1.py
from bottle import route, run, template
port = 9099
@route('/personal/<name>')
def homepage(name):
return template('Hi <b>{{name}}</b>!', name=name)
print("Try going to http://localhost:{}/personal/Tom".format(port))
print("Try going to http://localhost:{}/personal/Carl".format(port))
run(host='localhost', port=port)
```

Any command-line input or output is written as follows:

```
In: import numpy as np
from bokeh.plotting import figure, output_file, show
x = np.linspace(0, 5, 50)
y_cos = np.cos(x)
output_file("cosine.html")
p = figure()
p.line(x, y_cos, line_width=2)
show(p)
```

New terms and **important words** are shown in bold. Words that you see on the screen, for example, in menus or dialog boxes, appear in the text like this: "Once the Jupyter instance has opened in the browser, click on the **New** button."

Warnings or important notes appear in a box like this.

Tips and tricks appear like this.

Reader feedback

Feedback from our readers is always welcome. Let us know what you think about this book-what you liked or disliked. Reader feedback is important for us as it helps us develop titles that you will really get the most out of. To send us general feedback, simply e-mail feedback@packtpub.com, and mention the book's title in the subject of your message. If there is a topic that you have expertise in and you are interested in either writing or contributing to a book, see our author guide at www.packtpub.com/authors.

Customer support

Now that you are the proud owner of a Packt book, we have a number of things to help you to get the most from your purchase.

Downloading the example code

You can download the example code files for this book from your account at http://www.packtpub.com. If you purchased this book elsewhere, you can visit http://www.packtpub.com/support and register to have the files e-mailed directly to you.

You can download the code files by following these steps:

1. Log in or register to our website using your e-mail address and password.
2. Hover the mouse pointer on the **SUPPORT** tab at the top.
3. Click on **Code Downloads & Errata**.
4. Enter the name of the book in the **Search** box.
5. Select the book for which you're looking to download the code files.
6. Choose from the drop-down menu where you purchased this book from.
7. Click on **Code Download**.

Once the file is downloaded, please make sure that you unzip or extract the folder using the latest version of:

- WinRAR / 7-Zip for Windows
- Zipeg / iZip / UnRarX for Mac
- 7-Zip / PeaZip for Linux

The code bundle for the book is also hosted on GitHub at `https://github.com/PacktPubl ishing/Python-Data-Science-Essentials-Second-Edition`. We also have other code bundles from our rich catalog of books and videos available at `https://github.com/Packt Publishing/`. Check them out!

Downloading the color images of this book

We also provide you with a PDF file that has color images of the screenshots/diagrams used in this book. The color images will help you better understand the changes in the output. You can download this file from `http://www.packtpub.com/sites/default/files/downl oads/PythonDataScienceEssentialsSecondEdition_ColorImages.pdf`.

Errata

Although we have taken every care to ensure the accuracy of our content, mistakes do happen. If you find a mistake in one of our books-maybe a mistake in the text or the code-we would be grateful if you could report this to us. By doing so, you can save other readers from frustration and help us improve subsequent versions of this book. If you find any errata, please report them by visiting `http://www.packtpub.com/submit-errata`, selecting your book, clicking on the **Errata Submission Form** link, and entering the details of your errata. Once your errata are verified, your submission will be accepted and the errata will be uploaded to our website or added to any list of existing errata under the Errata section of that title.

To view the previously submitted errata, go to `https://www.packtpub.com/books/conten t/support` and enter the name of the book in the search field. The required information will appear under the **Errata** section.

Piracy

Piracy of copyrighted material on the Internet is an ongoing problem across all media. At Packt, we take the protection of our copyright and licenses very seriously. If you come across any illegal copies of our works in any form on the Internet, please provide us with the location address or website name immediately so that we can pursue a remedy.

Please contact us at `copyright@packtpub.com` with a link to the suspected pirated material.

We appreciate your help in protecting our authors and our ability to bring you valuable content.

Questions

If you have a problem with any aspect of this book, you can contact us at questions@packtpub.com, and we will do our best to address the problem.

1
First Steps

Whether you are an eager learner of data science or a well-grounded data science practitioner, you can take advantage of this essential introduction to Python for data science. You can use it to the fullest if you already have at least some previous experience in basic coding, in writing general-purpose computer programs in Python, or in some other data analysis-specific language such as MATLAB or R.

This book will delve directly into Python for data science, providing you with a straight and fast route to solve various data science problems using Python and its powerful data analysis and machine learning packages. The code examples that are provided in this book don't require you to be a master of Python. However, they will assume that you at least know the basics of Python scripting, including data structures such as lists and dictionaries, and the workings of class objects. If you don't feel confident about these subjects or have minimal knowledge of the Python language, before reading this book, we suggest that you take an online tutorial. There are many possible choices, but we suggest starting with the suggestions from the official beginner's guide to Python from the Python Foundation or directly going to the free Code Academy course at `https://www.codecademy.com/learn/python`. Using Code Academy's tutorial, or any other alternative you may find useful, in a matter of a few hours of study, you should acquire all the building blocks that will ensure you enjoy this book to the fullest. We have also prepared a tutorial of our own, which can be found in the last part of this book, in order to provide an integration of the two aforementioned free courses.

In any case, don't be intimidated by our starting requirements; mastering Python enough for data science applications isn't as arduous as you may think. It's just that we have to assume some basic knowledge on the reader's part because our intention is to go straight to the point of doing data science without having to explain too much about the general aspects of the language that we will be using.

Are you ready, then? Let's start!

In this introductory chapter, we will work out the basics to set off in full swing and go through the following topics:

- How to set up a Python data science toolbox
- Using your browser as an interactive notebook, to code with Python using Jupyter
- An overview of the data that we are going to study in this book

Introducing data science and Python

Data science is a relatively new knowledge domain, though its core components have been studied and researched for many years by the computer science community. Its components include linear algebra, statistical modeling, visualization, computational linguistics, graph analysis, machine learning, business intelligence, and data storage and retrieval.

Data science is a new domain and you have to take into consideration that currently its frontiers are still somewhat blurred and dynamic. Since data science is made of various constituent sets of disciplines, please also keep in mind that there are different profiles of data scientists depending on their competencies and areas of expertise.

In such a situation, what can be the best tool of the trade that you can learn and effectively use in your career as a data scientist? We believe that the best tool is Python, and we intend to provide you with all the essential information that you will need for a quick start.

In addition, other tools such as R and MATLAB provide data scientists with specialized tools to solve specific problems in statistical analysis and matrix manipulation in data science. However, Python really completes your data scientist skill set. This multipurpose language is suitable for both development and production alike; it can handle small- to large-scale data problems and it is easy to learn and grasp no matter what your background or experience is.

Created in 1991 as a general-purpose, interpreted, and object-oriented language, Python has slowly and steadily conquered the scientific community and grown into a mature ecosystem of specialized packages for data processing and analysis. It allows you to have uncountable and fast experimentations, easy theory development, and prompt deployment of scientific applications.

At present, the core Python characteristics that render it an indispensable data science tool are as follows:

- It offers a large, mature system of packages for data analysis and machine learning. It guarantees that you will get all that you may need in the course of a data analysis, and sometimes even more.
- Python can easily integrate different tools and offers a truly unifying ground for different languages, data strategies, and learning algorithms that can be fitted together easily and which can concretely help data scientists forge powerful solutions. There are packages that allow you to call code in other languages (in Java, C, Fortran, R, or Julia), outsourcing some of the computations to them and improving your script performance.
- It is very versatile. No matter what your programming background or style is (object-oriented, procedural, or even functional), you will enjoy programming with Python.
- It is cross-platform; your solutions will work perfectly and smoothly on Windows, Linux (even on small-sized distributions, suitable for IoT on tiny-PCs like Raspberry Pi, Arduino and so on), and Mac OS systems. You won't have to worry all that much about portability.
- Although interpreted, it is undoubtedly fast compared to other mainstream data analysis languages such as R and MATLAB (though it is not comparable to C, Java, and the newly emerged Julia language). Moreover, there are also static compilers such as *Cython* or just-in-time compilers such as *PyPy* that can transform Python code into C for higher performance.
- It can work with large in-memory data because of its minimal memory footprint and excellent memory management. The memory garbage collector will often save the day when you load, transform, dice, slice, save, or discard data using various iterations and reiterations of data wrangling.
- It is very simple to learn and use. After you grasp the basics, there's no better way to learn more than by immediately starting with the coding.
- Moreover, the number of data scientists using Python is continuously growing: new packages and improvements have been released by the community every day, making the Python ecosystem an increasingly prolific and rich language for data science.

Installing Python

First, let's proceed to introduce all the settings you need in order to create a fully working data science environment to test the examples and experiment with the code that we are going to provide you with.

Python is an open source, object-oriented, and cross-platform programming language. Compared to some of its direct competitors (for instance, C++ or Java), Python is very concise. It allows you to build a working software prototype in a very short time. Yet it has become the most used language in the data scientist's toolbox not just because of that. It is also a general-purpose language, and it is very flexible due to a variety of available packages that solve a wide spectrum of problems and necessities.

Python 2 or Python 3?

There are two main branches of Python: 2.7.x and 3.x. At the time of writing this second edition of the book, the Python Foundation (https://www.python.org/) is offering downloads for Python version 2.7.11 and 3.5.1. Although the third version is the newest, the *older* one is still the most used version in the scientific area, since a few packages (check the website at http://py3readiness.org/ for a compatibility overview) won't run otherwise yet.

In addition, there is no immediate backward compatibility between Python 3 and 2. In fact, if you try to run some code developed for Python 2 with a Python 3 interpreter, it may not work. Major changes have been made to the newest version, and that has affected past compatibility. Some data scientists, having built most of their work on Python 2 and its packages, are reluctant to switch to the new version.

In this second edition of the book, we intend to address a growing audience of data scientists, data analysts, and developers, who may not have such a strong legacy with Python 2. Thus, we agreed that it would be better to work with Python 3 rather than the older version. We suggest using a version such as Python 3.4 or above. After all, Python 3 is the present and the future of Python. It is the only version that will be further developed and improved by the Python Foundation and it will be the default version of the future on many operating systems.

Anyway, if you are currently working with version 2 and you prefer to keep on working with it, you can still use this book and all its examples. In fact, for the most part, our code will simply work on Python 2 after having the code itself preceded by these imports:

```
from __future__ import (absolute_import, division,
                        print_function, unicode_literals)
from builtins import *
from future import standard_library
standard_library.install_aliases()
```

The from __future__ import commands should always occur at the beginning of your scripts or else you may experience Python reporting an error.

As described in the Python-future website (http://python-future.org/), these imports will help convert several Python 3-only constructs to a form compatible with both Python 3 and Python 2 (and in any case, most Python 3 code should just simply work on Python 2 even without the aforementioned imports).

In order to run the upward commands successfully, if the future package is not already available on your system, you should install it (version >= 0.15.2) using the following command to be executed from a shell:

```
$> pip install -U future
```

If you're interested in understanding the differences between Python 2 and Python 3 further, we recommend reading the wiki page offered by the Python Foundation itself at: https://wiki.python.org/moin/Python2orPython3.

Step-by-step installation

Novice data scientists who have never used Python (who likely don't have the language readily installed on their machines) need to first download the installer from the main website of the project, www.python.org/downloads/, and then install it on their local machine.

This section provides you with full control over what can be installed on your machine. This is very useful when you have to set up single machines to deal with different tasks in data science. Anyway, please be warned that a step-by-step installation really takes time and effort. Instead, installing a ready-made scientific distribution, such as Anaconda, will lessen the burden of installation procedures and it may be well suited for first starting and learning because it saves you time and sometimes even trouble, though it will put a large number of packages (and we won't use most of them) on your computer all at once. Therefore, if you want to start immediately with an easy installation procedure, just skip this part and proceed to the section, *Scientific distributions*.

This being a multiplatform programming language, you'll find installers for machines that either run on Windows or Unix-like operating systems.

Remember that some of the latest versions of most Linux distributions (such as CentOS, Fedora, Red Hat Enterprise, Ubuntu, and some other minor ones) have Python 2 packaged in the repository. In such a case and in the case that you already have a Python version on your computer (since our examples run on Python 3), you first have to check what version you are exactly running. To do such a check, just follow these instructions:

1. Open a Python shell, type `python` in the terminal, or click on any Python icon you find on your system.

2. Then, after having Python started, to test the installation, run the following code in the Python interactive shell or REPL:

```
>>> import sys
>>> print (sys.version_info)
```

3. If you can read that your Python version has the `major=2` attribute, it means that you are running a Python 2 instance. Otherwise, if the attribute is valued 3, or if the `print` statement reports back to you something like v3.x.x (for instance v3.5.1), you are running the right version of Python and you are ready to move forward.

To clarify the operations we have just mentioned, when a command is given in the terminal command line, we prefix the command with $>. Otherwise, if it's for the Python REPL, it's preceded by >>> (**REPL** is an acronym that stands for **Read-Eval-Print-Loop**, a simple interactive environment which takes a user's single commands from an input line in a shell and returns the results by printing).

The installation of packages

Python won't come bundled with all you need, unless you take a specific premade distribution. Therefore, to install the packages you need, you can use either `pip` or `easy_install`. Both these two tools run in the command line and make the process of installation, upgrade, and removal of Python packages a breeze. To check which tools have been installed on your local machine, run the following command:

```
$> pip
```

 To install `pip`, follow the instructions given at `https://pip.pypa.io/en/latest/installing/`.

Alternatively, you can also run this command:

```
$> easy_install
```

If both of these commands end up with an error, you need to install any one of them. We recommend that you use `pip` because it is thought of as an improvement over `easy_install`. Moreover, `easy_install` is going to be dropped in future and pip has important advantages over it. It is preferable to install everything using pip because:

- It is the preferred package manager for Python 3. Starting with Python 2.7.9 and Python 3.4, it is included by default with the Python binary installers.
- It provides an uninstall functionality.
- It rolls back and leaves your system clear if, for whatever reason, the package installation fails.

Using easy_install in spite of the advantages of pip makes sense if you are working on Windows because pip won't always install pre-compiled binary packages. Sometimes it will try to build the package's extensions directly from C source, thus requiring a properly configured compiler (and that's not an easy task on Windows). This depends if the package is running on eggs, Python metadata files for distributing code as bundles, (and pip cannot directly use their binaries, but it needs to build from their source code) or wheels, the new standard for Python distribution of code bundles .(In this last case, pip can install binaries if available, as explained here: http://pythonwheels.com/). Instead, easy_install will always install available binaries from eggs and wheels. Therefore, if you are experiencing unexpected difficulties installing a package, easy_install can save your day (at some price anyway, as we just mentioned in the list).

The most recent versions of Python should already have pip installed by default. Therefore, you may have it already installed on your system. If not, the safest way is to download the get-pi.py script from https://bootstrap.pypa.io/get-pip.py and then run it using the following:

```
$> python get-pip.py
```

The script will also install the setup tool from https://pypi.python.org/pypi/setuptools, which also contains easy_install.

You're now ready to install the packages you need in order to run the examples provided in this book. To install the < package-name > generic package, you just need to run this command:

```
$> pip install < package-name >
```

Alternatively, you can run the following command:

```
$> easy_install < package-name >
```

Note that in some systems, pip might be named as pip3 and easy_install as easy_install-3 to stress the fact that both operate on packages for Python 3. If you're unsure, check the version of Python pip is operating on with:

```
$> pip -V
```

For `easy_install`, the command is slightly different:

```
$> easy_install --version
```

After this, the <pk> package and all its dependencies will be downloaded and installed. If you're not certain whether a library has been installed or not, just try to import a module inside it. If the Python interpreter raises an `ImportError` error, it can be concluded that the package has not been installed.

This is what happens when the NumPy library has been installed:

```
>>> import numpy
```

This is what happens if it's not installed:

```
>>> import numpy
Traceback (most recent call last):
File "<stdin>", line 1, in <module>
ImportError: No module named numpy
```

In the latter case, you'll need to first install it through `pip` or `easy_install`.

Take care that you don't confuse packages with modules. With `pip`, you install a package; in Python, you import a module. Sometimes, the package and the module have the same name, but in many cases, they don't match. For example, the sklearn module is included in the package named Scikit-learn.

Finally, to search and browse the Python packages available for Python, look at `https://py pi.python.org/pypi`.

Package upgrades

More often than not, you will find yourself in a situation where you have to upgrade a package because either the new version is required by a dependency or it has additional features that you would like to use. First, check the version of the library you have installed by glancing at the __version__ attribute, as shown in the following example, `numpy`:

```
>>> import numpy
>>> numpy.__version__ # 2 underscores before and after
'1.9.2'
```

Now, if you want to update it to a newer release, say the 1.11.0 version, you can run the following command from the command line:

```
$> pip install -U numpy==1.11.0
```

Alternatively, you can use the following command:

```
$> easy_install --upgrade numpy==1.11.0
```

Finally, if you're interested in upgrading it to the latest available version, simply run this command:

```
$> pip install -U numpy
```

You can alternatively run the following command:

```
$> easy_install --upgrade numpy
```

Scientific distributions

As you've read so far, creating a working environment is a time-consuming operation for a data scientist. You first need to install Python and then, one by one, you can install all the libraries that you will need. Sometimes, the installation procedures may not go as smoothly as you'd hoped for earlier, requiring the user to do extra steps, to install additional executables (like, in Linux boxes, gFortran for Scipy) or libraries (like libfreetype for Matplotlib). Usually, the backtrace of the error produced during the failed installation is clear enough to understand what went wrong and to take the correct resolving action, but at other times, the error is tricky or subtle, holding up the user for hours without advancing in the process.

If you want to save time and effort and want to ensure that you have a fully working Python environment that is ready to use, you can just download, install, and use the scientific Python distribution. Apart from Python, they also include a variety of preinstalled packages, and sometimes, they even have additional tools and an IDE. A few of them are very well known among data scientists, and in the sections that follow, you will find some of the key features of each of these packages.

We suggest that you first promptly download and install a scientific distribution, such as Anaconda (which is the most complete one), and after practicing the examples in the book, decide to fully uninstall the distribution and set up Python alone, which can be accompanied by just the packages you need for your projects.

Anaconda

Anaconda (`http://continuum.io/downloads`) is a Python distribution offered by Continuum Analytics that includes nearly 200 packages, which comprises NumPy, SciPy, pandas, Jupyter, Matplotlib, Scikit-learn, and NLTK. It's a cross-platform distribution (Windows, Linux, and Mac OS X) that can be installed on machines with other existing Python distributions and versions. Its base version is free; instead, add-ons that contain advanced features are charged separately. Anaconda introduces `conda`, a binary package manager, as a command-line tool to manage your package installations. As stated on the website, Anaconda's goal is to provide enterprise-ready Python distribution for large-scale processing, predictive analytics, and scientific computing.

Leveraging conda to install packages

If you've decided to install an Anaconda distribution, you can take advantage of the conda binary installer we mentioned previously. Anyway, conda is an open source package management system, and consequently it can be installed separately from an Anaconda distribution.

You can test immediately whether conda is available on your system. Open a shell and digit:

```
$> conda -V
```

If conda is available, there will appear the version of your conda; otherwise an error will be reported. If conda is not available, you can quickly install it on your system by going to `http://conda.pydata.org/miniconda.html` and installing the Miniconda software suitable for your computer. Miniconda is a minimal installation that only includes conda and its dependencies.

conda can help you manage two tasks: installing packages and creating virtual environments. In this section, we will explore how conda can help you easily install most of the packages you may need in your data science projects.

Before starting, please check that you have the latest version of conda at hand:

```
$> conda update conda
```

Now you can install any package you need. To install the `<package-name>` generic package, you just need to run the following command:

```
$> conda install <package-name>
```

You can also install a particular version of the package just by pointing it out:

```
$> conda install <package-name>=1.11.0
```

Similarly, you can install multiple packages at once by listing all their names:

```
$> conda install <package-name-1> <package-name-2>
```

If you just need to update a package that you previously installed, you can keep on using conda:

```
$> conda update <package-name>
```

You can update all the available packages simply by using the `--all` argument:

```
$> conda update --all
```

Finally, conda can also uninstall packages for you:

```
$> conda remove <package-name>
```

If you would like to know more about conda, you can read its documentation at `http://conda.pydata.org/docs/index.html`. In summary, as a main advantage, it handles binaries even better than `easy_install` (by always providing a successful installation on Windows without any need to compile the packages from source) but without its problems and limitations. With the use of conda, packages are easy to install (and installation is always successful), update, and even uninstall. On the other hand, conda cannot install directly from a git server (so it cannot access the latest version of many packages under development) and it doesn't cover all the packages available on PyPI as `pip` itself.

Enthought Canopy

Enthought Canopy (`https://www.enthought.com/products/canopy/`) is a Python distribution by Enthought Inc. It includes more than 200 preinstalled packages, such as NumPy, SciPy, Matplotlib, Jupyter, and pandas (more on these packages later). This distribution is targeted at engineers, data scientists, quantitative and data analysts, and enterprises. Its base version is free (which is named Canopy Express), but if you need advanced features, you have to buy a front version. It's a multiplatform distribution and its command-line install tool is `canopy_cli`.

PythonXY

PythonXY (`http://python-xy.github.io/`) is a free, open source Python distribution maintained by the community. It includes a number of packages, which include NumPy, SciPy, NetworkX, Jupyter, and Scikit-learn. It also includes Spyder, an interactive development environment inspired by the MATLAB IDE. The distribution is free. It works only on Microsoft Windows, and its command-line installation tool is `pip`.

WinPython

WinPython (`http://winpython.sourceforge.net/`) is also a free, open-source Python distribution maintained by the community. It is designed for scientists, and includes many packages such as NumPy, SciPy, Matplotlib, and Jupyter. It also includes Spyder as an IDE. It is free and portable. You can put WinPython into any directory, or even into a USB flash drive, and at the same time maintain multiple copies and versions of it on your system. It works only on Microsoft Windows, and its command-line tool is the **WinPython Package Manager (WPPM)**.

Explaining virtual environments

No matter whether you have chosen installing a standalone Python or instead you used a scientific distribution, you may have noticed that you are actually bound on your system to the Python's version you have installed. The only exception, for Windows users, is to use a WinPython distribution, since it is a portable installation and you can have as many different installations as you need.

A simple solution to break free of such a limitation is to use `virtualenv`, which is a tool to create isolated Python environments. That means that, by using different Python environments, you can easily achieve these things:

- Testing any new package installation or doing experimentation on your Python environment without any fear of breaking anything in an irreparable way. In this case, you need a version of Python that acts as a sandbox.

- Having at hand multiple Python versions (both Python 2 and Python 3), geared with different versions of installed packages. This can help you in dealing with different versions of Python for different purposes (for instance, some of the packages we are going to present on Windows OS only work using Python 3.4, which is not the latest release).
- Taking a replicable snapshot of your Python environment easily and having your data science prototypes work smoothly on any other computer or in production. In this case, your main concern is the immutability and replicability of your working environment.

You can find documentation about `virtualenv` at `http://virtualenv.readthedocs.io/en/stable/`, though we are going to provide you with all the directions you need to start using it immediately. In order to take advantage of `virtualenv`, you have first to install it on your system:

```
$> pip install virtualenv
```

After the installation completes, you can start building your virtual environments. Before proceeding, you have to take a few decisions:

- If you have more versions of Python installed on your system, you have to decide which version to pick up. Otherwise, virtualenv will take the Python version virtualenv was installed by on your system. In order to set a different Python version, you have to digit the argument `-p` followed by the version of Python you want or insert the path of the Python executable to be used (for instance, `-p python2.7`) or just point to a Python executable such as `-p c:\Anaconda2\python.exe`.
- With virtualenv, when required to install a certain package, it will install it from scratch, even if it is already available at a system level (on the Python directory you created the virtual environment from). This default behavior makes sense because it allows you to create a completely separated empty environment. In order to save disk space and limit the time of installation of all the packages, you may instead decide to take advantage of already available packages on your system by using the argument `--system-site-packages`.
- You may want to be able to later move around your virtual environment across Python installations, even among different machines. Therefore, you may want to make the functioning of all of the environment's scripts relative to the path it is placed in by using the argument `--relocatable`.

After deciding on the Python version, the linking to existing global packages, and the relocability of the virtual environment, in order to start, you just launch the command from a shell. Declare the name you would like to assign to your new environment:

```
$> virtualenv clone
```

`virtualenv` will just create a new directory using the name you provided, in the path from which you actually launched the command. To start using it, you just enter the directory and digit `activate`:

```
$> cd clone
$> activate
```

At this point, you can start working on your separated Python environment, installing packages and working with code.

If you need to install multiple packages at once, you may need some special function from pip—`pip freeze`—which will enlist all the packages (and their versions) you have installed on your system. You can record the entire list in a text file by this command:

```
$> pip freeze > requirements.txt
```

After saving the list in a text file, just take it into your virtual environment and install all the packages in a breeze with a single command:

```
$> pip install -r requirements.txt
```

Each package will be installed according to the order in the list (packages are listed in a case-insensitive sorted order). If a package requires other packages that are later in the list, that's not a big deal because pip automatically manages such situations. So if your package requires Numpy and Numpy is not yet installed, `pip` will install it first.

When you're finished installing packages and using your environment for scripting and experimenting, in order to return to your system defaults, just issue this command:

```
$> deactivate
```

If you want to remove the virtual environment completely, after deactivating and getting out of the environment's directory, you just have to get rid of the environment's directory itself by a recursive deletion. For instance, on Windows you just do this:

```
$> rd /s /q clone
```

On Linux and Mac, the command will be:

```
$> rm -r -f clone
```

If you are working extensively with virtual environments, you should consider using `virtualenvwrapper`, which is a set of wrappers for `virtualenv`, in order to help you manage multiple virtual environments easily. It can be found at `http://bitbucket.org/dhellmann/virtualenvwrapper`. If you are operating on a Unix system (Linux or OS X), another solution we have to quote is `pyenv` (which can be found at `https://github.com/yyuu/pyenv`), which lets you set your main Python version, allows installation of multiple versions and creates virtual environments. Its peculiarity is that it does not depend on Python to be installed and it works perfectly at the user-level (no need for `sudo` commands).

conda for managing environments

If you have installed the Anaconda distribution, or you have tried conda using a Miniconda installation, you can also take advantage of the conda command to run virtual environments as an alternative to virtualenv. Let's see in practice how to use conda for that. We can check what environments we have available like this:

```
>$ conda info -e
```

This command will report to you what environments you can use on your system based on conda. Most likely, your only environment will be just `root`, pointing to your Anaconda distribution's folder.

As an example, we can create an environment based on Python version 3.4, having all the necessary Anaconda-packaged libraries installed. That makes sense, for instance, for using the package Theano together with Python 3 on Windows (because of an issue we will explain in shortly). In order to create such an environment, just do this:

```
$> conda create -n python34 python=3.4 anaconda
```

The command asks for a particular Python Version 3.4 and requires the installation of all packages available on the Anaconda distribution (the argument `anaconda`). It names the environment as python34 using the argument `-n`. The complete installation will take a while, given the large number of packages in the Anaconda installation. After having completed all of the installation, you can activate the environment:

```
$> activate python34
```

If you need to install additional packages to your environment, when activated, you just do the following:

```
$> conda install -n python34 <package-name1> <package-name2>
```

That is, you make the list of the required packages follow the name of your environment. Naturally, you can also use pip install, as you would do in a `virtualenv` environment.

You can also use a file instead of listing all the packages by name yourself. You can create a list in an environment using the list argument and piping the output to a file:

```
$> conda list -e > requirements.txt
```

Then, in your target environment, you can install the entire list using:

```
$> conda install --file requirements.txt
```

You can even create an environment, based on a requirements list:

```
$> conda create -n python34 python=3.4 --file requirements.txt
```

Finally, after having used the environment, to close the session, you simply do this:

```
$> deactivate
```

Contrary to `virtualenv`, there is a specialized argument in order to completely remove an environment from your system:

```
$> conda remove -n python34 --all
```

A glance at the essential packages

We mentioned that the two most relevant characteristics of Python are its ability to integrate with other languages and its mature package system, which is well embodied by PyPI (see the Python Package Index at: `https://pypi.python.org/pypi`), a common repository for the majority of Python open source packages that is constantly maintained and updated.

The packages that we are now going to introduce are strongly analytical and they will constitute a complete data science toolbox. All the packages are made up of extensively tested and highly optimized functions for both memory usage and performance, ready to achieve any scripting operation with successful execution. A walkthrough on how to install them is provided in the following section.

Partially inspired by similar tools present in R and MATLAB environments, we will together explore how a few selected Python commands can allow you to efficiently handle data and then explore, transform, experiment, and learn from the same without having to write too much code or reinvent the wheel.

NumPy

NumPy, which is Travis Oliphant's creation, is the true analytical workhorse of the Python language. It provides the user with multidimensional arrays, along with a large set of functions to operate a multiplicity of mathematical operations on these arrays. Arrays are blocks of data arranged along multiple dimensions, which implement mathematical vectors and matrices. Characterized by optimal memory allocation, arrays are useful not just for storing data, but also for fast matrix operations (vectorization), which are indispensable when you wish to solve ad hoc data science problems:

- **Website**: http://www.numpy.org/
- **Version at the time of print**: 1.11.0
- **Suggested install command**: pip install numpy

As a convention largely adopted by the Python community, when importing NumPy, it is suggested that you alias it as np:

```
import numpy as np
```

We will be doing this throughout the course of this book.

SciPy

An original project by Travis Oliphant, Pearu Peterson, and Eric Jones, SciPy completes NumPy's functionalities, offering a larger variety of scientific algorithms for linear algebra, sparse matrices, signal and image processing, optimization, fast Fourier transformation, and much more:

- **Website**: http://www.scipy.org/
- **Version at time of print**: 0.17.1
- **Suggested install command**: pip install scipy

pandas

The pandas package deals with everything that NumPy and SciPy cannot do. Thanks to its specific data structures, namely DataFrames and Series, pandas allows you to handle complex tables of data of different types (which is something that NumPy's arrays cannot do) and time series. Thanks to Wes McKinney's creation, you will be able easily and smoothly to load data from a variety of sources. You can then slice, dice, handle missing elements, add, rename, aggregate, reshape, and finally visualize your data at will:

- **Website**: http://pandas.pydata.org/
- **Version at the time of print**: 0.18.1
- **Suggested install command**: pip install pandas

Conventionally, pandas is imported as pd:

```
import pandas as pd
```

Scikit-learn

Started as part of the **SciKits (SciPy Toolkits)**, Scikit-learn is the core of data science operations on Python. It offers all that you may need in terms of data preprocessing, supervised and unsupervised learning, model selection, validation, and error metrics. Expect us to talk at length about this package throughout this book. Scikit-learn started in 2007 as a Google Summer of Code project by David Cournapeau. Since 2013, it has been taken over by the researchers at **INRA (French Institute for Research in Computer Science and Automation)**:

- **Website**: http://scikit-learn.org/stable
- **Version at the time of print**: 0.17.1
- **Suggested install command**: pip install scikit-learn

 Note that the imported module is named sklearn.

Jupyter

A scientific approach requires the fast experimentation of different hypotheses in a reproducible fashion. Initially named IPython and limited to working only with the Python language, Jupyter was created by Fernando Perez in order to address the need for an interactive command shell for several languages (based on shell, web browser, and application interface), featuring graphical integration, customizable commands, rich history (in the JSON format), and computational parallelism for an enhanced performance. Jupyter is our favored choice throughout this book, and it is used to clearly and effectively illustrate operations with scripts and data and the consequent results. We will devote a section of this chapter to explain in detail the characteristics of its interface and describing how it can turn into a precious tool for any data scientist:

- **Website**: http://jupyter.org/
- **Version at the time of print**: 1.0.0 (ipykernel = 4.3.1)
- **Suggested install command**: `pip install jupyter`

Matplotlib

Originally developed by John Hunter, matplotlib is a library that contains all the building blocks that are required to create quality plots from arrays and to visualize them interactively.

You can find all the MATLAB-like plotting frameworks inside the pylab module:

- **Website**: http://matplotlib.org/
- **Version at the time of print**: 1.5.1
- **Suggested install command**: `pip install matplotlib`

You can simply import what you need for your visualization purposes with the following command:

```
import matplotlib.pyplot as plt
```

Downloading the example code

You can download the example code files from your account at
`www.packtpub.com` for all the Packt Publishing books you have purchased.
If you purchased this book elsewhere, you can visit
`www.packtpub.com/support` and register to have the files e-mailed directly
to you.

Statsmodels

Previously part of SciKits, statsmodels was thought to be a complement to SciPy's statistical
functions. It features generalized linear models, discrete choice models, time series analysis,
and a series of descriptive statistics as well as parametric and nonparametric tests:

- **Website**: `http://statsmodels.sourceforge.net/`
- **Version at the time of print**: 0.6.1
- **Suggested install command**: `pip install statsmodels`

Beautiful Soup

Beautiful Soup, a creation of Leonard Richardson, is a great tool to scrap out data from
HTML and XML files retrieved from the Internet. It works incredibly well, even in the case
of *tag soups* (hence the name), which are collections of malformed, contradictory, and
incorrect tags. After choosing your parser (the HTML parser included in Python's standard
library works fine), thanks to Beautiful Soup, you can navigate through the objects in the
page and extract text, tables, and any other information that you may find useful:

- **Website**: `http://www.crummy.com/software/BeautifulSoup`
- **Version at the time of print**: 4.4.1
- **Suggested install command**: `pip install beautifulsoup4`

Note that the imported module is named `bs4`.

NetworkX

Developed by the Los Alamos National Laboratory, NetworkX is a package specialized in the creation, manipulation, analysis, and graphical representation of real-life network data (it can easily operate with graphs made up of a million nodes and edges). Besides specialized data structures for graphs and fine visualization methods (2D and 3D), it provides the user with many standard graph measures and algorithms, such as the shortest path, centrality, components, communities, clustering, and PageRank. We will mainly use this package in Chapter 5, *Social Network Analysis*:

- **Website**: http://networkx.github.io/
- **Version at the time of print**: 1.11
- **Suggested install command**: pip install networkx

Conventionally, NetworkX is imported as nx:

```
import networkx as nx
```

NLTK

The **Natural Language Toolkit (NLTK)** provides access to corpora and lexical resources and to a complete suite of functions for statistical **Natural Language Processing (NLP)**, ranging from tokenizers to part-of-speech taggers and from tree models to named-entity recognition. Initially, Steven Bird and Edward Loper created the package as an NLP teaching infrastructure for their course at the University of Pennsylvania. Now, it is a fantastic tool that you can use to prototype and build NLP systems:

- **Website**: http://www.nltk.org/
- **Version at the time of print**: 3.2.1
- **Suggested install command**: pip install nltk

Gensim

Gensim, programmed by Radim Řehůřek, is an open source package that is suitable for the analysis of large textual collections with the help of parallel distributable online algorithms. Among advanced functionalities, it implements **Latent Semantic Analysis (LSA)**, topic modeling by **Latent Dirichlet Allocation (LDA)**, and Google's *word2vec*, a powerful algorithm that transforms text into vector features that can be used in supervised and unsupervised machine learning.

- **Website:** http://radimrehurek.com/gensim/
- **Version at the time of print:** 0.12.4
- **Suggested install command:** pip install gensim

PyPy

PyPy is not a package; it is an alternative implementation of Python 2.7.8 that supports most of the commonly used Python standard packages (unfortunately, NumPy is currently not fully supported). As an advantage, it offers enhanced speed and memory handling. Thus, it is very useful for heavy duty operations on large chunks of data and it should be part of your big data handling strategies:

- **Website:** http://pypy.org/
- **Version at time of print:** 5.1
- **Download page:** http://pypy.org/download.html

XGBoost

XGBoost is a scalable, portable, and distributed gradient boosting library (a tree ensemble algorithm). Initially created by Tianqi Chen from Washington University, it has been enriched by a Python wrapper by Bing Xu and an R interface by Tong He (you can read the story behind XGBoost directly from its principal creator at http://homes.cs.washington.edu/~tqchen/2016/03/10/story-and-lessons-behind-the-evolution-of-xgboost.html). XGBoost is available for Python, R, Java, Scala, Julia, and C++, and it can work on a single machine (leveraging multithreading) in both Hadoop and Spark clusters:

- **Website:** http://homes.cs.washington.edu/~tqchen/2016/03/10/story-and-lessons-behind-the-evolution-of-xgboost.html
- **Version at the time of print:** 0.4
- **Download page:** https://github.com/dmlc/xgboost

Detailed instructions for installing XGBoost on your system can be found at this page: `http s://github.com/dmlc/xgboost/blob/master/doc/build.md`.

The installation of XGBoost on both Linux and macOS is quite straightforward, whereas it is a little bit trickier for Windows users.

On a Posix system, you just have to build the executable with `make`, but on Windows things are a little bit more tricky.

For this reason, we provide specific installation steps to get XGBoost working on Windows:

1. First download and install Git for Windows (`https://git-for-windows.github .io/`).
2. Then you need a MINGW compiler present on your system. You can download it from `http://www.mingw.org/` accordingly to the characteristics of your system.
3. From the command line, execute:

```
$> git clone --recursive https://github.com/dmlc/xgboost
$> cd xgboost
$> git submodule init
$> git submodule update
```

4. Then, always from the command line, copy the configuration for 64-byte systems to be the default one:

```
$> copy make\mingw64.mk config.mk
```

5. Alternatively, you just copy the plain 32-byte version:

```
$> copy make\mingw.mk config.mk
```

6. After copying the configuration file, you can run the compiler, setting it to use four threads in order to speed up the compiling procedure:

```
$> mingw32-make -j4
```

7. In MinGW, the `make` command comes with the name mingw32-make. If you are using a different compiler, the previous command may not work; then you can simply try:

```
$> make -j4
```

8. Finally, if the compiler completes its work without errors, you can install the package in your Python with this:

```
$> cd python-package
$> python setup.py install
```

After following all the preceding instructions, if you try to import XGBoost in Python and yet it doesn't load and results in an error, it may well be that Python cannot find the MinGW's g++ runtime libraries.

You just need to find the location on your computer of MinGW's binaries (in our case, it was in `C:\mingw-w64\mingw64\bin`; just modify the next code to insert yours) and place the following code snippet before importing XGBoost:

```
import os
mingw_path = 'C:\\mingw-w64\\mingw64\\bin'
os.environ['PATH']=mingw_path + ';' + os.environ['PATH']
import xgboost as xgb
```

Depending on the state of the XGBoost project, similarly to many other projects under continuous development, the preceding installation commands may or may not temporarily work at the time you try them. Usually waiting for an update of the project or opening an issue with the authors of the package may solve the problem. In any case, we provide for our readers to download the version we have compiled on Windows and for those we used for the examples in this book. You can download it from Packt Publishing website (as pointed out in the preface).

Theano

Theano is a Python library that allows you to define, optimize, and evaluate mathematical expressions involving multi-dimensional arrays efficiently. Basically, it provides you with all the building blocks you need to create deep neural networks. Created by academics (an entire development team; you can read their names on their most recent paper at `http://ar xiv.org/pdf/1605.02688.pdf`), Theano has been used for large scale and intensive computations since 2007:

- **Website**: `http://deeplearning.net/software/theano/`
- **Release at the time of print**: 0.8.2

In spite of many installation problems experienced by users in the past (especially Windows users), the installation of Theano should be straightforward, the package being now available on PyPI:

```
$> pip install Theano
```

If you want the most updated version of the package, you can get it by GitHub cloning:

```
$> git clone git://github.com/Theano/Theano.git
```

Then you can proceed with direct Python installation:

```
$> cd Theano
$> python setup.py install
```

To test your installation, you can run the following commands from the shell/CMD and verify the reports:

```
$> pip install nose
$> pip install nose-parameterized
$> nosetests theano
```

If you are working on a Windows OS and the previous instructions don't work, you can try these steps using the conda command provided by the Anaconda distribution:

1. Install TDM GCC x64 (this can be found at http://tdm-gcc.tdragon.net/)
2. Open an Anaconda prompt interface and execute:

```
$> conda update conda
$> conda update --all
$> conda install mingw libpython
$> pip install git+git://github.com/Theano/Theano.git
```

Theano needs libpython, which isn't compatible yet with the version 3.5. So if your Windows installation is not working, this could be the likely cause. Anyway, Theano installs perfectly on Python version 3.4. Our suggestion in this case is to create a virtual Python environment based on version 3.4, install, and use Theano only on that specific version. Directions on how to create virtual environments are provided in the paragraph about virtualenv and conda create.

In addition, Theano's website provides some information to Windows users; it could support you when everything else fails: http://deeplearning.net/software/theano/install_windows.html.

An important requirement for Theano to scale out on GPUs is to install Nvidia CUDA drivers and SDK for code generation and execution on GPUs. If you do not know too much about the CUDA Toolkit, you can actually start from this web page in order to understand more about the technology being used: `https://developer.nvidia.com/cuda-toolkit`.

Therefore, if your computer has an NVidia GPU, you can find all the necessary instructions in order to install CUDA using this tutorial page from NVidia itself: `http://docs.nvidia.com/cuda/cuda-quick-start-guide/index.html#axzz4Msw9qwJZ`.

Keras

Keras is a minimalist and highly modular neural networks library, written in Python and capable of running on top of either Theano or TensorFlow (the source software library for numerical computation released by Google). Keras was created by François Chollet, a machine learning researcher working at Google:

- **Website**: `https://keras.io/`
- **Version at the time of print:** 1.0.3
- **Suggested installation from PyPI**: `$> pip install keras`

As an alternative, you can install the latest available version (which is advisable since the package is in continuous development) using the following command:

```
$> pip install git+git://github.com/fchollet/keras.git
```

Introducing Jupyter

As previously mentioned, Jupyter deserves more than a brief presentation. We are going to delve fully in detail about its history, installation, and usage for data science. Initially known as IPython, the project was initiated in 2001 as a free project by Fernando Perez. With this work, the author intended to address a deficiency in the Python stack and provide to the public a user-programming interface for data investigations that could easily incorporate the scientific approach (mainly meaning experimenting and interactively discovering) in the process of data discovery and development of data science solutions.

A scientific approach implies fast experimentation of different hypotheses in a reproducible fashion (as does data exploration and analysis in data science). When using this interface, you will be able more naturally to implement an explorative, iterative, trial and error research strategy during your code writing.

Recently (during Spring 2015), a large part of the IPython project was moved to a new one called Jupyter. This new project extends the potential usability of the original IPython interface to a wide range of programming languages, such as:

- Julia (http://github.com/JuliaLang/IJulia.jl)
- Scala (https://github.com/mattpap/IScala)
- R (https://github.com/IRkernel/IRkernel)

For a more complete list of available kernels for Jupyter, please visit the page at: https://github.com/ipython/ipython/wiki/IPython-kernels-for-other-languages.

For instance, once having installed Jupyter and its IPython kernel, you can easily add another useful kernel, such as the R kernel, in order to access through the same interface the R language. All you have to do is have an R installation, run your R interface, and enter the following commands:

```
install.packages(c('pbdZMQ', 'devtools'))
devtools::install_github('IRkernel/repr')
devtools::install_github('IRkernel/IRdisplay')
devtools::install_github('IRkernel/IRkernel')
IRkernel::installspec()
```

The commands will install the devtools library on your R, then pull and install all the necessary libraries from GitHub (you need to be connected to the Internet while running the other commands), and finally register the R kernel both in your R installation and on Jupyter. After that, every time you call the Jupyter notebook, you will have the choice of running either a Python or an R kernel, allowing you to use the same format and approach for all your data science projects.

You cannot mix the same notebook commands for different kernels; each notebook only refers to a single kernel, that is, the one it was initially created with. Consequently on the same notebook you cannot mix languages or even versions of the same language like Python2 and Python3.

Thanks to the powerful idea of kernels, programs that run the user's code communicated by the frontend interface and provide feedback on the results of the executed code to the interface itself, you can use the same interface and interactive programming style no matter what language you are using for development.

In such a context, IPython is the zero kernel, the original starting one, still existing but not intended to be used anymore to refer to the entire project (without the IPython kernel, Jupyter will not even function, even if you have installed another kernel and linked it).

Therefore, Jupyter can simply be described as a tool for interactive tasks operable by a console or by a web-based notebook, which offers special commands that help developers to better understand and build the code that is being currently written.

Contrary to an IDE—which is built around the idea of writing a script, running it afterwards, and finally evaluating its results—Jupyter lets you write your code in chunks, named cells, run each of them sequentially, and evaluate the results of each one separately, examining both textual and graphic outputs. Besides graphical integration, it provides you with further help, thanks to customizable commands, a rich history (in the JSON format), and computational parallelism for an enhanced performance when dealing with heavy numeric computations.

Such an approach is also particularly fruitful for tasks involving developing code based on data, since it automatically accomplishes the often neglected duty of documenting and illustrating how data analysis has been done, its premises and assumptions, and its intermediate and final results. If a part of your job is to also present your work and advocate it to an internal or external stakeholder in the project, Jupyter can really do the magic of storytelling for you with little additional effort.

You can easily combine code, comments, formulas, charts, interactive plots, and rich media such as images and videos, making each Jupyter Notebook a complete scientific sketchpad to find all your experimentations and their results together.

Jupyter works on your favorite browser (which could be Explorer, Firefox, or Chrome, for instance) and, when started, presents a cell waiting for code to be written in. Each block of code enclosed in a cell can be run and its results are reported in the space just after the cell. Plots can be represented in the notebook (inline plot) or in a separate window. In our example, we decided to plot our chart inline.

Moreover, written notes can be written easily using the Markdown language, a very easy and fast-to-grasp markup language (http://daringfireball.net/projects/markdown/). Math formulas can be handled using MathJax (https://www.mathjax.org/) to render any LaTeX script inside HTML/Markdown.

There are several ways to insert LaTeX code in a cell. The easiest way is to simply use the Markdown syntax, wrapping the equations with single $ (dollar sign) for an inline LaTeX formula, or with double dollar sign $$ for a one-line central equation. Remember that to have a correct output, the cell should be set as Markdown. Here's an example.

In Markdown:

```
This is a $\LaTeX$ inline equation: $x = Ax+b$

And this is a one-liner: $$x = Ax + b$$
```

This produces the following output:

> This is a $\LaTeX$ inline equation: $x = Ax + b$
>
> And this is a one-liner:
>
> $$x = Ax + b$$

If you're looking for something more elaborate, that is, a formula that spans for more than one line, a table, a series of equations that should be aligned, or simply a use of special LaTeX functions, then it's better to use the %%latex magic command offered by the Jupyter notebook. In this case, the cell must be in code mode and contain the magic command as the first line. The following lines must define a complete LaTeX environment that can be compiled by the LaTeX interpreter.

Here are a couple of examples showing what you can do:

```
In:
%%latex
\[
 |u(t)| =
  \begin{cases}
   u(t) & \text{if } t \geq 0 \\
   -u(t)        & \text{otherwise }
  \end{cases}
\]
```

Out:

$$\left| u\left(t \right) \right| = \begin{cases} u\left(t \right) & \text{if } t \geq 0 \\ -u\left(t \right) & \text{otherwise} \end{cases}$$

```
In:
%%latex
\begin{align}
f(x) &= (a+b)^2 \\
     &= a^2 + (a+b) + (a+b) + b^2 \\
     &= a^2 + 2\cdot (a+b) + b^2
\end{align}
```

Out:

$$f\left(x \right) = \left(a+b \right)^2$$
$$= a^2 + \left(a+b \right) + \left(a+b \right) + b^2$$
$$= a^2 + 2 \cdot \left(a+b \right) + b^2$$

Remember that by using the `%%latex` magic command, the whole cell must comply with the LaTeX syntax. Therefore, if you just need to write a few simple equations in text, we strongly advice you to use the Markdown method.

Being able to integrate technical formulas in Markdown is particularly fruitful for tasks involving development of code based on data, since it automatically accomplishes the often neglected duty of documenting and illustrating how data analysis has been managed as well as its premises, assumptions, and intermediate and final results. If a part of your job is to also present your work and persuade internal or external stakeholders in the project, Jupyter can really do the magic of storytelling for you with little additional effort.

On the web page `https://github.com/ipython/ipython/wiki/A-gallery-of-interesting-IPython-Notebooks`, there are many examples, some of which you may find inspiring for your work, as it did for ours. Actually, we have to confess that keeping a cleaned, up-to-date Jupyter Notebook has saved us uncountable times when meetings with managers/stakeholders have suddenly popped up, requiring us to present the state of our work hastily.

In short, Jupyter allows you to:

- See intermediate (debugging) results for each step of the analysis
- Run only some sections (or cells) of the code
- Store intermediate results in JSON format and have the ability to do version control on them
- Present your work (this will be a combination of text, code, and images), share it via the Jupyter Notebook Viewer service (`http://nbviewer.jupyter.org/`), and easily export it into a Python script, HTML, LaTeX, Markdown, PDF, or even slideshows (an HTML slideshow to be served by an HTTP server).

In the next section, we will discuss Jupyter's installation in more detail and show an example of its usage in a data science task.

Fast installation and first test usage

Jupyter is our favored choice throughout this book. It is used to clearly and effectively illustrate and *storytell* operations using scripts and data, and their consequent results.

Though we strongly recommend using Jupyter, if you are using a REPL or an IDE, you can use the same instructions and expect identical results (but for print formats and extensions of the returned results).

If you do not have Jupyter installed on your system, you can promptly set it up using this command:

```
$> pip install jupyter
```

You can find complete instructions about Jupyter installation (covering different operating systems) on this web page: http://jupyter.readthedocs.io/en/latest/install.html

After installation, you can immediately start using Jupyter by calling it from the command line:

```
$> jupyter notebook
```

Once the Jupyter instance has opened in the browser, click on the **New** button; in the Notebooks section, choose Python 3 (other kernels may be present in the section depending on what you installed).

At this point, your new empty notebook will look like the next screenshot and you can start entering the commands in the cells. For instance, you may start by typing in the cell:

```
In: print ("This is a test")
```

After writing in cells, you just press the play button (below the **Cell** tab) to run it and obtain an output. Then, another cell will appear for your input. As you are writing in a cell, if you press the plus button on the menu bar, you will get a new cell and you can move from one cell to another using the arrows on the menu.

Most of the other functions are quite intuitive and we invite you to try them. In order to know better how Jupyter works, you may use a quick start guide such as http://jupyter-notebook-beginner-guide.readthedocs.io/en/latest/ or get a book which specializes on Jupyter functionalities.

For a complete treatise of the full range of Jupyter functionalities when running the IPython kernel, refer to these two Packt Publishing books:

- *IPython Interactive Computing and Visualization Cookbook* by Cyrille Rossant, Packt Publishing, September 25, 2014
- *Learning IPython for Interactive Computing and Data Visualization* by Cyrille Rossant, Packt Publishing, April 25, 2013

For our illustrative purposes, just consider that every Jupyter block of instructions has a numbered input statement and an output one. So you will find the code presented in this book structured in two blocks, at least when the output is not trivial at all. Otherwise, expect only the input part:

```
In:   <the code you have to enter>
Out:  <the output you should get>
```

As a rule, you just have to type the code after `In:` in your cells and run it. You can then compare your output with the output that we may provide using `Out:` followed by the output that we actually obtained on our computers when we tested the code.

Jupyter magic commands

As a special tool for interactive tasks, Jupyter offers special commands that help to better understand the code that you are currently writing.

For instance, some of the commands are:

- `<object>?` and `<object>??`: This prints a detailed description (with `??` being even more verbose) of `<object>`
- `%<function>`: This uses the special `<magic function>`

Let's demonstrate the usage of these commands with an example. We first start the interactive console with the `jupyter` command, which is used to run Jupyter from the command line, as shown here:

```
$> jupyter console
Jupyter Console 4.1.1
In [1]: obj1 = range(10)
```

Then, in the first line of code, which is marked by Jupyter as `[1]`, we create a list of 10 numbers (from 0 to 9), assigning the output to an object named `obj1`:

```
In [2]: obj1?
Type:        range
String form: range(0, 10)
Length:      10
Docstring:
range(stop) -> range object
range(start, stop[, step]) -> range object
Return an object that produces a sequence of integers from start
(inclusive)
to stop (exclusive) by step.  range(i, j) produces i, i+1, i+2,
```

```
..., j-1.
start defaults to 0, and stop is omitted!  range(4) produces
0, 1, 2, 3.
These are exactly the valid indices for a list of 4 elements.
When step is given, it specifies the increment (or decrement).
In [3]: %timeit x=100
The slowest run took 184.61 times longer than the fastest.
This could mean that an intermediate result is being cached.
10000000 loops, best of 3: 24.6 ns per loop
In [4]: %quickref
```

In the next line of code, which is numbered [2], we inspect the obj1 object using the Jupyter command ?. Jupyter introspects the object, prints its details (obj is a range object that can generate the values [1, 2, 3..., 9] and elements), and finally prints some general documentation on the range objects. For complex objects, the usage of ?? instead of ? provides even more verbose output.

In line [3], we use the timeit magic function with a Python assignment (x=100). The timeit function runs this instruction many times and stores the computational time needed to execute it. Finally, it prints the average time that was taken to run the Python function.

We complete the overview with a list of all the possible special Jupyter functions by running the quickref helper function, as shown in line [4].

As you must have noticed, each time we use Jupyter, we have an input cell and, optionally, an output cell if there is something that has to be printed on stdout. Each input is numbered, so it can be referenced inside the Jupyter environment itself. For our purposes, we don't need to provide such references in the code of the book. Therefore, we will just report inputs and outputs without their numbers. However, we'll use the generic In: and Out: notations to point out the input and output cells. Just copy the commands after In: to your own Jupyter cell and expect an output that will be reported on the following Out:.

Therefore, the basic notations will be:

- The In: command
- The Out: output (wherever it is present and useful to be reported in the book)

Otherwise, if we expect you to operate directly on the Python console, we will use the following form:

```
>>> command
```

Wherever necessary, the command-line input and output will be written as follows:

```
$> command
```

Moreover, to run the bash command in the Jupyter console, prefix it with a ! (exclamation mark):

```
In: !ls
Applications     Google Drive     Public      Desktop      Develop
Pictures         env              temp
...
In: !pwd
/Users/mycomputer
```

How Jupyter Notebooks can help data scientists

The main goal of the Jupyter Notebook is easy storytelling. Storytelling is essential in data science because you must have the power to do the following:

- See intermediate (debugging) results for each step of the algorithm you're developing
- Run only some sections (or cells) of the code
- Store intermediate results and have the ability to version them
- Present your work (this will be a combination of text, code, and images)

Here comes Jupyter; it actually implements all the preceding actions:

1. To launch the Jupyter Notebook, run the following command:

   ```
   $> jupyter notebook
   ```

2. A web browser window will pop up on your desktop, backed by a Jupyter server instance. This is the how the main window looks:

3. Then, click on **New Notebook**. A new window will open, as shown in the following screenshot. You can start using the Notebook as soon as the kernel is ready. The small circle on the top right of the place, below the Python icon, indicates the state of the kernel: if it's filled, it means that the kernel is busy working; if it's empty (like the one in the screenshot) it means that the kernel is in idle, that is, ready to run any code

This is the web app that you'll use to compose your story. It's very similar to a Python IDE, with the bottom section (where you can write the code) composed of cells.

A cell can be either a piece of text (eventually formatted with a markup language) or a piece of code. In the second case, you have the ability to run the code, and any eventual output (the standard output) will be placed under the cell. The following is a very simple example of the same:

```
In: import random
a = random.randint(0, 100)
a
Out: 16
In: a*2
Out: 32
```

In the first cell, which is denoted by `In:`, we import the random module, assign a random value between 0 and 100 to the variable a, and print the value. When this cell is run, the output, which is denoted as `Out:`, is the random number. Then, in the next cell, we will just print the double of the value of the variable a.

As you can see, it's a great tool to debug and decide which parameter is best for a given operation. Now, what happens if we run the code in the first cell? Will the output of the second cell be modified since a is different? Actually, no, it won't. Each cell is independent and autonomous. In fact, after we run the code in the first cell, we end up with this inconsistent status:

```
In: import random
a = random.randint(0, 100)
a
Out: 56
In: a*2
Out: 32
```

Also note that the number in the squared parentheses has changed (from 1 to 3) since it's the third executed command (and its output) from the time the notebook started. Since each cell is autonomous, by looking at these numbers, you can understand their order of execution.

Jupyter is a simple, flexible, and powerful tool. However, as seen in the preceding example, you must note that when you update a variable that is going to be used later on in your Notebook, remember to run all the cells following the updated code so that you have a consistent state.

When you save a Jupyter Notebook, the resulting .ipynb file is JSON formatted, and it contains all the cells and their content plus the output. This makes things easier because you don't need to run the code to see the notebook (actually, you also don't need to have Python and its set of toolkits installed). This is very handy, especially when you have pictures featured in the output and some very time-consuming routines in the code. A downside of using the Jupyter Notebook is that its file format, which is JSON structured, cannot be easily read by humans. In fact, it contains images, code, text, and so on.

Now, let's discuss a data science-related example (don't worry about understanding it completely):

```
In:
%matplotlib inline
import matplotlib.pyplot as plt
from sklearn import datasets
from sklearn.feature_selection import SelectKBest, f_regression
from sklearn.linear_model import LinearRegression
from sklearn.svm import SVR
from sklearn.ensemble import RandomForestRegressor
```

In the following cell, some Python modules are imported:

```
In:
boston_dataset = datasets.load_boston()
X_full = boston_dataset.data
Y = boston_dataset.target
print (X_full.shape)
print (Y.shape)
Out:
(506, 13)
(506,)
```

Then, in cell [2], the dataset is loaded and an indication of its shape is shown. The dataset contains 506 house values that were sold in the suburbs of Boston, along with their respective data arranged in columns. Each column of the data represents a feature. A feature is a characteristic property of the observation. Machine learning uses features to establish models that can turn them into predictions. If you are from a statistical background, you can add features that can be intended as variables (values that vary with respect to the observations).

To see a complete description of the dataset, use `print (boston_dataset.DESCR)`.

After loading the observations and their features, in order to provide a demonstration of how Jupyter can effectively support the development of data science solutions, we will perform some transformations and analysis on the dataset. We will use classes, such as `SelectKBest`, and methods, such as `.getsupport()` or `.fit()`. Don't worry if these are not clear to you now; they will all be covered extensively later in this book. Try to run the following code:

```
In:
selector = SelectKBest(f_regression, k=1)
selector.fit(X_full, Y)
X = X_full[:, selector.get_support()]
print (X.shape)
Out:
(506, 1)
```

Here, we select a feature (the most discriminative one) of the `SelectKBest` class that is fitted to the data by using the `.fit()` method. Thus, we reduce the dataset to a vector with the help of a selection operated by indexing on all the rows and on the selected feature, which can be retrieved by the `.get_support()` method.

Since the target value is a vector, we can, therefore, try to see whether there is a linear relation between the input (the feature) and the output (the house value). When there is a linear relationship between two variables, the output will constantly react to changes in the input by the same proportional amount and direction:

```
In:
def plot_scatter(X, Y, R=None):
    plt.scatter(X, Y, s=32, marker='o', facecolors='white')
    if R is not None:
        plt.scatter(X, R, color='red', linewidth=0.5)
    plt.show()
In:
plot_scatter(X, Y)
```

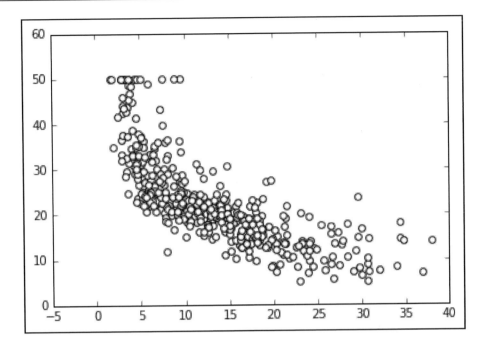

In our example, as X increases, Y decreases. However, this does not happen at a constant rate, because the rate of change is intense up to a certain X value and then it decreases and becomes constant. This is a condition of nonlinearity, and we can furthermore visualize it using a regression model. This model hypothesizes that the relationship between X and Y is linear in the form of $y=a+bX$. Its a and b parameters are estimated according to a certain criteria.

In the fourth cell, we scatter the input and output values for this problem:

```
In:
regressor = LinearRegression(normalize=True).fit(X, Y)
plot_scatter(X, Y, regressor.predict(X))
```

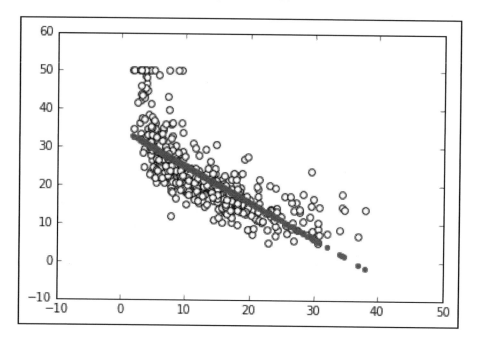

In the next cell, we create a regressor (a simple linear regression with feature normalization), train the regressor, and finally plot the best linear relation (that's the linear model of the regressor) between the input and output. Clearly, the linear model is an approximation that is not working well. We have two possible paths that we can follow at this point. We can transform the variables in order to make their relationship linear, or we can use a nonlinear model. **Support Vector Machine (SVM)** is a class of models that can easily solve nonlinearities. Also, **Random Forests** is another model for automatic solving of similar problems. Let's see them in action in Jupyter:

```
In:
regressor = SVR().fit(X, Y)
plot_scatter(X, Y, regressor.predict(X))
```

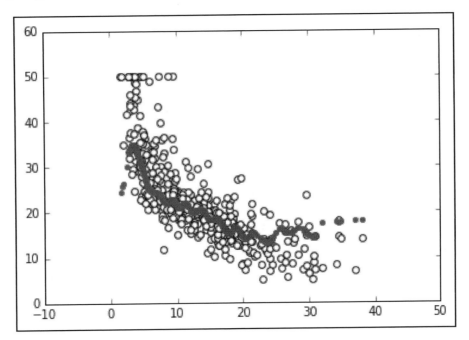

```
In:
regressor = RandomForestRegressor().fit(X, Y)
plot_scatter(X, Y, regressor.predict(X))
```

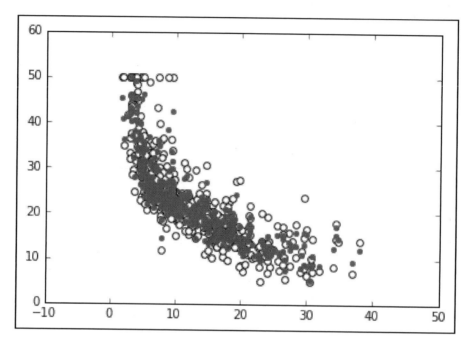

Finally, in the last two cells, we will repeat the same procedure. This time we will use two nonlinear approaches: an SVM and a Random Forest-based regressor.

This demonstrative code solves the nonlinearity problem. At this point, it is very easy to change the selected feature, regressor, and the number of features we use to train the model, and so on by simply modifying the cells where the script is. Everything can be done interactively, and according to the results we see, we can decide both what should be kept or changed and what is to be done next.

Alternatives to Jupyter

In case you may not prefer using Jupyter, there are actually a few alternatives that can help you in testing the code you will find in the book. If you have experience with R, the RStudio (http://www.rstudio.com/) layout may appeal more to you. In this case, Yhat, a company providing data science solutions for decision APIs, offers their data science IDE for Python free of charge. Named Rodeo (http://www.yhat.com/products/rodeo), it works using the IPython kernel of Jupyter under the hood. It is an interesting alternative given its different user interface. The main advantages of using Rodeo are as follows:

- A video layout is arranged in four windows: editor, console, plots, environment.
- Autocomple is provided for editor and console
- Plots are always visible inside the application in a specific window
- You can easily inspect the working variables in the environment window

Rodeo can be simply installed using the installer. You can download it from its website, or you can simply do this in the command line:

```
$> pip install rodeo
```

After the installation, you can immediately run the Rodeo IDE with this command:

```
$> rodeo .
```

Instead, if you have experience with MATLAB from Mathworks, you will find it easier to work with Spyder (http://pythonhosted.org/spyder/), a scientific IDE that can be found in major Scientific Python distributions (it is present in Anaconda, WinPython, and Python(x,y)—all distributions that we have suggested in the book). If you don't use a distribution, in order to install Spyder, you have to follow the instructions to be found at the web page: http://pythonhosted.org/spyder/installation.html. Spyder allows advanced editing, interactive editing, debugging, and introspection features and your scripts can be run in a Jupyter console or in a shell-like environment.

Datasets and code used in the book

As we progress through the concepts presented in the book, in order to facilitate the reader's understanding, learning, and memorizing processes, we will illustrate practical and effective data science Python applications on various explicative datasets. The reader will always be able to immediately replicate, modify, and experiment with the proposed instructions and scripts on the data that we will use in this book.

As for the code that you are going to find in this book, we will limit our discussions to the most essential commands in order to inspire you from the beginning of your data science journey with Python to do more with less by leveraging key functions from the packages we presented beforehand.

Given our previous introduction, we will present the code to be run interactively as it appears on a Jupyter console or Notebook.

All the presented code will be offered in the Notebooks, and is available on the Packt website (as pointed out in the *Preface*). As for the data, we will provide different examples of datasets.

Scikit-learn toy datasets

The Scikit-learn toy dataset module is embedded in the Scikit-learn package. Such datasets can easily be directly loaded into Python by the import command, and they don't require any download from any external Internet repository. Some examples of this type of dataset are the Iris, Boston, and Digits datasets, to name the principal ones mentioned in uncountable publications and books, and a few other classic ones for classification and regression.

Structured in a dictionary-like object, besides the features and target variables, they offer complete descriptions and contextualization of the data itself.

For instance, to load the Iris dataset, enter the following commands:

```
In:
from sklearn import datasets
iris = datasets.load_iris()
```

After loading, we can explore the data description and understand how the features and targets are stored. All Scikit-learn datasets present the following methods:

- `.DESCR`: This provides a general description of the dataset
- `.data`: This contains all the features
- `.feature_names`: This reports the names of the features
- `.target`: This contains the target values expressed as values or numbered classes

- `.target_names`: This reports the names of the classes in the target
- `.shape`: This is a method that you can apply to both `.data` and `.target`; it reports the number of observations (the first value) and features (the second value if present) that are present

Now, let's just try to implement them (no output is reported, but the print commands will provide you with plenty of information):

```
In:
print (iris.DESCR)
print (iris.data)
print (iris.data.shape)
print (iris.feature_names)
print (iris.target)
print (iris.target.shape)
print (iris.target_names)
```

Now, you should know something more about the dataset—how many examples and variables are present and what their names are.

Notice that the main data structures that are enclosed in the iris object are the two arrays, data and target:

```
In:
print (type(iris.data))
Out:
<class 'numpy.ndarray'>
```

Iris.data offers the numeric values of the variables named sepal length, sepal width, petal length, and petal width arranged in a matrix form (150,4), where 150 is the number of observations and 4 is the number of features. The order of the variables is the order presented in iris.feature_names.

Iris.target is a vector of integer values, where each number represents a distinct class (refer to the content of target_names; each class name is related to its index number and *setosa*, which is the zero element of the list, is represented as 0 in the target vector).

The Iris flower dataset was first used in 1936 by Ronald Fisher, who was one of the fathers of modern statistical analysis, in order to demonstrate the functionality of linear discriminant analysis on a small set of empirically verifiable examples (each of the 150 data points represented iris flowers). These examples were arranged into tree-balanced species classes (each class consisted of one-third of the examples) and were provided with four metric descriptive variables that, when combined, were able to separate the classes.

The advantage of using such a dataset is that it is very easy to load, handle, and explore for different purposes, from supervised learning to graphical representation due to the dataset's low dimensionality. Modeling activities take almost no time on any computer, no matter what its specifications are. Moreover, the relationship between the classes and the role of the explicative variables are well known. Therefore, the task is challenging, but it is not very arduous.

For example, let's just observe how classes can be easily separated when you wish to combine at least two of the four available variables by using a scatterplot matrix.

Scatterplot matrices are arranged in a matrix format, whose columns and rows are the dataset variables. The elements of the matrix contain single scatterplots whose x values are determined by the row variable of the matrix and y values by the column variable. The diagonal elements of the matrix may contain a distribution histogram or some other univariate representation of the variable at the same time in its row and column.

The pandas library offers an off-the-shelf function to quickly make up scatterplot matrices and start exploring relationship and distributions between the quantitative variables in a dataset:

```
In:
import pandas as pd
import numpy as np
colors = list()
palette = {0: "red", 1: "green", 2: "blue"}
In:
for c in np.nditer(iris.target): colors.append(palette[int(c)])
    # using the palette dictionary, we convert
    # each numeric class into a color string
dataframe = pd.DataFrame(iris.data,  columns=iris.feature_names)
In:
sc = pd.scatter_matrix(dataframe, alpha=0.3, figsize=(10, 10),
diagonal='hist', color=colors, marker='o', grid=True)
```

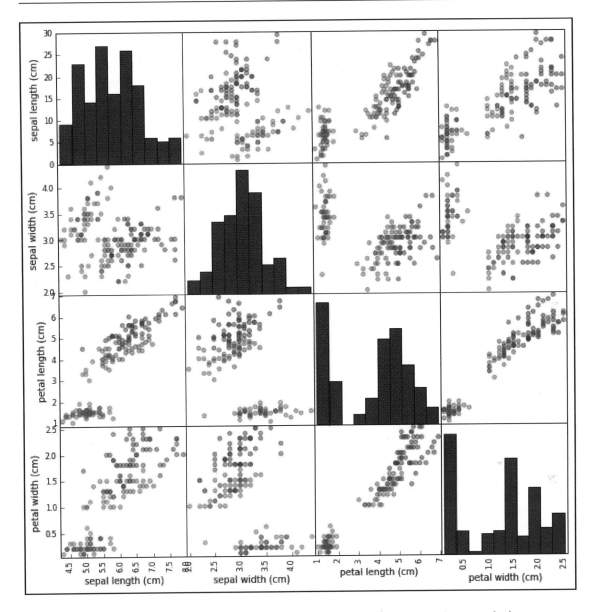

We encourage you to experiment a lot with this dataset and with similar ones before you work on other complex real data, because the advantage of focusing on an accessible, non-trivial data problem is that it can help you to quickly build your foundations on data science.

After a while anyway, though they are useful and interesting for your learning activities, toy datasets will start limiting the variety of different experimentations that you can achieve. In spite of the insights provided, in order to progress, you'll need to gain access to complex and realistic data science topics. Consequently, we will have to resort to some external data.

The MLdata.org public repository

The second type of example dataset that we will present can be downloaded directly from the machine learning dataset repository, or from the **LIBSVM** data website. Contrary to the previous dataset, in this case, you will need access to the Internet.

First, `mldata.org` is a public repository for machine learning datasets that is hosted by the TU Berlin University and supported by **Pattern Analysis, Statistical Modelling, and Computational Learning (PASCAL)**, a network funded by the European Union.

For example, if you need to download all the data related to earthquakes since 1972 as reported by the United States Geological Survey, in order to analyze the data to search for predictive patterns you will find the data repository at `http://mldata.org/repository/data/viewslug/global-earthquakes/` (here, you will find a detailed description of the data).

Note that the directory that contains the dataset is `global-earthquakes`; you can directly obtain the data using the following commands:

```
In:
from sklearn.datasets import fetch_mldata
earthquakes = fetch_mldata('global-earthquakes')
print (earthquakes.data)
print (earthquakes.data.shape)
Out:
(59209L, 4L)
```

As in the case of the Scikit-learn package toy dataset, the obtained object is a complex dictionary-like structure, where your predictive variables are `earthquakes.data` and your target to be predicted is `earthquakes.target`. This being the real data, in this case, you will have quite a lot of examples and just a few variables available.

LIBSVM data examples

LIBSVM Data (`http://www.csie.ntu.edu.tw/~cjlin/libsvmtools/datasets/`) is a page gathering data from many other collections. It offers different regression, binary, and multilabel classification datasets stored in the LIBSVM format. This repository is quite interesting if you wish to experiment with the support vector machines or any other machine learning algorithm.

If you want to load a dataset, first go to the web page where you can visualize the data on your browser. In the case of our example, visit `http://www.csie.ntu.edu.tw/~cjlin/lib svmtools/datasets/binary/a1a` and note down the address. Then, you can proceed by performing a direct download using that address:

```
In:
import urllib2
target_page =
'http://www.csie.ntu.edu.tw/~cjlin/libsvmtools/datasets/binary/a1a'
a2a = urllib2.urlopen(target_page)
In:
from sklearn.datasets import load_svmlight_file
X_train, y_train = load_svmlight_file(a2a)
print (X_train.shape, y_train.shape)
Out:
(1605, 119) (1605,)
```

In return, you will get two single objects: a set of training examples in a sparse matrix format and an array of responses.

Loading data directly from CSV or text files

Sometimes, you may have to download the datasets directly from their repository using a web browser or a `wget` command (on Linux systems).

If you have already downloaded and unpacked the data (if necessary) into your working directory, the simplest way to load your data and start working is offered by the NumPy and the pandas library with their respective `loadtxt` and `read_csv` functions.

For instance, if you intend to analyze the Boston housing data and use the version present at `http://mldata.org/repository/data/viewslug/regression-datasets-housing`, you first have to download the `regression-datasets-housing.csv` file in your local directory.

You can use this link for a direct download of the dataset: `http://mldata.org/repository /data/download/csv/regression-datasets-housing`.

Since the variables in the dataset are all numeric (13 continuous and one binary), the fastest way to load and start using it is by trying out the `loadtxt` NumPy function and directly loading all the data into an array.

Even in real-life datasets, you will often find mixed types of variables, which can be addressed by `pandas.read_table` or `pandas.read_csv`. Data can then be extracted by the `values` method; `loadtxt` can save a lot of memory if your data is already numeric. In fact, the `loadtxt` command doesn't require any in-memory duplication, something that is essential for large datasets, as other methods for loading a CSV file may use up all the available memory:

```
In:
housing = np.loadtxt('regression-datasets-housing.csv',
delimiter=',')
print (type(housing))
Out:
<class 'numpy.ndarray'>
In:
print (housing.shape)
Out:
(506, 14)
```

The `loadtxt` function expects, by default, a tabulation as a separator between the values on a file. If the separator is a comma (,) or a semicolon(;), you have to make it explicit using the parameter delimiter:

```
>>>   import numpy as np
>>> type(np.loadtxt)
<type 'function'>
>>> help(np.loadtxt)
```

Help on function `loadtxt` in module `numpy.lib.npyio`.

Another important default parameter is `dtype`, which is set to float.

 This means that `loadtxt` will force all of the loaded data to be converted into a floating-point number.

If you need to determinate a different type (for example, `int`), you have to declare it beforehand.

For instance, if you want to convert numeric data to `int`, use the following code:

```
In: housing_int =housing.astype(int)
```

Printing the first three elements of the row of the `housing` and `housing_int` arrays can help you understand the difference:

```
In:
print (housing[0,:3], '\n', housing_int[0,:3])
Out:
[  6.32000000e-03   1.80000000e+01   2.31000000e+00]
[ 0 18  2]
```

Frequently, though not always the case in our example, the data on files feature in the first line a textual header that contains the name of the variables. In this situation, the parameter that is skipped will point out the row in the `loadtxt` file from where it will start reading the data. Being the header on row 0 (in Python, counting always starts from 0), the parameter `skip=1` will save the day and allow you to avoid an error and fail to load your data.

The situation would be slightly different if you were to download the Iris dataset, which is present at `http://mldata.org/repository/data/viewslug/datasets-uci-iris/`. In fact, this dataset presents a qualitative target variable, `class`, which is a string that expresses the iris species. Specifically, it's a categorical variable with four levels.

Therefore, if you were to use the `loadtxt` function, you will get a value error because an array must have all its elements of the same type. The variable class is a string, whereas the other variables are constituted by floating-point values.

The pandas library offers the solution to this and many similar cases, thanks to its `DataFrame` data structure that can easily handle datasets in a matrix form (row per columns) that is made up of different types of variables.

First, just download the `datasets-uci-iris.csv` file and have it saved in your local directory.

The dataset can be downloaded from `http://archive.ics.uci.edu/ml/machine-learning-databases/iris/`.

At this point, using `read_csv` from pandas is quite straightforward:

```
In:
iris_filename = 'datasets-uci-iris.csv'
iris = pd.read_csv(iris_filename, sep=',', decimal='.',
\ header=None, names= ['sepal_length', 'sepal_width',
'petal_length', \ 'petal_width', 'target'])
print (type(iris))
Out:
< class 'pandas.core.frame.DataFrame'>
```

In order not to make the snippets of code printed in the book too cumbersome, we often wrap them and make them nicely formatted. In order to safely interrupt the code and wrap it to a new line, we use the backslash symbol (\) as in the preceding code. When rendering the code of the book by yourself, you can ignore backslash symbols and go on writing all of the instruction on the same line, or you can digit the backslash and start a new line with the remainder of the instruction. Please be warned that typing the backslash and then continuing the instruction on the same line will cause an execution error.

Apart from the filename, you can specify the separator (`sep`), the way the decimal points are expressed (decimal), whether there is a header (in this case, `header=None`; normally, if you have a header, then `header=0`), and the name of the variable where there is one (you can use a list; otherwise, pandas will provide some automatic naming).

 Also, we have defined names that use single words (instead of spaces, we used underscores). Thus, we can later directly extract single variables by calling them as we do for methods; for instance, `iris.sepal_length` will extract the sepal length data.

If, at this point, you need to convert the pandas `DataFrame` into a couple of NumPy arrays that contain the data and target values, this can be done easily in a couple of commands:

```
In:
iris_data = iris.values[:,:4]
iris_target, iris_target_labels = pd.factorize(iris.target)
print (iris_data.shape, iris_target.shape)
Out:
(150, 4) (150,)
```

Scikit-learn sample generators

As a last learning resource, the Scikit-learn package also offers the possibility to quickly create synthetic datasets for regression, binary and multilabel classification, cluster analysis, and dimensionality reduction.

The main advantage of recurring to synthetic data lies in its instantaneous creation in the working memory of your Python console. It is, therefore, possible to create bigger data examples without having to engage in long downloading sessions from the Internet (and saving a lot of stuff on your disk).

For example, you may need to work on a classification problem involving a million data points:

```
In:
from sklearn import datasets
X,y = datasets.make_classification(n_samples=10**6,
\ n_features=10, random_state=101)
print (X.shape,  y.shape)
Out: (1000000, 10) (1000000,)
```

After importing just the datasets module, we ask, using the `make_classification` command, for 1 million examples (the `n_samples` parameter) and 10 useful features (`n_features`). The `random_state` should be `101`, so we are assured that we can replicate the same datasets at a different time and in a different machine.

For instance, you can type the following command:

```
In: datasets.make_classification(1, n_features=4, random_state=101)
```

This will always give you the following output:

```
Out:(array([[-3.31994186, -2.39469384, -2.35882002,
1.40145585]]),  array([0]))
```

No matter what the computer and the specific situation are, `random_state` assures deterministic results that make your experimentations perfectly replicable, due to the fact that all the random numbers involved in this synthetic dataset are actually produced in a deterministic way, based on this number (sometime it's called seed).

Defining the `random_state` parameter using a specific integer number (in this case, it's `101`, but it may be any number that you prefer or find useful) allows easy replication of the same dataset on your machine, the way it is set up, on different operating systems, and on different machines.

By the way, did it take too long?

On an Intel i7 CPU @ 2.3GHz machine, it takes:

```
In:
%timeit X,y = datasets.make_classification(n_samples=10**6,
\ n_features=10, random_state=101)
Out: 1 loops, best of 3: 815 ms per loop
```

If it doesn't seem so on your machine and if you are ready, having set up and tested everything up to this point, we can start our data science journey.

Summary

In this introductory chapter, we installed everything that we will be using throughout this book, from Python packages to examples. They were installed either directly or by using a scientific distribution. We also introduced Jupyter notebooks and demonstrated how you can have access to the data run in the tutorials.

In the next chapter, *Data Munging*, we will have an overview of the data science pipeline and explore all the key tools to handle and prepare data before you apply any learning algorithm and set up your hypothesis experimentation schedule.

2
Data Munging

We are just getting into action with data! In this chapter, you'll learn how to munge data. What does munging data imply?

The term *munge* is a technical term coined about half a century ago by the students of the **Massachusetts Institute of Technology** (**MIT**). Munging means to change, in a series of well-specified and reversible steps, a piece of original data to a completely different (and hopefully more useful) one. Deep-rooted in hacker culture, munging is often described in the data science pipeline using other, almost synonymous, terms such as data wrangling or data preparation. It is a very important part of the data engineering pipeline.

Starting from this chapter, we will start mentioning more jargon and technicalities taken from the fields of probability and statistics (such as probability distributions, descriptive statistics, and hypothesis testing). Unfortunately, we cannot explain all of them in detail since our main purpose is to provide you with the essential Python concepts for handling data science projects and we should therefore presume that you are already familiar with some of them. In case you may need a refresh or even a straightforward introduction to any of the concepts dealt with in the chapter, we suggest you to refer to the MIT open-sourced course taught by Ramesh Sridharan and addressed to novice statisticians and social science researchers. You can find all the course's materials at `www.mit.edu/~6.s085/`.

Given such premises, in this chapter, the following topics will be covered:

- The data science process (so that you'll know what is going on and what's next)
- Uploading data from a file
- Selecting the data you need
- Handling any missing or wrong data

- Adding, inserting, and deleting data
- Grouping and transforming data to obtain new and meaningful information
- Managing to obtain a dataset matrix or an array to feed into the data modeling part of the pipeline

The data science process

Although every data science project is different, for our illustrative purposes, we can partition an ideal data science project into a series of reduced and simplified phases.

The process starts by obtaining data (a phase know as data ingestion or data acquisition), and as such implies a series of possible alternatives, from simply uploading data to assembling it from RDBMS or NoSQL repositories, or synthetically generating it or scraping it from the web APIs or HTML pages.

Especially when faced with novel challenges, uploading data can reveal itself as a critical part of a data scientist's work. Your data can arrive from multiple sources: databases, CSV or Excel files, raw HTML, images, sound recordings, APIs (`https://en.wikipedia.org/wiki/Application_programming_interface`) providing JSON files, and so on. Given the wide range of alternatives, we will just briefly touch upon this aspect by offering the basic tools to get your data (even if it is too big) into your computer memory by using either a textual file present on your hard disk or the Web or tables in RDBMS.

After successfully uploading your data comes the data munging phase. Although now available in-memory, inevitably, your data will surely be in a form unsuitable for any analysis and experimentation. Data in the real world is complex, messy, and is often even erroneous or missing. Yet, thanks to a bunch of basic Python data structures and commands, you'll address all the problematic data and feed it into the next phases of the project, appropriately transformed into a typical dataset that has observations in rows and variables in columns. Having a dataset is the basic requirement for any statistical and machine learning analysis and you may hear it being mentioned as flat file (when it is the result of joining together multiple relational tables from a database) or data matrix (when columns and rows are unlabeled and the values it contains are just numeric).

Though less rewarding than other intellectually stimulating phases (such as the application of algorithms or machine learning), data munging creates the foundations for every complex and sophisticated value-added analysis that you may have in mind to obtain. The success of your project heavily relies on it.

Having completely defined the dataset that you'll be working on, a new phase opens up. At this time, you'll start observing your data; then you will proceed to develop and test your hypothesis in a recurring loop. For instance, you'll explore your variables graphically. With the help of descriptive stats, you'll figure out how to create new variables by putting into action your domain knowledge. You'll address redundant and unexpected information (outliers, first of all) and select the most meaningful variables and effective parameters to be tested by a selection of machine learning algorithms (although, we have to pinpoint that there are times when conventional machine learning techniques are not appropriate for the problem at hand and we have to resort to graph analysis, or to some other data science methodology).

This phase is structured as a pipeline where your data is processed according to a series of steps. After that, a model is finally created, but you may realize that you have to reiterate and start again from data munging or somewhere in the data pipeline, supplying corrections or trying different experiments, until you have reached a meaningful result.

From our experience on the field, we can assure you that no matter how promising your plans were when starting to analyze the data, in the end your solution will be much different from any first envisioned idea. The confrontation with the experimental results you will obtain rules the kind of data munging, optimizations, models, and the overall number of iterations you have to go through before reaching a satisfactory end to your project. That is why if you want to be a successful data scientist, it won't suffice at all just to provide theoretically sound solutions. It is necessary to be able to quickly prototype a large number of possible solutions in the fastest time in order to ascertain which is the best path to take. It is our purpose to help you accelerate to the maximum by using the code snippets provided by this book in your data science process.

A result from your project is represented by an error or optimization measure (that you have chosen carefully in order to represent your business targets). Besides an error measurement, your achievement can also be communicated by an interpretable insight that has to be verbally or visually described to your data science project's sponsors or other data scientists. At this point, being able to visualize results and insights appropriately using tables, charts, and plots is indeed essential.

This process can also be described using the acronym **OSEMN (Obtain, Scrub, Explore, Model, iNterpret)**, as introduced by Hilary Mason and Chris Wiggins in a famous post to the blog *dataists* (http://www.dataists.com/2010/09/a-taxonomy-of-data-science/), describing a data science taxonomy. OSEMN is also quite memorable since it rhymes with the words *possum* and *awesome*.

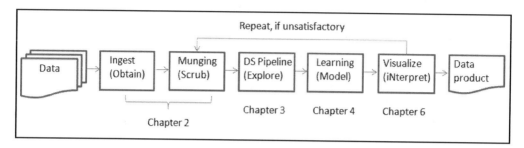

Naturally, the OSEMN taxonomy doesn't detail all the parts of a data science process, but, overall, it is a simple way of highlighting the key milestones of the process. For example, in the Explore phase, there is a key stage called "data discovery" where all the new or rehashed features come about, while the "data representation" that precedes it is also very important. The Learning phase (which will be dealt with in `Chapter 4`, *Machine Learning*), includes not just the model development but also the validation of it.

We won't ever get tired of remarking how everything starts with munging your data and that munging can easily require up to 80% of your efforts in a data project. Since even the longest journey starts with a single step, let's immediately step into this chapter and learn the building blocks of a successful munging phase!

Data loading and preprocessing with pandas

In the previous chapter, we discussed where to find useful datasets and examined basic import commands of Python packages. In this section, having kept your toolbox ready, you are about to learn how to structurally load, manipulate, process, and polish data using pandas and NumPy.

Fast and easy data loading

Let's start with a CSV file and pandas. The pandas library offers the most accessible and complete function to load tabular data from a file (or a URL). By default, it will store data in a specialized pandas data structure, index each row, separate variables by custom delimiters, infer the right data type for each column, convert data (if necessary), as well as parse dates, missing values, and erroneous values.

```
In: import pandas as pd
iris_filename = 'datasets-uci-iris.csv'
iris = pd.read_csv(iris_filename, sep=',', decimal='.', header=None,
names= ['sepal_length', 'sepal_width', 'petal_length',
'petal_width',
'target'])
```

You can specify the name of the file, the character used as a separator (sep), the character used for the decimal placeholder (decimal), whether there is a header (header), and the variable names (using names and a list). The settings of the sep=',' and decimal='.' parameters have default values, and they are redundant in this function. Anyway, for a European-style CSV, it is important to point out both since in many European countries (but also in some Asian countries), the separator character and the decimal placeholder are different from the default ones.

If the dataset is not available online, you can follow these steps to download it from the Internet:

```
import urllib
url = "http://aima.cs.berkeley.edu/data/iris.csv"
set1 = urllib.request.Request(url)
iris_p = urllib.request.urlopen(set1)
iris_other = pd.read_csv(iris_p, sep=',', decimal='.',
header=None, names= ['sepal_length', 'sepal_width',
'petal_length', 'petal_width', 'target'])
iris_other.head()
```

The resulting object, named `iris`, is a pandas DataFrame. It's more than a simple Python list or dictionary, and in the sections that follow, we will explore some of its features. To get an idea of its content, you can print the first (or the last) row(s), using the following commands:

```
In: iris.head()
Out:
```

	sepal_length	sepal_width	petal_length	petal_width	target
0	5.1	3.5	1.4	0.2	Iris-setosa
1	4.9	3.0	1.4	0.2	Iris-setosa
2	4.7	3.2	1.3	0.2	Iris-setosa
3	4.6	3.1	1.5	0.2	Iris-setosa
4	5.0	3.6	1.4	0.2	Iris-setosa

```
In: iris.tail()
[...]
```

The function, if called without arguments, will print five lines. If you want to get back a different number of rows, just call the function using the number of rows you want to see as an argument, as follows:

```
In: iris.head(2)
```

The preceding command will print only the first two lines. Now, to get the names of the columns, you can simply use the following method:

```
In: iris.columns
Out: Index(['sepal_length', 'sepal_width', 'petal_length',
'petal_width', 'target'], dtype='object')
```

The resulting object is a very interesting one. It looks like a list, but it actually is a pandas index. As suggested by the object's name, it indexes the columns' names. To extract the target column, for example, you can simply do the following:

```
In: Y = iris['target']
Y
Out:
0        Iris-setosa
1        Iris-setosa
2        Iris-setosa
3        Iris-setosa
```

```
. . .
149     Iris-virginica
Name: target, dtype: object
```

The type of the object Y is a pandas Series. Right now, think of it as a one-dimensional array with axis labels, as we will investigate it in depth later on. Now, we just understood that a pandas `Index` class acts like a dictionary index of the table's columns. Note that you can also get a list of columns referring to them by their indexes, as follows:

```
In: X = iris[['sepal_length', 'sepal_width']]
X
Out:
```

	sepal_length	sepal_width
0	5.1	3.5
1	4.9	3.0
2	4.7	3.2
3	4.6	3.1

146	6.3	2.5
147	6.5	3.0
148	6.2	3.4
149	5.9	3.0

```
[150 rows x 2 columns]
```

In this case, the result is a pandas DataFrame. Why such a difference in results when using the same function? In the first case, we asked for a column. Therefore, the output was a 1D vector (that is, a pandas Series). In the second example, we asked for multiple columns and we obtained a matrix-like result (and we know that matrices are mapped as pandas DataFrames). A novice reader can simply spot the difference by looking at the heading of the output; if the columns are labelled, then you are dealing with a pandas DataFrame. On the other hand, if the result is a vector and it presents no heading, then that is a pandas Series.

So far, we have learned some common steps from the data science process; after you load the dataset, you usually separate the features and target labels. In a classification problem, target labels are the discrete/nominal numbers or textual strings that indicate the class associated with every set of features.

Then, the following steps require you to get an idea of how large the problem is, and therefore, you need to know the size of the dataset. Typically, for each observation, we count a line, and for each feature, a column.

To obtain the dimensions of the dataset, just use the attribute shape on both a pandas DataFrame or Series, as shown in the following example:

```
In: print (X.shape)
Out: (150, 2)
In:  print (Y.shape)
Out: (150,)
```

The resulting object is a tuple that contains the size of the matrix/array in each dimension. Also, note that pandas Series follow the same format (that is, a tuple with only one element).

Dealing with problematic data

Now, you should be more confident with the basics of the process and be ready to face datasets that are more problematic since it is very common to have messy data in reality. Consequently, let's see what happens if the CSV file contains a header and some missing values and dates. For example, to make our example realistic, let's imagine the situation of a travel agency. According to the temperature of three popular destinations, they record whether the user picks the first, second, or third destination:

```
Date,Temperature_city_1,Temperature_city_2,Temperature_city_3,
Which_destination
20140910,80,32,40,1
20140911,100,50,36,2
20140912,102,55,46,1
20140912,60,20,35,3
20140914,60,,32,3
20140914,,57,42,2
```

In this case, all the numbers are integers and the header is in the file. In our first attempt to load this dataset, we can provide the following command:

```
In: import pandas as pd
In: fake_dataset = pd.read_csv('a_loading_example_1.csv',
sep=',') fake_dataset
Out:
```

	Date	Temperature_city_1	Temperature_city_2	Temperature_city_3	Which_destination
0	20140910	80.0	32.0	40	1
1	20140911	100.0	50.0	36	2
2	20140912	102.0	55.0	46	1
3	20140913	60.0	20.0	35	3
4	20140914	60.0	NaN	32	3
5	20140915	NaN	57.0	42	2

pandas automatically gave the columns their actual name after picking them from the first data row. We first detect a problem: all of the data, even the dates, has been parsed as integers (or, in other cases, as strings). If the format of the dates is not very strange, you can try the auto-detection routines that specify the column that contains the date data. In the next example, it works well using the following arguments:

```
In: fake_dataset = pd.read_csv('a_loading_example_1.csv',
parse_dates=[0])
fake_dataset
Out:
```

	Date	Temperature_city_1	Temperature_city_2	Temperature_city_3	Which_destination
0	2014-09-10	80.0	32.0	40	1
1	2014-09-11	100.0	50.0	36	2
2	2014-09-12	102.0	55.0	46	1
3	2014-09-13	60.0	20.0	35	3
4	2014-09-14	60.0	NaN	32	3
5	2014-09-15	NaN	57.0	42	2

Now, in order to get rid of the missing values that are indicated by NaN (which stands for **Not Any Number**), replace them with a more meaningful number (let's say, 50 Fahrenheit) which could be fine in certain situations (later in the chapter, we will offer a wider coverage of problems and remedies for missing data). We can execute our command in the following way:

```
In: fake_dataset.fillna(50)
Out:
```

	Date	Temperature_city_1	Temperature_city_2	Temperature_city_3	Which_destination
0	2014-09-10	80.0	32.0	40	1
1	2014-09-11	100.0	50.0	36	2
2	2014-09-12	102.0	55.0	46	1
3	2014-09-13	60.0	20.0	35	3
4	2014-09-14	60.0	50.0	32	3
5	2014-09-15	50.0	57.0	42	2

After that, all of the missing data is no more, replaced by the constant 50.0. Treating missing data can also require different approaches. As an alternative to the previous command, values can be replaced by a negative constant value to mark the fact that they are different from others (and leave the guessing to the learning algorithm):

```
In: fake_dataset.fillna(-1)
```

Note that this method only fills missing values in the view of the data (that is, it doesn't modify the original DataFrame). In order to actually change them, use the inplace=True argument.

NaN values can also be replaced by the column mean or median value as a way to minimize the guessing error:

```
In: fake_dataset.fillna(fake_dataset.mean(axis=0))
```

The .mean method calculates the arithmetic mean of the specified axis.

Note that `axis=0` implies a calculation of means that spans the rows; the consequently obtained means are derived from column-wise computations. Instead, `axis=1` spans columns and, therefore, row-wise results are obtained. This works in the same way for all other methods that require the axis parameter, both in pandas and NumPy.

The `.median` method is analogous to `.mean`, but it computes the median value, which is useful if the mean is not so well representative, given too skewed data (for instance, when there are many extreme values in your feature).

Another possible problem when handling real-world datasets is when loading a dataset containing errors or bad lines. In this case, the default behavior of the `load_csv` method is to stop and raise an exception. A possible workaround, which is feasible when erroneous examples are not the majority, is to ignore the lines causing exceptions. In many cases, such a choice has the sole implication of training the machine learning algorithm without the erroneous observations. As an example, let's say that you have a badly formatted dataset and you want to load just all the good lines and ignore the badly formatted ones.

Here is what you can do with the `error_bad_lines` option:

```
Val1,Val2,Val3
0,0,0
1,1,1
2,2,2,2
3,3,3
In: bad_dataset = pd.read_csv('a_loading_example_2.csv',
error_bad_lines=False)
bad_dataset
Out:
Skipping line 4: expected 3 fields, saw 4
```

	Val1	Val2	Val3
0	0	0	0
1	1	1	1
2	3	3	3

Dealing with big datasets

If the dataset you want to load is too big to fit in the memory, you can deal with it using a batch machine learning algorithm, which works with only a part of the data at once. Using a batch approach also makes sense if you just need a sample of the data (let's say that you want to take a peek at the data. Thanks to Python, you actually can load the data in chunks. This operation is also called data streaming since the dataset flows into a DataFrame or some other data structure as a continuous flow. As opposed to all the previous cases, the dataset has been fully loaded into the memory in a standalone step.

With pandas, there are two ways to chunk and load a file. The first way is by loading the dataset in chunks of the same size; each chunk is a piece of the dataset that contains all the columns and a limited number of lines, not more than as set in the function call (the `chunksize` parameter). Note that the output of the `read_csv` function in this case is not a pandas DataFrame but an iterator-like object. In fact, to get the results in memory, you need to iterate that object:

```
In:
import pandas as pd
iris_chunks = pd.read_csv(iris_filename, header=None,
names=['C1', 'C2', 'C3', 'C4', 'C5'], chunksize=10)
for chunk in iris_chunks:
    print ('Shape:', chunk.shape)
    print (chunk,'\n')
Out:Shape: (10, 5)    C1    C2    C3    C4         C50  5.1   3.5   1.4   0.2
Iris-setosa1   4.9   3.0   1.4   0.2   Iris-setosa2   4.7   3.2   1.3   0.2   Iris-
setosa3   4.6   3.1   1.5   0.2   Iris-setosa4   5.0   3.6   1.4   0.2   Iris-setosa5
5.4   3.9   1.7   0.4   Iris-setosa6   4.6   3.4   1.4   0.3   Iris-setosa7   5.0
3.4   1.5   0.2   Iris-setosa8   4.4   2.9   1.4   0.2   Iris-setosa9   4.9   3.1
1.5   0.1   Iris-setosa...
```

There will be 14 other pieces like these, each of them of shape (10, 5). The other method to load a big dataset is by specifically asking for an iterator of it. In this case, you can dynamically decide the length (that is, how many lines to get) you want for each piece of the pandas DataFrame:

```
In:  iris_iterator = pd.read_csv(iris_filename, header=None,
names=['C1', 'C2', 'C3', 'C4', 'C5'], iterator=True)
In:  print (iris_iterator.get_chunk(10).shape)
Out: (10, 5)
In:  print (iris_iterator.get_chunk(20).shape)
Out: (20, 5)
In:  piece = iris_iterator.get_chunk(2) piece
Out:
```

	C1	C2	C3	C4	C5
0	4.8	3.1	1.6	0.2	Iris-setosa
1	5.4	3.4	1.5	0.4	Iris-setosa

In this example, we first defined the iterator. Next, we retrieved a piece of data containing 10 lines. We then obtained 20 further rows, and finally the two rows that are printed at the end.

Besides pandas, you can also use the CSV package, which offers two functions to iterate small chunks of data from files: the `reader` and the `DictReader` functions. Let's illustrate such functions by importing the CSV package:

```
In:import csv
```

The `reader` inputs the data from disks to the Python lists. `DictReader` instead transforms the data into a dictionary. Both functions work by iterating over the rows of the file being read. The `reader` returns exactly what it reads, stripped of the return carriage and split into a list by the separator (which is a comma by default, but this can be modified). `DictReader` will map the list's data into a dictionary, whose keys will be defined by the first row (if a header is present) or the `fieldnames` parameter (using a list of strings that reports the column names).

The reading of lists in a native manner is not a limitation. For instance, it will be easier to speed up the code using a fast Python implementation such as PyPy. Moreover, we can always convert lists into NumPy `ndarrays` (a data structure that we are going to introduce soon). By reading the data into JSON-style dictionaries, it will be quite easy to get a DataFrame; this method of reading the data is highly effective if data is sparse and rows don't have all the features. In that case, the dictionary will contain just the non-null (or non-zero) entries, saving a lot of space. Then, moving from the dictionary to the DataFrame is a trivial operation.

Here is a simple example that uses such functionalities from the CSV package.

Let's pretend that our `datasets-uci-iris.csv` file that was downloaded from `http://ml data.org/` is a huge file that we cannot fully load in the memory (actually, we just pretend so because we remember having seen the file at the beginning of this chapter; it is made up of just 150 examples and the CSV lacks a header row).

Therefore, our only choice is to load it in chunks. Let's first conduct an experiment:

```
In:
with open(iris_filename, 'rt') as data_stream:
    # 'rt' mode
    for n, row in enumerate(csv.DictReader(data_stream,
        fieldnames = ['sepal_length', 'sepal_width',
        'petal_length', 'petal_width', 'target'],
        dialect='excel')):
            if n== 0:
                print (n,row)
            else:
                break
Out:
0 {'petal_width': '0.2', 'target': 'Iris-setosa', 'sepal_width': '3.5',
'sepal_length': '5.1', 'petal_length': '1.4'}
```

What does the preceding code accomplish? First, it opens a read-binary connection to the file that aliases it as `data_stream`. Using the `with` command assures that the file is closed after the commands placed in the preceding indentation are completely executed.

Then, it iterates (for...in...) and it enumerates a `csv.DictReader` call, which wraps the flow of the data from `data_stream`. Since we don't have a header row in the file, `fieldnames` provides information about the fields' names. `dialect` just specifies that we are calling the standard comma-separated CSV (later, we'll provide some hints on how to modify this parameter).

Inside the iteration, if the row being read is just the first, then it is printed. Otherwise, the loop is stopped by a `break` command. The `print` command presents us with the row number 0 and a dictionary. Therefore, you can recall every piece of data of the row by just calling the keys bearing the variables' names.

Similarly, we can make the same code work for the `csv.reader` command, as follows:

```
In: with open(iris_filename, 'rt') as data_stream:
    for n, row in enumerate(csv.reader(data_stream,
        dialect='excel')):
            if n==0:
                print (row)
            else:
                break
Out: ['5.1', '3.5', '1.4', '0.2', 'Iris-setosa']
```

Here, the code is even more straightforward and the output is simpler, providing a list that contains the row values in a sequence.

At this point, based on this second piece of code, we can create a generator callable from a for loop. This retrieves the data on the fly from the file in the blocks of the size defined by the batch parameter of the function:

```
In:
def batch_read(filename, batch=5):
    # open the data stream
    with open(filename, 'rt') as data_stream:
        # reset the batch
        batch_output = list()
        # iterate over the file
        for n, row in enumerate(csv.reader(data_stream,
        dialect='excel')):
            # if the batch is of the right size
            if n > 0 and n % batch == 0:
                # yield back the batch as an ndarray
                yield(np.array(batch_output))
                # reset the batch and restart
                batch_output = list()
            # otherwise add the row to the batch
            batch_output.append(row)
    # when the loop is over, yield what's
    leftyield(np.array(batch_output))
```

Similar to the previous example, the data is drawn out, thanks to the `csv.reader` function wrapped by the `enumerate` function that accompanies the extracted list of data along with the example number (which starts from zero). Based on the example number, a batch list is either appended with the data list or returned to the main program using the generative `yield` function. This process is repeated until the entire file is read and returned in batches:

```
In:
import numpy as np
for batch_input in batch_read(iris_filename, batch=3):
    print (batch_input)
    break
Out:
[['5.1' '3.5' '1.4' '0.2' 'Iris-setosa']
 ['4.9' '3.0' '1.4' '0.2' 'Iris-setosa']
 ['4.7' '3.2' '1.3' '0.2' 'Iris-setosa']]
```

Such a function can provide the basic functionality for learning with stochastic gradient descent, as will be presented in *Chapter 4, Machine Learning*, where we will come back to this piece of code and expand the example by introducing some more advanced examples.

Accessing other data formats

So far, we have worked on CSV files only. The pandas package offers similar functionality (and functions) in order to load MS Excel, HDFS, SQL, JSON, HTML, and Stata datasets. Since they're not used in all data science projects, the understanding of how one can load and handle each of them is left to you, and you can refer to the verbose documentation available on the website. A basic example on how to load a SQL table is available in the code that accompanies the book.

Finally, pandas DataFrames can be created by merging series or other list-like data. Note that scalars are transformed into lists, as follows:

```
In: import pandas as pd
my_own_dataset = pd.DataFrame({'Col1': range(5), 'Col2':
[1.0]*5, 'Col3': 1.0, 'Col4': 'Hello World!'})
my_own_dataset
Out:
```

	Col1	Col2	Col3	Col4
0	0	1.0	1.0	Hello World!
1	1	1.0	1.0	Hello World!
2	2	1.0	1.0	Hello World!
3	3	1.0	1.0	Hello World!
4	4	1.0	1.0	Hello World!

It can be said easily that for each of the columns you want stacked together, you provide their names (as the dictionary key) and values (as the dictionary value for that key). As seen in the preceding example, Col2 and Col3 are created in two different ways but they provide the same resulting column of values. In this way, you can create a pandas DataFrame that contains multiple types of data with a very simple function.

In this process, please ensure that you don't mix lists of different sizes; otherwise an exception will be raised, as shown here:

```
In: my_wrong_own_dataset = pd.DataFrame({'Col1': range(5),
'Col2': 'string', 'Col3': range(2)})
...
ValueError: arrays must all be same length
```

To check the type of data present in each column, check the `dtypes` attribute:

```
In: my_own_dataset.dtypes
Col1       int64
Col2     float64
Col3     float64
Col4      object
dtype: object
```

The last method seen in the example is very handy if you wish to check whether a datum is categorical, integer numerical, or a floating point, and its precision. In fact, sometimes it is possible to increase the processing speed by rounding up floats to integers and casting double-precision floats to single-precision floats, or by using only a single type of data. Let's see how you can cast the type in the following example. This example can also be seen as a broad example on how to reassign column data:

```
In:  my_own_dataset['Col1'] = my_own_dataset['Col1'].astype(float)
my_own_dataset.dtypes
Out: Col1     float64
Col2     float64
Col3     float64
Col4      object
dtype: object
```

Data preprocessing

We are now able to import the dataset, even a big, problematic one. Now, we need to learn the basic preprocessing routines in order to make it feasible for the next data science step.

First, if you need to apply a function to a limited section of rows, you can create a **mask**. A mask is a series of Boolean values (that is, True or False) that tells whether the line is selected or not.

For example, let's say we want to select all the lines of the iris dataset that have a `sepal length` greater than 6. We can simply do the following:

```
In: mask_feature = iris['sepal_length'] > 6.0
In: mask_feature
0       False
1       False
...
146      True
147      True
148      True
149     False
```

In the preceding simple example, we can immediately see which observations are `True` and which are not (`False`), and which ones fit the selection query.

Now, let's check how you can use a selection mask on another example. We want to substitute the `Iris-virginica` target label with the `New label` label. We can do this by using the following two lines of code:

```
In: mask_target = iris['target'] == 'Iris-virginica'
In: iris.loc[mask_target, 'target'] = 'New label'
```

You'll see that all occurrences of `Iris-virginica` are now replaced by `New label`. The `.loc()` method is explained in the following. Just think of it as a way to access the data of the matrix with the help of row-column indexes.

To see the new list of the labels in the target column, we can use the `unique()` method. This method is very handy if initially you want to evaluate the dataset:

```
In: iris['target'].unique()
Out: array(['Iris-setosa', 'Iris-versicolor', 'New label'],
dtype=object)
```

If you want to see some statistics about each feature, you can group each column accordingly; eventually, you can also apply a mask. The pandas method `groupby` will produce a similar result to the GROUP BY clause in a SQL statement. The next method to apply should be an aggregate method on one or multiple columns. For example, the `mean()` pandas aggregate method is the counterpart of the AVG() SQL function to compute the mean of the values in the group; the pandas aggregate method `var()` calculates the variance, `sum()` the summation, `count()` the number of rows in the group, and so on. Note that the result is still a pandas DataFrame; therefore multiple operations can be chained together. As a next step, we can try a couple of examples of `groupby` in action. Grouping observations by target (that is, label) we can check the difference between the average value and the variance of the features for each group:

```
In: grouped_targets_mean = iris.groupby(['target']).mean()
grouped_targets_mean
Out:
```

	sepal_length	sepal_width	petal_length	petal_width
target				
Iris-setosa	5.006	3.418	1.464	0.244
Iris-versicolor	5.936	2.770	4.260	1.326
New label	6.588	2.974	5.552	2.026

```
In: grouped_targets_var = iris.groupby(['target']).var()
grouped_targets_var
Out:
```

	sepal_length	sepal_width	petal_length	petal_width
target				
Iris-setosa	0.124249	0.145180	0.030106	0.011494
Iris-versicolor	0.266433	0.098469	0.220816	0.039106
New label	0.404343	0.104004	0.304588	0.075433

Later, if you need to sort the observations using a function, you can use the
`.sort_index()` method, as follows:

```
In: iris.sort_index(by='sepal_length').head()
Out:
```

	sepal_length	sepal_width	petal_length	petal_width	target
13	4.3	3.0	1.1	0.1	Iris-setosa
42	4.4	3.2	1.3	0.2	Iris-setosa
38	4.4	3.0	1.3	0.2	Iris-setosa
8	4.4	2.9	1.4	0.2	Iris-setosa
41	4.5	2.3	1.3	0.3	Iris-setosa

Finally, if your dataset contains a time series (for example, in the case of a numerical target) and you need to apply a rolling operation to it (in the case of noisy data points), you can simply do the following:

```
In: smooth_time_series = pd.rolling_mean(time_series, 5)
```

This can be performed for a rolling average of the values. Alternatively, you can give the following command:

```
In: median_time_series = pd.rolling_median(time_series, 5)
```

Instead, this can be performed in order to obtain a rolling median of the values. In both of these cases, the window had five sample sizes.

More generically, the apply() pandas method is able to perform any row-wise or column-wise operation programmatically. apply() should be called directly on the DataFrame; the first argument is the function to be applied row-wise or column-wise; the second the axis to apply it on. Note that the function can be a built-in, library-provided, lambda or any other user-defined function.

As an example of this powerful method, let's now try to count how many non-zero elements there are in each line. With the apply method, this is simple:

```
In: iris.apply(np.count_nonzero, axis=1).head()
Out: 0      5
     1      5
     2      5
     3      5
     4      5
     dtype: int64
```

Similarly, to compute the non-zero elements feature-wise (that is, per column), you just need to change the second argument and set it to 0:

```
In: iris.apply(np.count_nonzero, axis=0)
Out: sepal_length      150
     sepal_width       150
     petal_length      150
     petal_width       150
     target            150
     dtype: int64
```

Finally, to operate element-wise, the applymap() method should be used on the DataFrame. In this case, just one argument should be provided: the function to apply.

For example, let's assume you're interested in the length of the string representation of each cell. To obtain that value, you should first cast each cell to a string value, and then compute the length. With `applymap`, this operation is very easy:

```
In: iris.applymap(lambda el:len(str(el))).head()
Out:
```

	sepal_length	sepal_width	petal_length	petal_width	target
0	3	3	3	3	11
1	3	3	3	3	11
2	3	3	3	3	11
3	3	3	3	3	11
4	3	3	3	3	11

Data selection

The last topic on pandas that we'll focus on is data selection. Let's start with an example. We might come across a situation where the dataset contains an index column. How do we properly import it with pandas? And then, can we actively exploit it to make our job simpler?

We will use a very simple dataset that contains an index column (this is just a counter and not a feature). To make the example very generic, let's start the index from 100. So, the index of the row number 0 is 100:

```
n,val1,val2,val3
100,10,10,C
101,10,20,C
102,10,30,B
103,10,40,B
104,10,50,A
```

When trying to load a file the classic way, you'll find yourself in a situation where you have n as a feature (or a column). Nothing is practically incorrect, but an index should not be used by mistake as a feature. Therefore, it is better to keep it separated. If instead, by chance it is used during the learning phase of your model, you may possibly incur a case of "leakage", which is one of the major sources of error in machine learning.

In fact, if the index is a random number, no harm will be done to your model's efficacy. However, if the index contains progressive, temporal, or even informative elements (for example, certain numeric ranges may be used for positive outcomes, and others for the negative ones), you might incorporate into the model leaked information. That will be impossible to replicate when using your model on fresh data (as the index will be missing):

```
In: import pandas as pd
In: dataset = pd.read_csv('a_selection_example_1.csv') dataset
Out:
```

	n	val1	val2	val3
0	100	10	10	C
1	101	10	20	C
2	102	10	30	B
3	103	10	40	B
4	104	10	50	A

Therefore, while loading such a dataset, we might want to specify that n is the index column. Since the index n is the first column, we can give the following command:

```
In: dataset = pd.read_csv('a_selection_example_1.csv',
index_col=0) dataset
Out:
```

n	val1	val2	val3
100	10	10	C
101	10	20	C
102	10	30	B
103	10	40	B
104	10	50	A

Here, the dataset is loaded and the index is correct. Now, to access the value of a cell, there are a few ways. Let's list them one by one.

First, you can simply specify the column and the line (by using its index) you are interested in.

To extract the val3 of the fifth line (indexed with n=104), you can give the following command:

```
In: dataset['val3'][104]
Out: 'A'
```

Apply this operation carefully since it's not a matrix and you might be tempted to first input the row and then the column. Remember that it's actually a pandas DataFrame, and the [] operator works first on columns and then on the element of the resulting pandas Series.

To have something similar to the preceding method of accessing data, you can use the .loc() method:

```
In: dataset.loc[104, 'val3']
Out: 'A'
```

In this case, you should first specify the index and then the columns you're interested in. The solution is equivalent to the one provided by the .ix() method. The latter works with all kinds of indexes (labels or positions), and is more flexible.

 Note that ix() has to guess what are you referring to. Therefore, if you don't want to mix labels and positional indexes, loc and iloc are preferred to create a more structured approach.

```
In: dataset.ix[104, 'val3']
Out: 'A'
In: dataset.ix[104, 2]
Out: 'A'
```

Finally, a full-optimized function that specifies the positions (as in a matrix) is iloc(). With it, you must specify the cell by using the row number and column number:

```
In: dataset.iloc[4, 2]
Out: 'A'
```

The retrieving of sub-matrixes is a very intuitive operation; you simply need to specify the lists of indexes instead of scalars:

```
In: dataset[['val3', 'val2']][0:2]
```

This command is equivalent to this:

```
In: dataset.loc[range(100, 102), ['val3', 'val2']]
```

It is also equivalent to the following:

```
In: dataset.ix[range(100, 102), ['val3', 'val2']]
```

The following command is identical to the preceding commands:

```
In: dataset.ix[range(100, 102), [2, 1]]
```

As is the following command as well:

```
In: dataset.iloc[range(2), [2,1]]
```

In all the cases, the resulting DataFrame is:

Out:

	val3	val2
n		
100	C	10
101	C	20

Working with categorical and text data

Typically, you'll find yourself dealing with two main kinds of data: categorical and numerical. Numerical data, such as temperature, amount of money, days of usage, or house number, can be composed of either floating-point numbers (such as 1.0, -2.3, 99.99, and so on) or integers (such as -3, 9, 0, 1, and so on). Each value that the data can assume has a direct relation with others since they're comparable. In other words, you can say that a feature with a value of 2.0 is greater (actually, it is double) than a feature that assumes a value of 1.0. This type of data is very well-defined and comprehensible, with binary operators such as equal to, greater than, and less than.

 A key aspect of numerical data is that basic stats are meaningful for it (for example, averages). This does not apply to any other category, making it an important characteristic of this data type

The other type of data you might see in your career is the categorical type (also known as nominal data). A categorical datum expresses an attribute that cannot be measured and assumes values in a finite or infinite set of values, often named levels. For example, the weather is a categorical feature since it takes values in the discrete set (sunny, cloudy, snowy, rainy, and foggy). Other examples are features that contain URLs, IPs, items you put in your e-commerce cart, device IDs, and so on. On this data, you cannot define the equal to, greater than, and less than binary operators and therefore, you cannot rank them.

A plus point for both categorical and numerical values is Booleans. In fact, they can be seen as categorical (presence/absence of a feature) or, on the other hand, as the probability of a feature having an exhibit (has displayed, has not displayed). Since many machine learning algorithms do not allow the input to be categorical, Boolean features are often used to encode categorical features as numerical values.

Let's continue the example of the weather. If we want to map a feature, that contains the current weather and which takes values in the set [sunny, cloudy, snowy, rainy, and foggy] and encodes them to binary features, we should create five True/False features, with one for each level of the categorical feature. Now, the map is straightforward:

```
Categorical_feature = sunny   binary_features = [1, 0, 0, 0, 0]
Categorical_feature = cloudy  binary_features = [0, 1, 0, 0, 0]
Categorical_feature = snowy   binary_features = [0, 0, 1, 0, 0]
Categorical_feature = rainy   binary_features = [0, 0, 0, 1, 0]
Categorical_feature = foggy   binary_features = [0, 0, 0, 0, 1]
```

Only one binary feature reveals the presence of the categorical feature; the others remain 0. By this easy step, we moved from the categorical world to a numerical one. The price of this operation is its complexity in terms of memory and computations; instead of a single feature, we now have five features. Generically, instead of a single categorical feature with N possible levels, we will create N features, each with two numerical values (1/0). This operation is named dummy coding, or, more technically, binarization of nominal features.

The pandas package helps us in this operation, making the mapping easy with one command:

```
In: import pandas as pd
categorical_feature = pd.Series(['sunny', 'cloudy', 'snowy',
'rainy', 'foggy'])
mapping = pd.get_dummies(categorical_feature)
mapping
Out:
```

	cloudy	foggy	rainy	snowy	sunny
0	0.0	0.0	0.0	0.0	1.0
1	1.0	0.0	0.0	0.0	0.0
2	0.0	0.0	0.0	1.0	0.0
3	0.0	0.0	1.0	0.0	0.0
4	0.0	1.0	0.0	0.0	0.0

The output is a DataFrame that contains the categorical levels as column labels and the respective binary features along the column. To map a categorical value to a list of numerical ones, just use the power of pandas:

```
In: mapping['sunny']
Out:
0    1.0
1    0.0
2    0.0
3    0.0
4    0.0
Name: sunny, dtype: float64
In: mapping['cloudy']
Out:
0    0.0
1    1.0
2    0.0
3    0.0
4    0.0
Name: cloudy, dtype: float64
```

As seen in this example, sunny is mapped into the list of Boolean values (1, 0, 0, 0, 0), cloudy to (0, 1, 0, 0, 0), and so on.

The same operation can be done with another toolkit, scikit-learn. It's somehow more complex since you must first convert text to categorical indices, but the result is the same. Let's take a peek at the previous example again:

```
In:
from sklearn.preprocessing import OneHotEncoder
from sklearn.preprocessing import LabelEncoder
le = LabelEncoder()
ohe = OneHotEncoder()
levels = ['sunny', 'cloudy', 'snowy', 'rainy', 'foggy']
fit_levs = le.fit_transform(levels)
ohe.fit([[fit_levs[0]], [fit_levs[1]], [fit_levs[2]], [fit_levs[3]],
[fit_levs[4]]])
print (ohe.transform([le.transform(['sunny'])]).toarray())
print (ohe.transform([le.transform(['cloudy'])]).toarray())
Out:
[[ 0.  0.  0.  0.  1.]]
[[ 1.  0.  0.  0.  0.]]
```

Basically, `LabelEncoder` maps the text to a 0-to-*N* integer number (note that in this case, it's still a categorical variable since it makes no sense to rank it). Now, these five values are mapped to five binary variables.

A special type of data – text

Let's introduce another type of data. Text is a frequently used input for machine learning algorithms since it contains a natural representation of data in our language. It's so rich that it also contains the answer to what we're looking for. The most common approach when dealing with text is to use a bag of words. According to this approach, every word becomes a feature and the text becomes a vector that contains non-zero elements for all the features (that is, the words) in its body. Given a text dataset, what's the number of features? It is simple. Just extract all the unique words in it and enumerate them. For a very rich text that uses all the English words, that number is around 600,000. If you're not going to further process it (removal of third person, abbreviations, contractions, and acronyms), you might find yourself dealing with more than that, but that's a very rare case. In a plain and simple approach, which is the target of this book, we just let Python do its best.

The dataset used in this section is textual; it's the famous *20newsgroup* (for more information about this, visit `http://qwone.com/~jason/20Newsgroups/`). It is a collection of about 20,000 documents that belong to 20 topics of newsgroups. It's one of the most frequently used (if not the top most used) datasets presented while dealing with text classification and clustering. To import it, we're going to use only its restricted subset, which contains all the science topics (medicine and space):

```
In: from sklearn.datasets import fetch_20newsgroups
categories = ['sci.med', 'sci.space'] twenty_sci_news =
fetch_20newsgroups(categories=categories)
```

The first time you run this command, it automatically downloads the dataset and places it in the `$HOME/scikit_learn_data/20news_home/` default directory. You can query the dataset object by asking for the location of the files, their content, and the label (that is, the topic of the discussion where the document was posted). They're located in the `.filenames`, `.data`, and `.target` attributes of the object respectively:

```
In: print(twenty_sci_news.data[0])
Out: From: flb@flb.optiplan.fi ("F.Baube[tm]") Subject:
Vandalizing the sky
X-Added: Forwarded by Space Digest
Organization: [via International Space University]
Original-Sender: isu@VACATION.VENARI.CS.CMU.EDU
Distribution: sci
Lines: 12
```

```
From: "Phil G. Fraering" <pgf@srl03.cacs.usl.edu> [...]
In: twenty_sci_news.filenames
Out: array([
'/Users/datascientist/scikit_learn_data/20news_home/20news-bydate-
train/sci.space/61116',
'/Users/datascientist/scikit_learn_data/20news_home/20news- bydate-
train/sci.med/58122',
'/Users/datascientist/scikit_learn_data/20news_home/20news- bydate-
train/sci.med/58903',          ...,
'/Users/datascientist/scikit_learn_data/20news_home/20news- bydate-
train/sci.space/60774', [...]
In: print (twenty_sci_news.target[0])
print (twenty_sci_news.target_names[twenty_sci_news.target[0]])
Out:
1
sci.space
```

The target is categorical, but it's represented as an integer (0 for `sci.med` and 1 for `sci.space`). If you want to read it out, check against the index of the `twenty_sci_news.target` array.

The easiest way to deal with the text is by transforming the body of the dataset into a series of words. This means that for each document, the number of times a specific word appears in the body will be counted.

For example, let's make a small, easy-to-process dataset:

- `Document_1`: We love data science
- `Document_2`: Data science is great

In the entire dataset, which contains `Document_1` and `Document_2`, there are only six different words: we, `love`, `data`, `science`, `is`, and `great`. Given this array, we can associate each document with a feature vector:

```
Feature_Document_1 = [1 1 1 1 0 0]
Feature_Document_2 = [0 0 1 1 1 1]
```

Note that we're discarding the positions of the words and retaining only the number of times the word appears in the document. That's all.

In the *20newsletter* database, with Python, this can be done in a simple way:

```
In:
from sklearn.feature_extraction.text import CountVectorizer
count_vect = CountVectorizer()
word_count = count_vect.fit_transform(twenty_sci_news.data)
```

```
word_count.shape
Out: (1187, 25638)
```

First, we instantiate a `CountVectorizer` object. Then, we call the method to count the terms in each document and produce a feature vector for each of them (`fit_transform`). We then query the matrix size. Note that the output matrix is sparse because it's very common to have only a limited selection of words for each document (since the number of non-zero elements in each line is very low and it makes no sense to store all the redundant zeros). Anyway, the output shape is (1187, 25638). The first value is the number of observations in the dataset (the number of documents), while the latter is the number of features (the number of unique words in the dataset).

After the `CountVectorizer` transforms, each document is associated with its feature vector. Let's take a look at the first document:

```
In: print (word_count[0])
Out:
  (0, 10827)   2
  (0, 10501)   2
  (0, 17170)   1
  (0, 10341)   1
  (0, 4762)    2
  (0, 23381)   2
  (0, 22345)   1
  (0, 24461)   1
  (0, 23137)   7
  [...]
```

You can notice that the output is a sparse vector where only non-zero elements are stored. To check the direct correspondence to words, just try the following code:

```
In: word_list = count_vect.get_feature_names()
for n in word_count[0].indices:
    print ('Word "%s" appears %i times' % (word_list[n],
    word_count[0, n])) Out:  Word: from appears 2 times
Word: flb appears 2 times
Word: optiplan appears 1 times
Word: fi appears 1 times
Word: baube appears 2 times
Word: tm appears 2 times
Word: subject appears 1 times
Word: vandalizing appears 1 times
Word: the appears 7 times
[...]
```

So far, everything has been pretty simple, hasn't it? Let's move forward to another task of increasing complexity and effectiveness. Counting words is good, but we can manage more. Let's compute their frequency. It's a measure that you can compare across differently sized datasets. It gives an idea whether a word is a stop word (that is, a very common word such as a, an, the, or is) or a rare, unique one. Typically, these terms are the most important because they're able to characterize an instance and the features based on these words, which are very discriminative in the learning process. To retrieve the frequency of each word in each document, try the following code:

```
In:
from sklearn.feature_extraction.text import TfidfVectorizer
tf_vect = TfidfVectorizer(use_idf=False, norm='l1')
word_freq = tf_vect.fit_transform(twenty_sci_news.data)
word_list = tf_vect.get_feature_names()
for n in word_freq[0].indices:
    print ('Word "%s" has frequency %0.3f' % (word_list[n],
    word_freq[0, n]))
  Out:
Word "from" has frequency 0.022
Word "flb" has frequency 0.022
Word "optiplan" has frequency 0.011
Word "fi" has frequency 0.011
Word "baube" has frequency 0.022
Word "tm" has frequency 0.022
Word "subject" has frequency 0.011
Word "vandalizing" has frequency 0.011
Word "the" has frequency 0.077
[...]
```

The sum of the frequencies is 1 (or close to 1 due to the approximation). This happens because we chose the l1 norm. In this specific case, the word frequency is a probability distribution function. Sometimes, it's nice to increase the difference between rare and common words. In such cases, you can use the l2 norm to normalize the feature vector.

An even more effective way to vectorize text data is by using `Tfidf`. In brief, you can multiply the term frequency of the words that compose a document by the inverse document frequency of the word itself (that is, in the number of documents it appears, or in its logarithmically scaled transformation). This is very handy to highlight words that effectively describe each document and which are a powerful discriminative element among the dataset. `Tfidf` gained a lot of popularity since computers have started to process text data. The vast majority of search engines and information retrieval software have used it mainly for its effective way to measure sentence similarity and distance, making it an optimal solution to retrieve documents from a user-inserted text search query.

```
In:
from sklearn.feature_extraction.text import TfidfVectorizer
tfidf_vect = TfidfVectorizer() # Default: use_idf=True
word_tfidf = tfidf_vect.fit_transform(twenty_sci_news.data)
word_list = tfidf_vect.get_feature_names()
for n in word_tfidf[0].indices:
    print ('Word "%s" has tf-idf %0.3f' % (word_list[n],
    word_tfidf[0, n]))
Out:
Word "fred" has tf-idf 0.089
Word "twilight" has tf-idf 0.139
Word "evening" has tf-idf 0.113
Word "in" has tf-idf 0.024
Word "presence" has tf-idf 0.119
Word "its" has tf-idf 0.061
Word "blare" has tf-idf 0.150
Word "freely" has tf-idf 0.119
Word "may" has tf-idf 0.054
Word "god" has tf-idf 0.119
Word "blessed" has tf-idf 0.150
Word "is" has tf-idf 0.026
Word "profiting" has tf-idf 0.150
[...]
```

In this example, the four most information-rich words of the first documents are `caste`, `baube`, `flb`, and `tm` (they have the highest `tf-idf` score). This means that their term frequency within the document is high, whereas they're pretty rare in the remaining documents. In terms of information theory, their entropy is high within the document, while it's lower considering all the documents.

So far, for each word, we have generated a feature. What about taking a couple of words together? That's exactly what happens when you consider bigrams instead of unigrams. With bigrams (or generically, n-grams), the presence or absence of a word—as well as its neighbors—matters (that is, the words near it and their disposition). Of course, you can mix unigrams and n-grams and create a rich feature vector for each document. In a simple example, let's test how n-grams work:

```
In:
text_1 = 'we love data science'
text_2 = 'data science is hard'
documents = [text_1, text_2]
documents
Out: ['we love data science', 'data science is hard']
In: # That is what we say above, the default one
count_vect_1_grams = CountVectorizer(ngram_range=(1, 1),
stop_words=[], min_df=1)
word_count = count_vect_1_grams.fit_transform(documents)
word_list = count_vect_1_grams.get_feature_names()
print ("Word list = ", word_list)
print ("text_1 is described with", [word_list[n] + "(" +
str(word_count[0, n]) + ")" for n in word_count[0].indices])
Out:
Word list =  ['data', 'hard', 'is', 'love', 'science', 'we']
text_1 is described with ['we(1)', 'love(1)', 'data(1)',
'science(1)']
In: # Now a bi-gram count vectorizer
count_vect_1_grams = CountVectorizer(ngram_range=(2, 2))
word_count = count_vect_1_grams.fit_transform(documents)
word_list = count_vect_1_grams.get_feature_names()
print ("Word list = ", word_list)
print ("text_1 is described with", [word_list[n] + "(" +
str(word_count[0, n]) + ")" for n in word_count[0].indices])
 Out:
Word list =  ['data science', 'is hard', 'love data',
'science is', 'we love']
text_1 is described with ['we love(1)', 'love data(1)',
'data science(1)']
In: # Now a uni- and bi-gram count vectorizer
count_vect_1_grams = CountVectorizer(ngram_range=(1, 2))
word_count = count_vect_1_grams.fit_transform(documents)
word_list = count_vect_1_grams.get_feature_names()
print ("Word list = ", word_list)
print ("text_1 is described with", [word_list[n] + "(" +
str(word_count[0, n]) + ")" for n in word_count[0].indices])
Out:
Word list =  ['data', 'data science', 'hard', 'is', 'is hard',
'love', 'love data', 'science', 'science is', 'we', 'we love']
```

```
text_1 is described with ['we(1)', 'love(1)', 'data(1)',
'science(1)', 'we love(1)', 'love data(1)', 'data science(1)']
```

The preceding example very intuitively combines the first and second approach we previously presented. In this case, we used a `CountVectorizer`, but this approach is very common with a `TfidfVectorizer`. Note that the number of features explodes exponentially when you use n-grams.

If you have too many features (the dictionary may be too rich, there may be too many n-grams, or the computer may be just limited), you can use a trick that lowers the complexity of the problem (but you should first evaluate the trade-off performance / trade-off complexity). It's common to use the hashing trick where many words (or n-grams) are hashed and their hashes collide (which makes a bucket of words). Buckets are sets of semantically unrelated words but with colliding hashes. With `HashingVectorizer()`, as shown in the following example, you can decide the number of buckets of words you want. The resulting matrix, of course, reflects your setting:

```
In: from sklearn.feature_extraction.text import HashingVectorizer
hash_vect = HashingVectorizer(n_features=1000)
word_hashed = hash_vect.fit_transform(twenty_sci_news.data)
word_hashed.shape
Out: (1187, 1000)
```

Note that you can't invert the hashing process (since it's an irreversible summarization process). Therefore, after this transformation, you will have to work on the hashed features as they are. Hashing presents quite a few advantages: allowing quick transformation of a bag of words into vectors of features (hash buckets are our features in this case), easily accommodating never-previously-seen words among the features, and avoiding overfitting by having unrelated words collide together in the same feature.

Scraping the Web with Beautiful Soup

In the last section, we discussed how to operate on textual data, given the fact that we already have the dataset. What if we need to scrape a web page and download it manually?

This process happens more often than you might expect; and it's a very popular topic of interest in data science. For example:

- Financial institutions scrape the Web to extract fresh details and information about the companies in their portfolio. Newspapers, social networks, blogs, forums, and corporate websites are the ideal targets for these analyses.

- Advertisement and media companies analyze sentiment and the popularity of many pieces of the Web to understand people's reactions.
- Companies specialized in insight analysis and recommendation scrape the Web to understand patterns and model user behaviors.
- Comparison websites use the web to compare prices, products, and services, offering the user an updated synoptic table of the current situation.

Unfortunately, understanding websites is a very hard work since each website is built and maintained by different people, with different infrastructures, locations, languages, and structures. The only common aspect among them is represented by the standard exposed language, which, most of the time, is HTML.

That's why the vast majority of the web scrapers, available as of today, are only able to understand and navigate HTML pages in a general-purpose way. One of the most used web parsers is named Beautiful Soup. It's written in Python, and it's very stable and simple to use. Moreover, it's able to detect errors and pieces of malformed code in the HTML page (always remember that web pages are often human-made products and prone to errors).

A complete description of Beautiful Soup would require an entire book; here we will see just a few bits. First at all, Beautiful Soup is not a crawler. In order to download a web page, we should use the `urllib` library, for example.

Let's now download the code behind the William Shakespeare page on Wikipedia:

```
In: import urllib.request
url = 'https://en.wikipedia.org/wiki/William_Shakespeare'
request = urllib.request.Request(url)
response = urllib.request.urlopen(request)
```

It's time to instruct Beautiful Soup to read the resource and parse it using the HTML parser:

```
In: from bs4 import BeautifulSoup
soup = BeautifulSoup(response, 'html.parser')
```

Now the `soup` is ready, and can be queried. To extract the title, we can simply ask for the title attribute:

```
In: soup.title
Out: <title>William Shakespeare - Wikipedia, the free encyclopedia</title>
```

As you can see, the whole title tag is returned, allowing a deeper investigation of the nested HTML structure. What if we want to know the categories associated with the Wikipedia page of William Shakespeare? It can be very useful to create a graph of the entry, simply recurrently downloading and parsing adjacent pages. We should first manually analyze the HTML page itself to figure out what's the best HTML tag containing the information we're looking for. Remember here the "no free lunch" theorem in data science: there are no auto-discovery functions, and furthermore, things can change if Wikipedia modifies its format.

After a manual analysis, we discover that categories are inside a div named "mw-normal-catlinks"; excluding the first link, all the others are okay. Now it's time to program. Let's put into code what we've observed, printing for each category, the title of the linked page and the relative link to it:

```
In:
section = soup.find_all(id='mw-normal-catlinks')[0]
for catlink in section.find_all("a")[1:]:
    print(catlink.get("title"), "->", catlink.get("href"))
Out:
Category:William Shakespeare -> /wiki/Category:William_Shakespeare
Category:1564 births -> /wiki/Category:1564_births
Category:1616 deaths -> /wiki/Category:1616_deaths
Category:16th-century English male actors -> /wiki/Category:16th-
century_English_male_actors
Category:English male stage actors ->
/wiki/Category:English_male_stage_actors
Category:16th-century English writers -> /wiki/Category:16th-
century_English_writers
```

We've used the find_all method twice to find all the HTML tags with the text contained in the argument. In the first case, we were specifically looking for an ID; in the second case, we were looking for all the "a" tags.

Given the output then, and using the same code with the new URLs, it's possible to download recursively the Wikipedia category pages, arriving at this point at the ancestor categories.

A final note about scraping: always remember that this practice is not always allowed, and when so, remember to tune down the rate of the download (at high rates, the website's server may think you're doing a small-scale DoS attack and will probably blacklist/ban your IP address). For more information, you can read the terms and conditions of the website, or simply contact the administrators. Downloading data from various sites where there are copyright laws in place is bound to get you into real legal trouble. That's also why most companies that employ web scraping use external vendors for this task, or have a special arrangement with the site owners.

Data processing with NumPy

Having introduced the essential pandas commands to upload and preprocess your data in memory completely, in smaller batches, or even in single data rows, at this point of the data science pipeline you'll have to work on it in order to prepare a suitable data matrix for your supervised and unsupervised learning procedures.

As a best practice, we advise that you divide the task between a phase of your work when your data is still heterogeneous (a mix of numerical and symbolic values) and another phase when it is turned into a numeric table of data. A table of data, or matrix, is arranged in rows that represent your examples, and columns that contain the characteristic observed values of your examples, which are your variables.

Following our advice, you have to wrangle between two key Python packages for scientific analysis, pandas and NumPy, and their two pivotal data structures, DataFrame and `ndarray`. But your data science pipeline will be more efficient and fast.

Since the target data structure that we want to feed into the following machine learning phase is a matrix represented by the `NumPy ndarray` object, let's start from the result we want to achieve, that is, how to generate an `ndarray` object.

NumPy's n-dimensional array

Python presents native data structures such as lists and dictionaries, which you should use to the best of your ability. Lists, for example, can store sequentially heterogeneous objects (for instance, you can save numbers, texts, images, and sounds in the same list). On the other hand, being based on a lookup table (a hash table), dictionaries can recall content. The content can be any Python object, and often it is a list of another dictionary. Thus, dictionaries allow you to access complex, multidimensional data structures.

Anyway, lists and dictionaries have their own limitations. First, there's the problem with memory and speed. They are not really optimized for using nearly contiguous chunks of memory, and this may become a problem when trying to apply highly optimized algorithms or multiprocessor computations, because the memory handling may turn into a bottleneck. Then, they are excellent for storing data but not for operating on it. Therefore, whatever you may want to do with your data, you have to first define custom functions and iterate or map over the list or dictionary elements. Iterating may often prove suboptimal when working on a large amount of data.

NumPy offers an `ndarray` object class (n-dimensional array) that has the following attributes:

- It is memory optimal (and, besides other aspects, configured to transmit data to C or Fortran routines in the best-performing layout of memory blocks)
- It allows fast linear algebra computations (vectorization) and element-wise operations (broadcasting) without any need to use iterations with for loops, which is generally computationally expensive in Python
- Critical libraries, such as SciPy or scikit-learn, expect arrays as an input for their functions to operate correctly

All of this comes with some limitations. In fact, `ndarray` objects have the following drawbacks:

- They usually store only elements of a single, specific data type, which you can define beforehand (but there's a way to define complex data and heterogeneous data types, though they could be very difficult to handle for analysis purposes).
- After they are initialized, their size is fixed. If you want to change their shape, you have to create them anew.

The basics of NumPy ndarray objects

In Python, an array is a block of memory-contiguous data of a specific type with a header that contains the indexing scheme and the data type descriptor.

Thanks to the indexing scheme, an array can represent a multidimensional data structure where each element is indexed with a tuple of n integers, where n is the number of dimensions. Therefore, if your array is unidimensional, that is, a vector of sequential data, the index will start from zero (as in Python lists).

If it is bidimensional, you'll have to use two integers as an index (a tuple of coordinates of the type x, y); if there are three dimensions, the number of integers used will be three (a tuple x, y, z), and so on.

At each indexed location, the array will contain data of the specified data type. An array can store many numerical data types, as well as strings, and other Python objects. It is also possible to create custom data types and therefore handle data sequences of different types, though we advise against it and we suggest that you should use the pandas DataFrame in such cases. pandas data structures are indeed much more flexible for any intensive usage of heterogeneous data types as necessary for a data scientist. Consequently, in this book we will consider only NumPy arrays of a specific, defined type and leave pandas to deal with heterogeneity.

Since the type (and the memory space it occupies in terms of bytes) of an array should be defined from the beginning, the array creation procedure reserves the exact memory space to contain all the data. The access, modification, and computation of the elements of an array are therefore quite fast, though this also consequently implies that the array is fixed and cannot be changed in its structure.

The Python list data structure is actually very cumbersome and slow, being a collection of pointers linking the list structure to the scattered memory locations containing the data itself. Instead, as depicted in the following figure, a NumPy ndarray is made of just a pointer addressing a single memory location where data, arranged sequentially, is stored. When you access the data in a NumPy ndarray you'll actually require fewer operations and less access to different memory parts than when using a list, hence the major efficiency and speed when working with large amounts of data. As a drawback, data connected to a NumPy array cannot be changed; it has to be recreated when inserting or removing data.

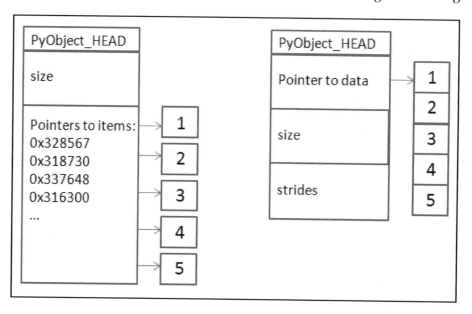

No matter the dimensions of the NumPy array, data will always be arranged as a continuous sequence of values (a contiguous block of memory). It is the knowledge of the size of the array and of the strides (telling us how many bytes we have to skip in memory to move to the next position along a certain axis) that makes it easy to correctly represent and operate on the array.

In contrast, list data structures, when they require representing multiple dimensions, cannot but turn themselves into nested lists, thus increasing both overhead and memory fragmentation when accessing data.

That may sound like a computer scientist's blabbering, after all data scientists do care just about getting Python do something useful and quickly. That's surely true, but doing something quickly from a syntactic point of view, sometimes doesn't automatically equate into doing something quick from the point of view of the execution itself. If you can grasp the internals of NumPy and pandas, you could really make your code speed up and achieve more in your project in less time. We have experience of synthetically correct data munging code using NumPy and pandas that, by the right refactoring, reduced its execution time by 95%!

For our purposes, it is also very important to understand that when accessing or transforming an array, we may be just viewing it or we may be copying it. When we are *viewing* an array, we actually call a procedure that allows us to convert the data present in its structure into something else, but the sourcing array is unaltered. Based on the previous example, when viewing, we are just changing the size attribute of an `ndarray`; the data is left untouched. Consequently, any data transformation experienced when viewing an array is merely ephemeral, unless we fix it into a new array.

Instead, when we are *copying* an array, we are effectively creating a new array with a different structure (thus occupying fresh memory). We do not just change the parameter relative to the size of the array; we are also reserving another sequential chunk of memory and copying our data there.

All pandas DataFrames are actually made of one-dimensional NumPy arrays. For this reason, they inherit the speed and memory efficiency of `ndarrays` when you operate by columns (since each column is a NumPy array). When operating by rows, DataFrames are more inefficient because you are accessing sequentially different columns, that is, different NumPy arrays. For the same reason, it is speedier to address portions of a pandas DataFrame by a positional index, not by a pandas index, because NumPy arrays work using integer numbers as positions. Using pandas indexes (which can be also textual, not just numerical) actually requires a transformation of the index into its corresponding position in order for the DataFrame to operate correctly on the data.

Creating NumPy arrays

There is more than one way to create NumPy arrays. The following are some of the ways:

- Transforming an existing data structure into an array
- Creating an array from scratch and populating it with default or calculated values
- Uploading some data from a disk into an array

If you are going to transform an existing data structure, the odds are in favor of you working with a structured list or a pandas DataFrame.

From lists to unidimensional arrays

One of the most common situations you will encounter when working with data is the transforming of a list into an array.

When operating such a transformation, it is important to consider the objects the lists contain because this will determine the dimensionality and the dtype of the resulting array.

Let's start with the first example of a list containing just integers:

```
In: import numpy as np
In:  # Transform a list into a uni-dimensional array
list_of_ints = [1,2,3]
Array_1 = np.array(list_of_ints)
In: Array_1
Out: array([1, 2, 3])
```

Remember that you can access a one-dimensional array as you do with a standard Python list (the indexing starts from zero):

```
In: Array_1[1] # let's output the second value
Out: 2
```

We can ask for further information about the type of the object and the type of its elements (the effectively resulting type depends on whether your system is 32-bit or 64-bit):

```
In: type(Array_1)
Out: numpy.ndarray
In: Array_1.dtype
Out: dtype('int64')
```

The default `dtype` depends on the system you're operating.

Our simple list of integers will turn into a one-dimensional array, that is, a vector of 32-bit integers (ranging from -231 to 231-1, the default integer on the platform we used for our examples).

Controlling the memory size

You may think that it is a waste of memory to use an `int64` data type if the range of your values is so limited.

In fact, conscious of data-intensive situations, you can calculate how much memory space your `Array_1` object is taking:

```
In: import numpy as np
In: Array_1.nbytes
Out: 24
```

Note that on 32-bit platforms (or when using a 32-bit Python version on a 64-bit platform), the result is 12.

In order to save memory, you can specify beforehand the type that best suits your array:

```
In: Array_1 = np.array(list_of_ints, dtype= 'int8')
```

Now, your simple array occupies just a fourth of the previous memory space. It may seem an obvious and overly simplistic example, but when dealing with millions of rows and columns, defining the best data type for your analysis can really save the day, allowing you to fit everything nicely into memory.

For your reference, here are a few tables that present the most common data types for data science applications and their memory usage for a single element:

Type	Size in bytes	Description
bool	1	**Boolean (**True **or** False**) stored as a byte**
int_	4	Default integer type (normally int32 or int64)
int8	1	Byte (-128 to 127)
int16	2	Integer (-32,768 to 32,767)
int32	4	Integer (-2**31 to 2**31-1)
int64	8	Integer (-2**63 to 2**63-1)
uint8	1	Unsigned integer (0 to 255)
uint16	2	Unsigned integer (0 to 65,535)
uint32	3	Unsigned integer (0 to 2**32-1)
uint64	4	Unsigned integer (0 to 2**64-1)
float_	8	Shorthand for float64
float16	2	Half-precision float (exponent 5 bits, mantissa 10 bits)
float32	4	Single-precision float (exponent 8 bits, mantissa 23 bits)
float64	8	Double-precision float (exponent 11 bits, mantissa 52 bits)

There are some more numerical types, such as complex number, that are less usual but which may be required by your application (for example, in a spectrogram). You can get the complete idea from the NumPy user guide at http://docs.scipy.org/doc/numpy/user/basics.types.html.

If an array has a type that you want to change, you can easily create a new array by casting a new specified type:

```
In: Array_1b = Array_1.astype('float32')
Array_1b
Out: array([ 1.,   2.,   3.], dtype=float32)
```

In case your array is quite memory consuming, note that the .astype method will copy the array, and thus it always creates a new array.

Heterogeneous lists

What if the list were made of heterogeneous elements, such as integers, floats, and strings? This gets trickier. A quick example can describe the situation to you:

```
In: import numpy as np
complex_list = [1,2,3] + [1.,2.,3.] + ['a','b','c']
Array_2 = np.array(complex_list[:3]) # at first the input list
is just ints
print ('complex_list[:3]', Array_2.dtype)
Array_2 = np.array(complex_list[:6]) # then it is ints and floats
print ('complex_list[:6]', Array_2.dtype)
Array_2 = np.array(complex_list) # finally we add strings
print ('complex_list[:] ',Array_2.dtype)
Out:
complex_list[:3] int64
complex_list[:6] float64
complex_list[:]   <U32
```

As explicated by our output, it seems that float types prevail over int types and strings (<U32 means a unicode string of size 32 or less) take over everything else.

While creating an array using lists, you can mix different elements, and the most Pythonic way to check the results is by questioning the dtype of the resulting array.

Be aware that if you are uncertain about the contents of your array, you really have to check. Otherwise, you may later find it impossible to operate on your resulting array and you may incur an error (unsupported operand type):

```
In: # Check if a NumPy array is of the desired numeric type
print (isinstance(Array_2[0],np.number))
Out: False
```

In our data munging process, unintentionally finding out an array of the string type as output would mean that we forgot to transform all the variables into numeric ones in the previous steps—for example, when all the data was stored in a pandas DataFrame. In the section, *Working with categorical and text data*, we provided some simple and straightforward ways to deal with such situations.

Before that, let's complete our overview of how to derive an array from a list object. As we mentioned before, the type of objects in the list influences the dimensionality of the array, too.

From lists to multidimensional arrays

If a list containing numeric or textual objects is rendered into a unidimensional array (that could represent a coefficient vector, for instance), a list of lists translates into a two-dimensional array and a list of list of lists becomes a three-dimensional one:

```
In: import numpy as np
# Transform a list into a bidimensional array
a_list_of_lists = [[1,2,3],[4,5,6],[7,8,9]]
Array_2D = np.array(a_list_of_lists )
Array_2D
Out:
array([[1, 2, 3],
       [4, 5, 6],
       [7, 8, 9]])
```

As mentioned before, you can call out single values with indices, as in a list, though here you'll have two indices—one for the row dimension (also called axis 0) and one for the column dimension (axis 1):

```
In: Array_2D[1,1]
Out: 5
```

Two-dimensional arrays are usually the norm in data science problems, though three-dimensional arrays may be found when a dimension represents time, for instance:

```
In: # Transform a list into a multi-dimensional array
a_list_of_lists_of_lists = [[[1,2],[3,4],[5,6]],
[[7,8],[9,10],[11,12]]]
Array_3D = np.array(a_list_of_lists_of_lists)
Array_3D
Out:
array([[[ 1,  2],
        [ 3,  4],
        [ 5,  6]],
       [[ 7,  8],
        [ 9, 10],
        [11, 12]]])
```

To access single elements of a three-dimensional array, you just have to point out three indexes:

```
In: Array_3D[0,2,0] # Accessing the 5th element
Out: 5
```

Arrays can be made from tuples in a way that is similar to the method of creating lists. Also, dictionaries can be turned into two-dimensional arrays thanks to the `.items()` method, which returns a copy of the dictionary's list of key-value pairs:

```
In: np.array({1:2,3:4,5:6}.items()) Out:
array([[1, 2],      [3, 4],      [5, 6]])
```

Resizing arrays

Earlier, we mentioned how you can change the type of the elements of an array. We will now stop a while to examine the most common instructions to modify the shape of an existing array.

Let's start with an example that uses the `.reshape` method, which accepts as a parameter an *n*-tuple containing the size of the new dimensions:

```
In: import numpy as np
# Restructuring a NumPy array shape
original_array = np.array([1, 2, 3, 4, 5, 6, 7, 8])
Array_a = original_array.reshape(4,2)
Array_b = original_array.reshape(4,2).copy()
Array_c = original_array.reshape(2,2,2)
# Attention because reshape creates just views, not copies
original_array[0] = -1
```

Our original array is a unidimensional vector of integer numbers from one to eight.

- We assign `Array_a` to a reshaped `original_array` of size 4 x 2
- We do the same with `Array_b`, though we append the `.copy()` method, which will copy the array into a new one
- We assign `Array_c` to a reshaped array in three dimensions of size 2 x 2 x 2
- After having done this, the first element of `original_array` is changed in value from 1 to –1

Now, if we check the content of our arrays, we will notice that `Array_a` and `Array_c`, though they have the desired shape, are characterized by –1 as the first element. That's because they dynamically mirror the original array they are a view from:

```
In: Array_a
Out:
array([[-1, 2],
       [3, 4],
```

```
        [5, 6],
        [7, 8]])
In: Array_c
Out:
array([[[-1,  2],
        [3,  4]],
       [[ 5,  6],
        [7,  8]]])
```

Only the `Array_b` array, having been copied before mutating the original array, has a first element with a value of 1:

```
In: Array_b
Out:
array([[1, 2],
       [3, 4],
       [5, 6],
       [7, 8]])
```

If it is necessary to change the shape of the original array, then the `resize` method is to be favored.

```
In: original_array.resize(4,2)      original_array
Out:   array([[-1,  2],
        [ 3,  4],
        [ 5,  6],
        [ 7,  8]])
```

The same results may be obtained by acting on the `.shape` value and assigning a tuple of values representing the size of the intended dimensions:

```
In: original_array.shape = (4,2)
```

Instead, if your array is two-dimensional and you need to exchange the rows with the columns, that is, to transpose the array, the `.T` or `.transpose()` methods will help you obtain such a kind of transformation (which is a view, like `.reshape`):

```
In: original_array
Out:
array([[-1,  2],
       [ 3,  4],
       [ 5,  6],
       [ 7,  8]])
```

Arrays derived from NumPy functions

If you need a vector or a matrix characterized by particular numeric series (zeros, ones, a series of ordinal numbers, and random numbers from particular statistical distributions), NumPy functions provide you with quite a large range of choices.

First, creating a NumPy array of ordinal values (integers) is straightforward if you use the `arange` function, which returns integer values in a given interval (usually from zero) and reshapes its results:

```
In: import numpy as np
In: ordinal_values = np.arange(9).reshape(3,3)
ordinal_values
Out:
array([[0, 1, 2],
       [3, 4, 5],
       [6, 7, 8]])
```

If the array has to be reversed in the order of values, use the following command:

```
In: np.arange(9)[::-1] Out: array([8, 7, 6, 5, 4, 3, 2, 1, 0])
```

If the integers are just random (with no order and possibly repeated), provide the following command:

```
In: np.random.randint(low=1,high=10,size=(3,3)).reshape(3,3)
```

Other useful arrays either are made of just zeros and ones, or are identity matrices:

```
In: np.zeros((3,3))
In: np.ones((3,3))
In: np.eye(3)
```

If the array will be used for a grid-search to search optimal parameters, fractional values in an interval or a logarithmic growth should prove most useful:

```
In: fractions = np.linspace(start=0, stop=1, num=10)
In: growth = np.logspace(start=0, stop=1, num=10, base=10.0)
```

Also, statistical distributions such as normal or uniform may be handy for the initialization of a vector or matrix of coefficients.

A 3 x 3 matrix of standardized normal values (mean=0, std=1):

```
In: std_gaussian = np.random.normal(size=(3,3))
```

If you need to specify a different mean and standard deviation, just give the following command:

```
In: gaussian = np.random.normal(loc=1.0, scale= 3.0, size=(3,3))
```

The `loc` parameter stands for the mean and the `scale` is actually the standard deviation.

Another frequent choice for a statistical distribution that is used to initialize a vector is certainly the uniform distribution:

```
In: rand = np.random.uniform(low=0.0, high=1.0, size=(3,3))
```

Getting an array directly from a file

NumPy arrays can also be created directly from the data present in a file.

Let's use an example from the previous chapter:

```
In: import numpy as np
housing = np.loadtxt('regression-datasets-
housing.csv',delimiter=',', dtype=float)
```

NumPy `loadtxt`, given a `filename`, `delimiter`, and `dtype`, will upload the data to an array, unless the `dtype` is wrong; for instance, there's a `string` variable and the required array type is a `float`, as shown in the following example:

```
In: np.loadtxt('datasets-uci-iris.csv',delimiter=',',dtype=float)
Out: ValueError: could not convert string to float: Iris-setosa
```

Extracting data from pandas

Interacting with pandas is quite easy. In fact, with pandas being built upon NumPy, arrays can easily be extracted from DataFrame objects, and they can be transformed into DataFrames themselves.

First, let's upload some data into a DataFrame. The `BostonHouse` example we downloaded in the previous chapter from the ML repository is suitable:

```
In: import pandas as pd
import numpy as np
housing_filename = 'regression-datasets-housing.csv'
housing = pd.read_csv(housing_filename, header=None)
```

This example assumes, of course, that you are operating on the same directory as the data file. In case you are operating on a different directory, you should add the directory path in the `housing_filename` variable. Depending on your system, which could be Windows (thus using \ backslashes) or Unix/Mac (using / the forward slash), you have to write the correct full address. Luckily, the `os.path.join()` function can make your code compatible across platforms and your job easier (since it outputs the right solution for the system it is run in). For instance, if your file is in the `mydir` directory, just change the code snippet to:

```
In: import pandas as pd
import os
import numpy as np
housing_filename = os.path.join('mydir',
                    'regression-datasets-housing.csv')
housing = pd.read_csv(housing_filename, header=None)
```

As demonstrated in the *Heterogeneous lists* section, at this point the `.values` method will extract an array of a type that accommodates all the different types present in the DataFrame:

```
In: housing_array = housing.values
housing_array.dtype
Out: dtype('float64')
```

In such a case, the selected type is `float64` because the float type prevails over the `int` type:

```
In: housing.dtypes
Out:  0        float64
1          int64
2        float64
3          int64
4        float64
5        float64
6        float64
7        float64
8          int64
9          int64
10         int64
11       float64
12       float64
13       float64
dtype: object
```

Asking for the types used by the DataFrame object before extracting your NumPy array by using the `.dtypes` method on the DataFrame allows you to anticipate the `dtype` of the resulting array. Consequently, it allows you to decide whether to transform or change the type of the variables in the DataFrame object before proceeding (please consult the *Working with categorical and text data* section of this chapter).

NumPy's fast operations and computations

When arrays need to be manipulated by mathematical operations, you just need to apply the operation on the array with respect to a numerical constant (a scalar) or an array of the same shape:

```
In: import numpy as np
In: a =  np.arange(5).reshape(1,5)
In: a += 1
In: a*a
Out: array([[ 1,   4,   9, 16, 25]])
```

As a result, the operation is to be performed element-wise; that is, every element of the array is operated by either the scalar value or the corresponding element of the other array.

When operating on arrays of different dimensions, it is still possible to obtain element-wise operations without having to restructure the data if one of the corresponding dimensions is 1. In fact, in such a case, the dimension of size 1 is stretched until it matches the dimension of the corresponding array. This conversion is called **broadcasting**. This is NumPy's way of performing mathematical operations between arrays with different shapes and has the main benefits of helping you to write more elegant and better performing code.

For instance:

```
In: a = np.arange(5).reshape(1,5) + 1 b = np.arange(5).reshape(5,1)
+ 1 a * b
Out:  array([[ 1,   2,   3,   4,   5],        [ 2,   4,   6,   8, 10],
        [ 3,   6,   9, 12, 15],        [ 4,   8, 12, 16, 20],
        [ 5, 10, 15, 20, 25]])
```

The preceding code is equivalent to the following:

```
In: a2 = np.array([1,2,3,4,5] * 5).reshape(5,5)
b2 = a2.T
a2 * b2
```

However, it won't require an expansion of memory of the original arrays in order to obtain pair-wise multiplication.

Furthermore, there exists a wide range of NumPy functions that can operate element-wise on arrays: abs(), sign(), round(), floor(), sqrt(), log(), and exp().

Other usual operations that could be operated by NumPy functions are sum() and prod(), which provide the summation and product of the array rows or columns on the basis of the specified axis:

```
In: print (a2)
Out:
[[1 2 3 4 5]
 [1 2 3 4 5]
 [1 2 3 4 5]
 [1 2 3 4 5]
 [1 2 3 4 5]]
In: np.sum(a2, axis=0)
Out: array([ 5, 10, 15, 20, 25])
In: np.sum(a2, axis=1)
Out: array([15, 15, 15, 15, 15])
```

When operating on your data, remember that operations and NumPy functions on arrays are extremely fast when compared to simple Python lists. Let's try out a couple of experiments. First, let's try to compare a list comprehension to an array when dealing with a sum of a constant:

```
In:  %timeit -n 1 -r 3 [i+1.0 for i in range(10**6)]
%timeit -n 1 -r 3 np.arange(10**6)+1.0
Out:  1 loops, best of 3: 158 ms per loop
1 loops, best of 3: 6.64 ms per loop
```

On IPython, %time allows you to easily benchmark operations. The -n 1 parameter just requires the benchmark to execute the code snippet for only one loop; -r 3 requires you to retry the execution of the loops (in this case, just one loop) three times and report the best performance recorded from such repetitions.

Results on your computer may vary depending on your configuration and operating system. Anyway, the difference between the standard Python operations and the NumPy ones will remain quite large. Though unnoticeable when working on small datasets, this difference can really impact your analysis when dealing with larger data or looping over and over the same analysis pipeline for parameter or variable selection.

This also happens when applying sophisticated operations, such as finding a square root:

```
In:   import math
%timeit -n 1 -r 3 [math.sqrt(i) for i in range(10**6)]
Out:
1 loops, best of 3: 222 ms per loop
In:   %timeit -n 1 -r 3 np.sqrt(np.arange(10**6))
Out:  1 loops, best of 3: 6.9 ms per loop
```

Matrix operations

Apart from element-wise calculations using the np.dot() function, you can also apply multiplications to your two-dimensional arrays based on matrix calculations such as vector-matrix and matrix-matrix multiplications:

```
In: import numpy as np
M = np.arange(5*5, dtype=float).reshape(5,5)
M
Out:
 array([[  0.,    1.,    2.,    3.,    4.],
        [  5.,    6.,    7.,    8.,    9.],
        [ 10.,   11.,   12.,   13.,   14.],
        [ 15.,   16.,   17.,   18.,   19.],
        [ 20.,   21.,   22.,   23.,   24.]])
```

As an example, we create a 5 x 5 two-dimensional array of ordinal numbers from 0 to 24.

We will then define a vector of coefficients and an array column stacking the vector and its reverse:

```
In: coefs = np.array([1., 0.5, 0.5, 0.5, 0.5])
coefs_matrix = np.column_stack((coefs,coefs[::-1]))
print (coefs_matrix)
Out:
[[ 1.    0.5]
 [ 0.5  0.5]
 [ 0.5  0.5]
 [ 0.5  0.5]
 [ 0.5  1. ]]
```

We can now multiply the array with the vector using the np.dot function:

```
In: np.dot(M,coefs)
Out: array([  5.,   20.,   35.,   50.,   65.])
```

Or the vector by the array:

```
In: np.dot(coefs,M)
Out: array([ 25.,   28.,   31.,   34.,   37.])
```

Or the array by the stacked coefficient vectors (which is a 5 x 2 matrix):

```
In: np.dot(M,coefs_matrix)
Out:   array([[  5.,    7.],
         [ 20.,   22.],
         [ 35.,   37.],
         [ 50.,   52.],
         [ 65.,   67.]])
```

NumPy also offers an object class, matrix, which is actually a subclass of ndarray, inheriting all its attributes and methods. NumPy matrices are exclusively two-dimensional (as arrays are actually multi-dimensional) by default. When multiplied, they apply matrix products, not element-wise ones (the same happens when raising powers), and they have some special matrix methods (.H for the conjugate transpose and .I for the inverse). Apart from the convenience of operating in a fashion that is similar to that of MATLAB, they do not offer any other advantage. You may risk confusion in your scripts since you'll have to handle different product notations for matrix objects and arrays.

Since Python 3.5, a new operator, the @ (at) operator, dedicated to matrix multiplication, has been introduced in Python (the change is for all the packages in Python, not just NumPy). The introduction of this new operator brings a couple of advantages.

First, there won't be any more cases when the * operator will be meant to be used for matrix multiplication. The * operator will be used exclusively for element-wise operations—those operations where, having two matrices (or vectors) of the same dimension, you apply the operation between the elements having the same position in the two matrices.

Then, code that is representing formulas will gain in readability, thus becoming much easier to read and interpret. You won't have to evaluate operators (+, −, /, and *) and methods (.dot) together anymore, but only operators (+, −, /, *, and @).

You can learn more (this is just formal introduction, all you need to do is check the `.dot` method works with the operator @) and look at some examples of the application by reading the **Python Enhancement Proposal (PEP)** 465 at the Python Foundation website: `https://www.python.org/dev/peps/pep-0465/`

Slicing and indexing with NumPy arrays

Indexing allows us to take a view of an `ndarray` by pointing out what to visualize: either a slice of columns and rows, or an index.

Let's define a working array:

```
In: import numpy as np
M = np.arange(100, dtype=int).reshape(10,10)
```

Our array is a 10 x 10 two-dimensional array. We can initially start by slicing it to a single dimension. The notation for a single dimension is the same as that in Python lists:

```
[start_index_included:end_index_exclude:steps]
```

Let's say that we want to extract even rows from 2 to 8:

```
In: M[2:9:2,:]
Out:  array([[20, 21, 22, 23, 24, 25, 26, 27, 28, 29],
        [40, 41, 42, 43, 44, 45, 46, 47, 48, 49],
        [60, 61, 62, 63, 64, 65, 66, 67, 68, 69],
        [80, 81, 82, 83, 84, 85, 86, 87, 88, 89]])
```

After slicing the rows, we can furthermore slice the columns by taking only the columns from index 5:

```
In: M[2:9:2,5:]
Out:
array([[25, 26, 27, 28, 29],
        [45, 46, 47, 48, 49],
        [65, 66, 67, 68, 69],
        [85, 86, 87, 88, 89]])
```

As in the lists, it is possible to use negative index values in order to start counting from the end. Moreover, a negative number for parameters such as steps reverses the order of the output array, as in the following example, where the counting starts from column index 5 but in the reverse order and goes towards the index 0:

```
In: M[2:9:2,5::-1]
Out:
array([[25, 24, 23, 22, 21, 20],
       [45, 44, 43, 42, 41, 40],
       [65, 64, 63, 62, 61, 60],
       [85, 84, 83, 82, 81, 80]])
```

We can also create Boolean indexes that point out which rows and columns to select. Therefore, we can replicate the previous example by using a row_index and a col_index variable:

```
In: row_index = (M[:,0]>=20) & (M[:,0]<=80)
col_index = M[0,:]>=5
M[row_index,:][:,col_index]
Out:
array([[25, 26, 27, 28, 29],
       [35, 36, 37, 38, 39],
       [45, 46, 47, 48, 49],
       [55, 56, 57, 58, 59],
       [65, 66, 67, 68, 69],
       [75, 76, 77, 78, 79],
       [85, 86, 87, 88, 89]])
```

We cannot contextually use Boolean indexes on both columns and rows in the same square brackets, though we can apply the usual indexing to the other dimension using integer indexes. Consequently, we have to first operate a Boolean selection on rows and then reopen the square brackets and operate a second selection on the first, this time focusing on the columns.

If we need a global selection of elements in the array, we can also use a mask of Boolean values, as follows:

```
In: mask = (M>=20) & (M<=90) & ((M / 10.) % 1 >= 0.5)
M[mask]
Out:
array([25, 26, 27, 28, 29, 35, 36, 37, 38, 39, 45, 46, 47, 48,
49, 55, 56, 57, 58, 59, 65, 66, 67, 68, 69, 75, 76, 77, 78, 79,
85, 86, 87, 88, 89])
```

This approach is particularly useful if you need to operate on the partition of the array selected by the mask (for example, `M[mask]=0`).

Another way to point out which elements need to be selected from your array is by providing a row or column index consisting of integers. Such indexes may be defined either by a `np.where()` function that transforms a Boolean condition on an array into indexes, or by simply providing a sequence of integer indexes, where integers may be in a particular order or might even be repeated. Such an approach is called *fancy indexing*:

```
In: row_index = [1,1,2,7]
col_index = [0,2,4,8]
```

Having defined the indexes of your rows and columns, you have to apply them contextually to select elements whose coordinates are given by the tuple of values of both the indexes:

```
In: M[row_index,col_index]
Out: array([10, 12, 24, 78])
```

In this way, the selection will report the following points: $(1, 0), (1, 2), (2, 4)$, and $(7, 8)$. Otherwise, as seen before, you just have to select the rows first and then the columns, which are separated by square brackets:

```
In: M[row_index,:][:,col_index]
Out:
array([[10, 12, 14, 18],
       [10, 12, 14, 18],
       [20, 22, 24, 28],
       [70, 72, 74, 78]])
```

Finally, please remember that slicing and indexing are just views of the data. If you need to create new data from such views, you have to use the `.copy` method on the slice and assign it to another variable. Otherwise, any modification to the original array will be reflected on your slice and vice versa, a consequence that is usually highly undesirable. The `copy` method is shown here:

```
In: N = M[2:9:2,5:].copy()
```

Stacking NumPy arrays

When operating with two-dimensional data arrays, there are some common operations, such as the adding of data and variables, that NumPy functions can render easily and quickly.

The most common such operation is the addition of more rows to your array.

Let's create an array to start off with:

```
In: import numpy as np
dataset = np.arange(50).reshape(10,5)
```

Now, let's add a single row and a bunch of rows to be concatenated after each other:

```
In: single_line = np.arange(1*5).reshape(1,5)
a_few_lines = np.arange(3*5).reshape(3,5)
```

We can first try to add a single line:

```
In: np.vstack((dataset,single_line))
```

All you have to do is to provide a tuple containing the vertical array preceding it and the one following it. In our example, the same command can work if you have more lines to be added:

```
In: np.vstack((dataset,a_few_lines))
```

Or, if you want to add the same single line more than once, the tuple can represent the sequential structure of your newly concatenated array:

```
In: np.vstack((dataset,single_line,single_line))
```

Another common situation is when you have to add a new variable to an existing array. In this case, you have to use `hstack` (h stands for horizontal) instead of the just-presented `vstack` command (where v is vertical).

Let's pretend that you have to add a `bias` of unit values to your original array:

```
In: bias = np.ones(10).reshape(10,1) np.hstack((dataset,bias))
```

Without reshaping `bias` (this, therefore, can be any data sequence of the same length as the rows of the array), you can add it as a sequence using the `column_stack()` function, which obtains the same result but with fewer concerns regarding data reshaping:

```
In: bias = np.ones(10)
np.column_stack((dataset,bias))
```

Adding rows and columns to two-dimensional arrays is basically all that you need to effectively wrangle your data in data science projects. Now, let's see a couple of more specific functions for slightly different data problems.

First, though two-dimensional arrays are the norm, you can also operate on a three-dimensional data structure. So `dstack()`, which is analogous to `hstack()` and `vstack()` but operates on the third axis (depth wise), will come in quite handy:

```
In: np.dstack((dataset*1,dataset*2,dataset*3))
```

In this example, the third dimension offers the original two-dimensional array with a multiplicand, presenting a progressive rate of change (a time or change dimension).

A further problematic variation could be the insertion of a row or, more frequently, a column to a specific position into your array. As you may recall, arrays are contiguous chunks of memory. Insertion actually requires the recreation of a new array, splitting the original array. The NumPy `insert` command helps you to do so in a fast and hassle-free way:

```
In:   np.insert(dataset, 3, bias, axis=1)
```

You just have to define the array where you wish to insert (`dataset`), the position (index 3), the sequence you want to insert (in this case, the array `bias`), and the axis along which you would like to operate the insertion (axis 1 is the vertical axis).

Naturally, you can insert entire arrays (not just vectors), such as bias, by ensuring that the array to be inserted is aligned with the dimension along which we are operating the insertion. In this example, in order to insert the same array into itself, we have to transpose it as an inserted element:

```
In: np.insert(dataset, 3, dataset.T, axis=1)
```

You can also make insertions on different axes (in the following case, axis 0, which is the horizontal one, but you can also operate on any dimension of an array that you may have):

```
In: np.insert(dataset, 3, np.ones(5), axis=0)
```

What is being done is that the original array is split at the specified position along the chosen axis. Then, the split data is concatenated with the new data to be inserted.

Summary

In this chapter, we discussed how pandas and NumPy can provide you with all the tools to load and effectively munge your data.

We started with pandas and its data structures, DataFrames and Series, and conducted you through to the final NumPy two-dimensional array, a data structure suitable for subsequent experimentation and machine learning. In doing so, we touched upon subjects such as the manipulation of vectors and matrices, categorical data encoding, textual data processing, fixing missing data and errors, slicing and dicing, merging, and stacking.

pandas and NumPy surely offer many more functions than the essential building blocks we presented here—the commands and procedures illustrated. You can now take any available raw data and apply all the cleaning and shaping transformations necessary for your data science project.

In the next chapter, we will take our data operations to the next step. In this chapter, we overviewed all the essential data munging operations necessary for a machine learning process to work. In the next chapter, we will discuss all the operations that can potentially improve or even boost your results.

3
The Data Pipeline

So far, we've explored how to load data into Python and process it to create a bi-dimensional NumPy array containing numerical values (your dataset). Now, we are ready to immerse ourselves fully in data science, extract meaning from data, and develop potential data products. This chapter on data treatment and transformations and the next one on machine learning are the most challenging sections of the entire book.

In this chapter, you will learn how to:

- Briefly explore data and create new features
- Reduce the dimensionality of data
- Spot and treat outliers
- Decide on the best score or loss metrics for your project
- Apply scientific methodology and effectively test the performance of your machine learning hypothesis
- Reduce the complexity of the data science problem by decreasing the number of features
- Optimize your learning parameters

Introducing EDA

Exploratory Data Analysis (EDA), or data exploration, is the first step in the data science process. John Tukey coined this term in 1977, when he wrote a book emphasizing the importance of EDA. EDA is required to understand a dataset better, check its features and its shape, validate an initial hypothesis, and get a preliminary idea about the next step that you want to pursue in the following data science tasks.

In this section, you will work on the iris dataset, which was already used in the previous chapter. First, let's load the dataset:

```
In: import pandas as pd
iris_filename = 'datasets-uci-iris.csv'
iris = pd.read_csv(iris_filename, header=None,
names= ['sepal_length', 'sepal_width',
'petal_length', 'petal_width', 'target'])
iris.head()
Out:
```

	sepal_length	sepal_width	petal_length	petal_width	target
0	5.1	3.5	1.4	0.2	Iris-setosa
1	4.9	3.0	1.4	0.2	Iris-setosa
2	4.7	3.2	1.3	0.2	Iris-setosa
3	4.6	3.1	1.5	0.2	Iris-setosa
4	5.0	3.6	1.4	0.2	Iris-setosa

Great! Using a few commands, you have already loaded the dataset. Now, the investigation phase starts. Some great insights are provided by the .describe() method, which can be used as follows:

```
In: iris.describe()
Out:
```

	sepal_length	sepal_width	petal_length	petal_width
count	150.000000	150.000000	150.000000	150.000000
mean	5.843333	3.054000	3.758667	1.198667
std	0.828066	0.433594	1.764420	0.763161
min	4.300000	2.000000	1.000000	0.100000
25%	5.100000	2.800000	1.600000	0.300000
50%	5.800000	3.000000	4.350000	1.300000
75%	6.400000	3.300000	5.100000	1.800000
max	7.900000	4.400000	6.900000	2.500000

For all numerical features, you have the number of observations, their respective average value, standard deviation, minimum and maximum values, and some routinely reported quantiles (at 25 percent, 50 percent, and 75 percent), the so-called quartiles. This provides you with a good idea about the distribution of each feature. If you want to visualize this information, just use the `boxplot()` method, as follows:

```
In: boxes = iris.boxplot(return_type='axes')
Out:
```

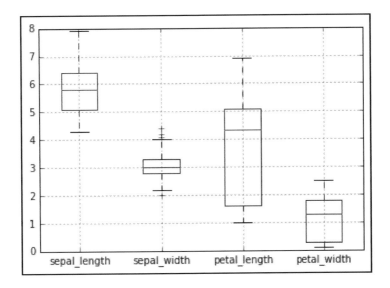

 Sometimes, graphs and screenshots presented in this chapter might be slightly different from the ones obtained on your local computer because graphical layout initialization is made with random parameters.

If you need to know about other quantile values, you can use the `.quantile()` method. For example, if you need the values at 10 percent and the 90 percent of the distribution of values, you can try out the following code:

```
In: iris.quantile([0.1, 0.9])
Out:
```

	sepal_length	sepal_width	petal_length	petal_width
0.1	4.8	2.50	1.4	0.2
0.9	6.9	3.61	5.8	2.2

Finally, to calculate the median, you can use the `.median()` method. Similarly, to obtain the mean and standard deviation, the `.mean()` and `.std()` methods are used respectively. In the case of categorical features, to get information about the levels present in a feature (that is, the different values the feature assumes), you can use the `.unique()` method, as follows:

```
In: iris.target.unique()
Out: array(['Iris-setosa', 'Iris-versicolor', 'Iris-virginica'],
dtype=object)
```

To examine the relation between features, you can create a co-occurrence matrix, or similarity matrix. In the following example, we will count the number of times the `petal_length` feature appears more than the average against the same count for the `petal_width` feature. To do this, you need to use the `crosstab` method, as follows:

```
In: pd.crosstab(iris['petal_length'] > 3.758667, iris['petal_width']
> 1.198667)
Out:
```

petal_width	False	True
petal_length		
False	56	1
True	4	89

As a result, you will notice that the features will always occur almost conjointly. Consequently, you can suppose a strong relationship between the two events. Graphically, you can check such a hypothesis using the following code:

```
In:
scatterplot = iris.plot(kind='scatter', x='petal_width',
y='petal_length', s=64, c='blue', edgecolors='white')
Out:
```

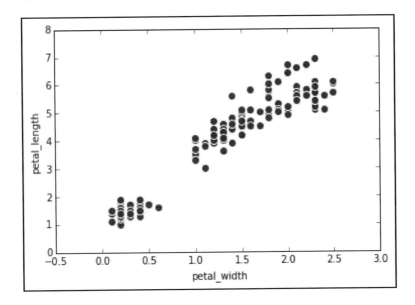

The trend is quite marked; we deduce that x and y are strongly related. The last operation that you usually perform during an EDA is checking the distribution of the feature. To manage this with pandas, you can approximate the distribution using a histogram, which can be done thanks to the following snippet:

```
In: distr = iris.petal_width.plot(kind='hist', alpha=0.5, bins=20)
Out:
```

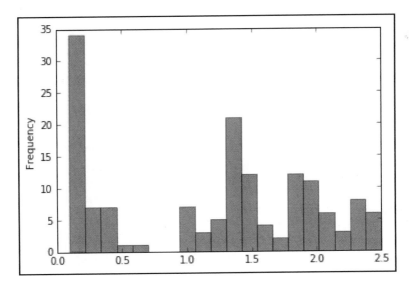

We chose 20 bins after a careful search. In other situations, 20 bins might be an extremely low or high value. As a rule of thumb, when drawing a distribution histogram, the starting value is the square root of the number of observations. After the initial visualization, you will then need to modify the number of bins until you recognize a well-known shape in the distribution.

We suggest that you explore all the features in order to check their relations and estimate their distribution. In fact, given its distribution, you may decide to treat each feature differently in order to subsequently achieve maximum classification or regression performance.

Building new features

Sometimes, you'll find yourself in a situation when features and target variables are not really related. In this case, you can modify the input dataset. You can apply linear or nonlinear transformations to improve the accuracy of the system, and so on. It's a very important step for the overall process because it completely depends on the skills of the data scientist, who is the one responsible for artificially changing the dataset and shaping the input data to better fit the learning model. Although this steps intuitively just adds complexity, this approach often boosts the performance of the learner; that's why it is used by bleeding-edge techniques, such as deep learning.

For example, if you're trying to predict the value of a house and you know the height, width, and the length of each room, you can artificially build a feature that represents the volume of the house. This is strictly not an observed feature, but it's a feature built on the top of the existing ones. Let's start with some code:

```
In: import numpy as np
from sklearn import datasets
from sklearn.cross_validation import train_test_split
from sklearn.metrics import mean_squared_error
cali = datasets.california_housing.fetch_california_housing()
X = cali['data']
Y = cali['target']
X_train, X_test, Y_train, Y_test = train_test_split(X, Y,
train_size=0.8)
```

We imported the dataset containing house prices in California. This is a regression problem because the target variable is the house price (that is, a real number). Applying a simple regressor straightaway, called KNN Regressor (take it as an example of a simple learner; an in-depth description of regressors will be provided in `Chapter 4`, *Machine Learning*), supplies a **Mean Absolute Error** (**MAE**) of around 1.15 on the test dataset. Don't worry if you cannot fully understand the code; MAE and other regressors are described later on in the book. Right now, assume that MAE represents the error. Thus, the lower the value of MAE, the better the solution:

```
In: from sklearn.neighbors import KNeighborsRegressor
regressor = KNeighborsRegressor()
regressor.fit(X_train, Y_train)
Y_est = regressor.predict(X_test)
print ("MAE=", mean_squared_error(Y_test, Y_est))
Out: MAE= 1.15752795578
```

A MAE result of 1.16 could seem good, but let's strive to do better. We're going to normalize the input features using Z-scores and compare the regression tasks on this new feature set. Z-normalization is simply the mapping of each feature to a new one with a null mean and unitary variance. With Scikit-learn, it is achieved in the following way:

```
In: from sklearn.preprocessing import StandardScaler
scaler = StandardScaler()
X_train_scaled = scaler.fit_transform(X_train)
X_test_scaled = scaler.transform(X_test)
regressor = KNeighborsRegressor()
regressor.fit(X_train_scaled, Y_train)
Y_est = regressor.predict(X_test_scaled)
print ("MAE=", mean_squared_error(Y_test, Y_est))
Out: MAE= 0.432334179429
```

With the help of this easy step, we dropped the MAE by more than a half, which now has a value of about 0.43.

Note that we didn't use the original features; we used their linear modification, which is more suitable for learning with a KNN regressor.

Instead of Z-normalization, we can use a scaling function on those features more robust to outliers, namely, **RobustScaler.** Such a scaler, instead of using mean and standard deviation, uses median and IQR (Inter-Quartile Range, that is, the first and the third quartile) to scale each feature independently. It is more robust to outliers, since median and IQR are not influenced as much as mean and variance if a few points (eventually just one) are far away from the center, for example, due to a faulty reading, a transmission error, or a broken sensor. Its usage is straightforward and usually leads to better results, as in the following example, reduces the MAE from the previous example of about 5% without introducing additional complexity:

```
In: from sklearn.preprocessing import RobustScaler
scaler2 = RobustScaler()
X_train_scaled = scaler2.fit_transform(X_train)
X_test_scaled = scaler2.transform(X_test)
regressor = KNeighborsRegressor()
regressor.fit(X_train_scaled, Y_train)
Y_est = regressor.predict(X_test_scaled)
print ("MAE=", mean_squared_error(Y_test, Y_est))
Out: MAE=0.418179216189
```

Now, let's try to add a nonlinear modification to a specific feature. We can assume that the output is related roughly to the number of occupiers of a house. In fact, there is a big difference between the price of a house occupied by a single person and the price for three persons staying in the same house. However, the difference between the price for the same 10 people living there and the price for 12 people is not that great (though there is still a difference of two). So, let's try to add another feature built as a nonlinear transform of another one:

```
In: non_linear_feat = 5 # AveOccup
X_train_new_feat = np.sqrt(X_train[:,non_linear_feat])
X_train_new_feat.shape = (X_train_new_feat.shape[0], 1)
X_train_extended = np.hstack([X_train, X_train_new_feat])
X_test_new_feat = np.sqrt(X_test[:,non_linear_feat])
X_test_new_feat.shape = (X_test_new_feat.shape[0], 1)
X_test_extended = np.hstack([X_test, X_test_new_feat])
scaler = StandardScaler()
X_train_extended_scaled = scaler.fit_transform(X_train_extended)
X_test_extended_scaled = scaler.transform(X_test_extended)
regressor = KNeighborsRegressor()
regressor.fit(X_train_extended_scaled, Y_train)
Y_est = regressor.predict(X_test_extended_scaled)
print ("MAE=", mean_squared_error(Y_test, Y_est))
Out: MAE= 0.363402604306
```

By adding this new feature, we have additionally reduced the MAE and finally obtained a more satisfying regressor. Of course, we may try out more other transformations in order to improve, but this straightforward example should hint at how important it is for your analysis the application of linear and nonlinear transformations found by EDA and obtain features that are conceptually more related to the output variable.

Dimensionality reduction

Oftentimes, you will have to deal with a dataset containing a large number of features, many of which may be unnecessary. This is a typical problem where some features are very inform the prediction, some are somehow related, and some are completely unrelated (that is, they only contain noise or irrelevant information). Keeping only the interesting features is a way to not only make your dataset more manageable but also have predictive algorithms work better instead of being fooled in their predictions by the noise in the data.

Hence, dimensionality reduction is the operation of eliminating some features of the input dataset and creating a restricted set of features that contains all of the information you need to predict the target variable in a more effective and reliable way. As mentioned, reducing the number of features usually also reduces the output variability and complexity of the learning process (as well as the time required).

The main hypothesis behind many algorithms used in the reduction is the one pertaining to **Additive White Gaussian Noise (AWGN)** noise. We suppose an independent Gaussian-shaped noise has been added to every feature of the dataset. Consequently, reducing the dimensionality also reduces the energy of the noise since you're decreasing its span set.

The covariance matrix

The covariance matrix provides you with an idea about the correlation between all the different pairs of features. It's usually the first step in dimensionality reduction because it gives you an idea of the number of features that are strongly related (and therefore, the number of features that you can discard) and the ones that are independent. Using the iris dataset, where each observation has four features, a correlation matrix can be computed easily and you can understand its results with the help of a simple graphical representation, which can be obtained with the help of the following code:

```
In: from sklearn import datasets
import numpy as np
iris = datasets.load_iris()
cov_data = np.corrcoef(iris.data.T)
```

```
print (iris.feature_names)
print (cov_data)
Out:
['sepal length (cm)', 'sepal width (cm)', 'petal length (cm)',
'petal width (cm)']
[[ 1.          -0.10936925  0.87175416  0.81795363]
 [-0.10936925  1.          -0.4205161  -0.35654409]
 [ 0.87175416 -0.4205161   1.          0.9627571 ]
 [ 0.81795363 -0.35654409  0.9627571   1.         ]]
```

Using a `heatmap`, let's now visualize the covariance matrix in a graphical form:

```
In: import matplotlib.pyplot as plt
img = plt.matshow(cov_data, cmap=plt.cm.rainbow)
plt.colorbar(img, ticks=[-1, 0, 1], fraction=0.045)
for x in range(cov_data.shape[0]):
  for y in range(cov_data.shape[1]):
    plt.text(x, y, "%0.2f" % cov_data[x,y],
      size=12, color='black', ha="center", va="center")
plt.show()
Out:
```

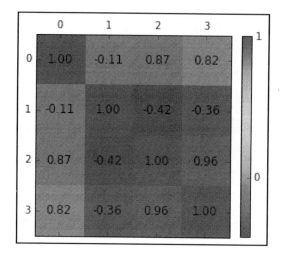

From the previous figure, you can see that the value of the primary diagonal is 1. This is so because we're using the normalized version of the covariance matrix (normalizing each feature covariance to 1.0). We can also notice a high correlation between the first and the third, the first and the fourth, and the third and the fourth features. In addition, we can verify that only the second feature is almost independent of the others; all the other features are somehow correlated to each other.

We now have an idea about the potential number of features in the reduced set, imagining the duplicated information being compressed, as pointed out by the correlation matrix; we can reduce everything simply to two features.

Principal Component Analysis (PCA)

PCA is a technique that helps define a smaller and more relevant set of features. The new features obtained from a PCA are linear combinations (that is, rotation) of the current features, even if they are binary. After rotation of the input space, the first vector of the output set contains most of the signal's energy (or, in other words, its variance). The second is orthogonal to the first, and it contains most of the remaining energy; the third is orthogonal to the first two vectors and contains most of the remaining energy, and so on. It's just like restructuring the information in the dataset by aggregating as much as possible of the information onto the initial vectors produced by the PCA.

In the (ideal) case of AWGN, the initial vectors contain all of the information of the input signal; the ones towards the end only contain noise. Moreover, since the output basis is orthogonal, you can decompose and synthesize an approximate version of the input dataset. The key parameter, which is used to decide how many basis vectors one can use, is the energy. Since the algorithm, under the hood, is for singular value decomposition, eigenvectors (the basis vectors) and eigenvalues (the standard deviation associated with that vector) are two terms that are often referred to when reading about PCA. Typically, the cardinality of the output set is the one that guarantees the presence of 95 percent (in some cases, 90 or 99 percent are needed) of the input energy (or variance). A rigorous explanation of PCA is beyond the scope of this book, and hence we will just provide you with guidelines on how to use this powerful tool in Python.

Here's an example on how to reduce the dataset to two dimensions. In the previous section, we deduced that 2 was a good choice for a dimensionality reduction; let's check if we were right:

```
In: from sklearn.decomposition import PCA
pca_2c = PCA(n_components=2)
X_pca_2c = pca_2c.fit_transform(iris.data)
X_pca_2c.shape
Out: (150, 2)
In: plt.scatter(X_pca_2c[:,0], X_pca_2c[:,1], c=iris.target,
alpha=0.8, s=60, marker='o', edgecolors='white')
plt.show()
pca_2c.explained_variance_ratio_.sum()
Out:
0.97763177502480336
```

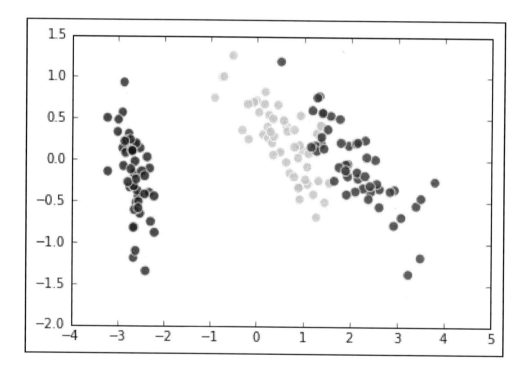

We can immediately see that, after applying the PCA, the output set has only two features. This is so because the PCA() object was called with the n_components parameter set to 2. An alternative way to obtain the same result would be to run PCA() for 1, 2, and 3 components and then conclude from the explained variance ratio and the visual inspection that, for n_components = 2, we got the best result. Then, we will have evidence that, using two basis vectors, the output dataset contains almost 98 percent of the energy of the input signal, and in the schema the classes are pretty much neatly separable. Each color is located in a different area of the 2-dimensional Euclidean space.

> Note that this process is automatic and you don't need to provide labels while training PCA. In fact, PCA is an unsupervised algorithm, and it does not require data related to the independent variable to rotate the projection basis.

For curious readers, the transformation matrix (which turns the initial dataset into the PCA-restructured one) can be seen with the help of the following code:

```
In: pca_2c.components_
Out:
array([[ 0.36158968, -0.08226889,  0.85657211,  0.35884393],
       [-0.65653988, -0.72971237,  0.1757674 ,  0.07470647]])
```

The transformation matrix comprises four columns (the number of input features) and two rows (the number of the reduced ones).

Sometimes, you will find yourself in a situation where PCA is not effective enough, especially when dealing with high dimensionality data, since the features may be very correlated and, at the same time, the variance is unbalanced A possible solution for such a situation is to try to whiten the signal (or make it more spherical). In this occurrence, eigenvectors are forced to unit component-wise variances. Whitening removes information, but sometimes it improves the accuracy of the machine learning algorithms that will be used after the PCA reduction. Here's how the code looks when resorting to whitening (in our example, it doesn't change anything except for the scale of the dataset with the reduced output):

```
In: pca_2cw = PCA(n_components=2, whiten=True)
X_pca_1cw = pca_2cw.fit_transform(iris.data)
plt.scatter(X_pca_1cw[:,0], X_pca_1cw[:,1], c=iris.target,
alpha=0.8, s=60, marker='o', edgecolors='white')
plt.show()
pca_2cw.explained_variance_ratio_.sum()
Out:
0.97763177502480336
```

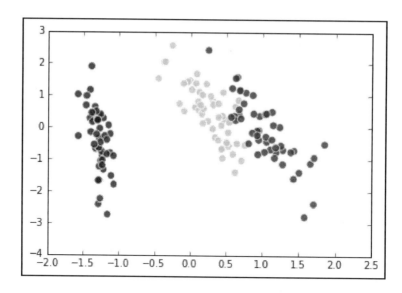

Now, let's try to see what happens if we project the input dataset on an 1D space generated with PCA as follows:

```
In: pca_1c = PCA(n_components=1)
X_pca_1c = pca_1c.fit_transform(iris.data)
plt.scatter(X_pca_1c[:,0], np.zeros(X_pca_1c.shape), c=iris.target,
alpha=0.8, s=60, marker='o', edgecolors='white')
plt.show()
```

```
pca_1c.explained_variance_ratio_.sum()
Out: 0. 9246162071742684
```

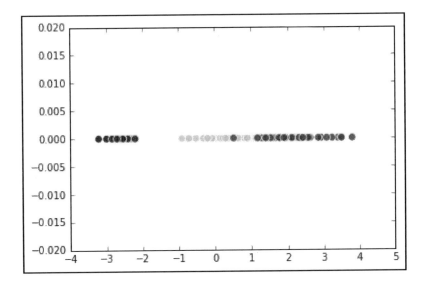

In this case, the output energy is lower (92.4 percent of the original signal), and the output points are added to the mono-dimensional Euclidean space. This might not be a great feature reduction step since many points with different labels are mixed together.

Finally, here's a trick. To ensure that you generate an output set containing at least 95 percent of the input energy, you can just specify this value to the PCA object during its first call. A result equal to the one with two vectors can be obtained with the following code:

```
In: pca_95pc = PCA(n_components=0.95)
X_pca_95pc = pca_95pc.fit_transform(iris.data)
print (pca_95pc.explained_variance_ratio_.sum())
print (X_pca_95pc.shape)
Out: 0.977631775025
(150, 2)
```

PCA for big data – RandomizedPCA

The main issue with PCA is the complexity of the underlying **Singular Value Decomposition (SVD)** algorithm, which makes the reduction work and renders the whole process very difficult to scale. There is, anyway, a faster algorithm in Scikit-Learn based on Randomized SVD. It is a lighter but approximate iterative decomposition method. Using Randomized SVD, the full-rank reconstruction is not perfect, and the basis vectors are optimized locally during every iteration. On the other hand, it requires only a few steps to get a good approximation, demonstrating much faster than classical SVD algorithms. Therefore, this reduction algorithm is a great choice if the training dataset is big. In the following code, we will apply it to the iris dataset. The output is pretty close to the classical PCA since the size of the problem is very small. However, the results vary significantly when the algorithm is applied to large datasets:

```
In: from sklearn.decomposition import RandomizedPCA
rpca_2c = RandomizedPCA(n_components=2)
X_rpca_2c = rpca_2c.fit_transform(iris.data)
plt.scatter(X_rpca_2c[:,0], X_rpca_2c[:,1], c=iris.target,
alpha=0.8, s=60, marker='o', edgecolors='white')
plt.show()
rpca_2c.explained_variance_ratio_.sum()
Out: 0.97763177502480414
```

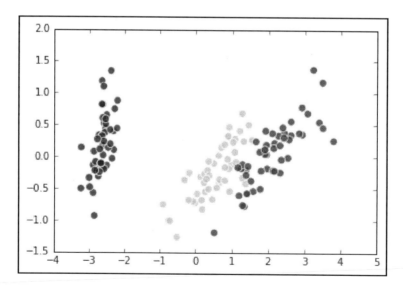

Latent Factor Analysis (LFA)

Latent factor analysis is another technique that helps you reduce the dimensionality of the dataset. The overall idea is similar to PCA. However, in this case, there's no orthogonal decomposition of the input signal, and therefore no output basis. Some data scientists think that LFA is a generalization of PCA that removes the constraint of orthogonality. Generally, latent factor analysis is used when a latent factor or a construct is expected to be present in the system. Under such a hypothesis, all the features are observations of variables derived or influenced by the latent factor that is transformed linearly and which has an **Arbitrary Waveform Generator** (AWG) noise. It is generally assumed that the latent factor has a Gaussian distribution and a unitary covariance. Therefore, in this case, instead of collapsing the energy/variance of the signal, the covariance among the variables is explained in the output dataset. The Scikit-learn toolkit implements an iterative algorithm, making it suitable for large datasets.

Here's the code to lower the dimensionality of the iris dataset by assuming two latent factors in the system:

```
In: from sklearn.decomposition import FactorAnalysis
fact_2c = FactorAnalysis(n_components=2)
X_factor = fact_2c.fit_transform(iris.data)
plt.scatter(X_factor[:,0], X_factor[:,1], c=iris.target,
alpha=0.8, s=60, marker='o', edgecolors='white')
plt.show()
Out:
```

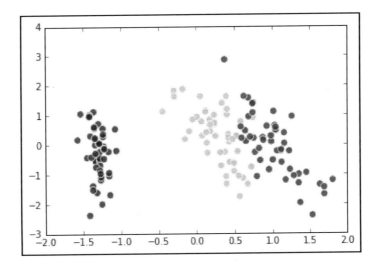

Linear Discriminant Analysis (LDA)

Strictly speaking, LDA is a classifier (a classical statistical method developed by Ronald Fisher, the father of modern statistics), but it is often used for dimensionality reduction. It doesn't scale so well to larger datasets (like many statistical methods) but it is something to be tried as it could bring better results than other classification methods such as logistic regression. Since it's a supervised approach, it requires the label set to optimize the reduction step. LDA outputs linear combinations of the input features, trying to model the difference between the classes that best discriminate them (since LDA uses label information). Compared to PCA, the output dataset that is obtained with the help of LDA contains neat distinctions between classes. However, it cannot be used in regression problems, since it is derived from a classification process.

Here's the application of LDA on the iris dataset:

```
In: from sklearn.lda import LDA
lda_2c = LDA(n_components=2)
X_lda_2c = lda_2c.fit_transform(iris.data, iris.target)
plt.scatter(X_lda_2c[:,0], X_lda_2c[:,1], c=iris.target,
alpha=0.8,  edgecolors='none'); plt.show()
Out:
```

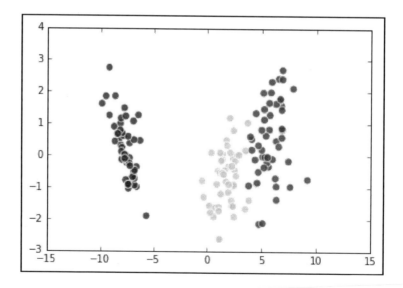

Latent Semantical Analysis (LSA)

Typically, LSA is applied to text after it has been processed by `TfidfVectorizer` or `CountVectorizer`. Compared to PCA, it applies SVD to the input dataset (which is usually a sparse matrix), producing semantic sets of words usually associated with the same concept. This is why LSA is used when the features are homogeneous (that is, all the words are in the documents) and are present in large numbers.

An example of this on Python with text and `TfidfVectorizer` is as follows. The output shows part of the content of a latent vector:

```
In: from sklearn.datasets import fetch_20newsgroups
categories = ['sci.med', 'sci.space']
twenty_sci_news = fetch_20newsgroups(categories=categories)
from sklearn.feature_extraction.text import TfidfVectorizer
tf_vect = TfidfVectorizer()
word_freq = tf_vect.fit_transform(twenty_sci_news.data)
from sklearn.decomposition import TruncatedSVD
tsvd_2c = TruncatedSVD(n_components=50)
tsvd_2c.fit(word_freq)
np.array(tf_vect.get_feature_names())
[tsvd_2c.components_[20].argsort()[-10:][::-1]]
Out: array(['jupiter', 'sq', 'comet', 'of', 'gehrels',
'zisfein', 'jim', 'gene', 'are', 'omen'], dtype='<U79')
```

Independent Component Analysis (ICA)

As you can guess from the name, ICA is an approach where you try to derive independent components from the input signal. In fact, ICA is a technique that allows you to create maximally independent additive subcomponents from the initial multivariate input signal. The main hypothesis of this technique focuses on the statistical independence of the subcomponents and their non-Gaussian distribution. ICA has a lot of applications in neurological data and is widely used in the neuroscience domain.

A typical scenario that may require the usage of ICA is blind source separation. For example, two or more microphones will record two sounds (for instance, a person speaks and a song plays at the same time). In this case, ICA is able to separate the two sounds into two output features.

The Scikit-learn package offers a faster version of the algorithm (`sklearn.decomposition.FastICA`), whose usage is similar to the other techniques presented so far.

Kernel PCA

Kernel PCA is a technique that uses a kernel to map the signal on a (typically) nonlinear space and makes it linearly separable (or close to attaining this). It's an extension of PCA, where the mapping is an actual projection on a linear subspace. There are many well-known kernels (and of course, you can always build your own on the fly), but the most used ones are *linear*, *poly*, *RBF*, *sigmoid*, and *cosine*. They all serve different configurations of input datasets as they are able to linearize only some selected types of data. For example, let's imagine having a disk-shaped dataset, like the one created with the following code:

```
In: def circular_points (radius, N):
      return np.array([[np.cos(2*np.pi*t/N)*radius,
      np.sin(2*np.pi*t/N)*radius] for t in range(N)])
N_points = 50
fake_circular_data = np.vstack([circular_points(1.0, N_points),
circular_points(5.0, N_points)])
fake_circular_data += np.random.rand(*fake_circular_data.shape)
fake_circular_target = np.array([0]*N_points + [1]*N_points)
plt.scatter(fake_circular_data[:,0], fake_circular_data[:,1],
c=fake_circular_target, alpha=0.8, s=60, marker='o',
edgecolors='white')
plt.show()
Out:
```

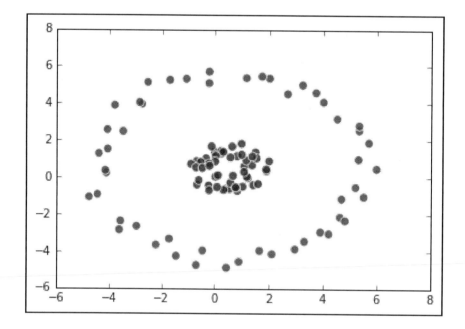

With this input dataset, all the linear transformations will fail to separate blue and red dots since the dataset contains circumference-shaped classes. Now, let's try this with Kernel PCA by using a RBF kernel and see what happens:

```
In: from sklearn.decomposition import KernelPCA
kpca_2c = KernelPCA(n_components=2, kernel='rbf')
X_kpca_2c = kpca_2c.fit_transform(fake_circular_data)
plt.scatter(X_kpca_2c[:,0], X_kpca_2c[:,1], c=fake_circular_target,
alpha=0.8, s=60, marker='o', edgecolors='white')
plt.show()
Out:
```

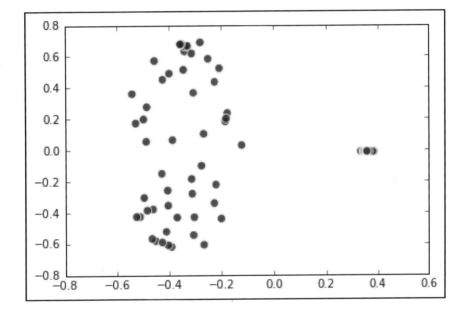

 Graphs in this chapter can be different from those obtained on your local computer because graphical layout initialization is made with random parameters.

We achieved our goal—the blue dots are on the left and the red dots are on the right. Thanks to Kernel PCA's transformation, you can now deal with this dataset using linear techniques.

T-SNE

PCA is a wide-spread technique for dimensionality reduction; yet, when we deal with large data presenting many features, we first need to understand *what's going on* in the feature space. In fact, usually, in the EDA phase you'll do several scatterplots of the data to understand what the coarse relation between features is. At this point T-SNE comes to your help, since it has been designed with the goal of embedding high dimensional data in a 2D or 3D space, to make the most of a scatterplot. The core of the algorithm is based on two rules: the first is that recurrent similar observations must have a greater contribution to the output (achieved with a probability distribution function); second, the distribution in the high dimensional space must be similar to the one in the small space (achieved minimized the KL, Kullback-Leibler, divergence between the two probability distribution functions). The output is visually nice, and allows us to guess non-linear interactions between features.

Let's now explore a simple example, applying the T-SNE to the Iris dataset and plotting it to a 2-dimensional space:

```
In: from sklearn.manifold import TSNE
from sklearn.datasets import load_iris
iris = load_iris()
X, y = iris.data, iris.target
X_tsne = TSNE(n_components=2).fit_transform(X)
plt.scatter(X_tsne[:, 0], X_tsne[:, 1], c=y, alpha=0.8, s=60,
marker='o', edgecolors='white')
plt.show()
Out:
```

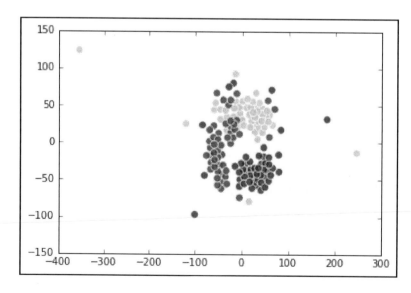

Restricted Boltzmann Machine (RBM)

RBM is another technique that, composed of linear functions (which are usually called hidden units or neurons), creates a nonlinear transformation of the input data. The hidden units represent the status of the system and the output dataset is actually the status of that layer.

The main hypothesis of this technique is that the input dataset is composed of features that represent probability (binary values or real values in the [0,1] range) since RBM is a probabilistic approach. In the following example, we will feed the RBM using binarized pixels of images as features (1=white, 0=black), and we will print the latent components of the system. These components represent different generic faces that appear in the original images:

```
In: from sklearn import preprocessing
from sklearn.neural_network import BernoulliRBM
n_components = 64 # Try with 64, 100, 144
olivetti_faces = datasets.fetch_olivetti_faces()
X = preprocessing.binarize(preprocessing.scale(olivetti_faces.data.astype
(float)), 0.5)
rbm = BernoulliRBM(n_components=n_components, learning_rate=0.01,
n_iter=100)
rbm.fit(X)
plt.figure(figsize=(4.2, 4))
for i, comp in enumerate(rbm.components_):
  plt.subplot(int(np.sqrt(n_components+1)),
  int(np.sqrt(n_components+1)), i + 1)
  plt.imshow(comp.reshape((64, 64)), cmap=plt.cm.gray_r,
  interpolation='nearest')
  plt.xticks(()); plt.yticks(())
plt.suptitle(str(n_components) + ' components extracted by RBM',
fontsize=16)
plt.subplots_adjust(0.08, 0.02, 0.92, 0.85, 0.08, 0.23)
plt.show()
Out:
```

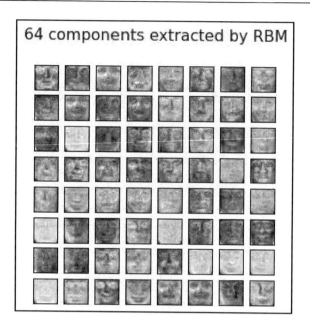

Note that Scikit-learn contains just the base layer of RBM processing; if you are working on big datasets, you are better off using GPU-based toolkits (such as the ones built on top of CUDA or OpenCL) since RBMs are highly parallelizable

The detection and treatment of outliers

In data science, examples are at the core of learning from data processes. If unusual, inconsistent, or erroneous data is fed into the learning process, the resulting model may be unable to correctly generalize the accommodating of any new data. An unusually high value present in a variable, apart from skewing descriptive measures such as the mean and variance, may also distort how many machine learning algorithms learn from data, causing distorted predictions as a result.

When a data point deviates markedly from the others in a sample, it is called an *outlier*. Any other expected observation is labeled an *inlier*.

A data point may be an outlier due to the following three general causes (and each one implies different remedies):

- The point represents a rare occurrence, but it is yet a possible value given the fact that the available data is just a sample of the original data distribution. In such an occurrence, the generative underlying process is the same for all the points, but the outlying point may be deemed unsuitable for a generalization by machine learning due to its rarity. In such a case, the point is commonly removed or underweighted. Another solution is to increase the sample number, thus making the unusual value less relevant in the dataset.

- The point represents the usual occurrence of another distribution. When similar situations occur, it is plausible to imagine an error or a misspecification that affected the generation of the sample. In any case, your learning algorithm is going to learn from data coming from an extraneous distribution that is not the focus of interest of your data science project (the focus is on the generalization). In such a case, the outlier has simply to be removed.

- The point is clearly some kind of a mistake. For some reason, there has been a data entry error or a problem with data integrity that modified the original value and replaced it with an inconsistent value. The best course of action is to remove the value and treat it as a value that is missing at random. In this case, it is common to replace the outlier with a mean or the most common class depending on whether it is a regression or a classification problem. If it is not convenient or possible to do so, then we suggest that you just remove the example from the dataset.

Univariate outlier detection

To explain the reason behind why a data point is an outlier, you are first required to locate the possible outliers in your data. There are quite a few approaches-some are univariate (you can observe each singular variable at once) and the others are multivariate (they consider more variables at the same time). The univariate methods are usually based on EDA and visualizations such as boxplots (introduced at the beginning of the present chapter; we will discuss boxplots more specifically in Chapter 6, *Visualization, Insights, and Results*).There are a couple of rules of thumb to keep in mind when chasing outliers by examining single variables. In fact outliers may be spotted as extreme values:

- If you are observing Z-scores, observations with scores higher than 3 in absolute value have to be considered as suspect outliers.
- If you are observing a description of data, you can consider as suspect outliers the observations that are smaller than the 25th percentile value minus the IQR (the interquartile range, that is, the difference between the 75th and 25th percentile values) *1.5 and those greater that the 75th percentile value plus the IQR * 1.5. Usually, you can achieve such distinction with the help of a boxplot graph.

In order to present how we can easily detect some outliers using Z-scores, let's load and explore the Boston House Prices dataset. As pointed out by the description of the dataset (which you can get with the help of `boston.DESCR`), the variable CHAS, which is indexed 3, is a binary one. Therefore, it makes little sense to use it while detecting anomalous values. In fact, such a variable can have just a value of either 0 or 1:

```
In: from sklearn.datasets import load_boston
boston = load_boston()
continuous_variables = [n for n in range(boston.data.shape[1])
if n!=3]
```

Now, let's quickly standardize all the continuous variables using the `StandardScaler` function from sklearn. Our target is the fancy indexing of `boston.data` `boston.data[:,continuous_variables]` in order to create another array containing all the variables except the previous one that was indexed 3.

`StandardScaler` automatically standardizes to zero mean and unit variance. This is a necessary routine operation that should be performed before feeding the data to the learning phase. Otherwise, many algorithms won't work properly (such as linear models powered by gradient descent and support vector machines).

Finally, let's locate the values that are above the absolute value of 3 standard deviations:

```
In:
import numpy as np
from sklearn import preprocessing
normalized_data = preprocessing.StandardScaler().fit_transform(boston.data
[:, continuous_variables])
outliers_rows, outliers_columns = np.where(np.abs(normalized_data)>3)
```

The `outliers_rows` and `outliers_columns` variables contain the row and column indexes of the suspect outliers. We can print the index of the examples:

```
In: print (outliers_rows)
Out: [ 55   56   57 102 141 199 200 201 202 203 204 225 256
257 262 283 284 347 ...
```

Alternatively, we can display the tuple of the row/column coordinates in the array:

```
In: print (list(zip(outliers_rows, outliers_columns)))
Out: [(55, 1), (56, 1), (57, 1), (102, 10), (141, 11),
(199, 1), (200, 1), (201, 1), ...
```

The univariate approach can reveal quite a lot of potential outliers. Anyway, it won't disclose an outlier that does not have an extreme value but instead it is characterized by an unusual combination of values in two or more variables. In such cases, the values of the involved variables may not even be extreme ones, and therefore, the outlier may slip away unnoticed by a univariate inspection. These outliers are called multivariate outliers.

In order to discover multivariate outliers, you can use a dimensionality reduction algorithm, such as the previously illustrated PCA, and then check the absolute values of the components that are beyond three standard deviations or visually inspect bivariate plots in order to locate isolated clusters of data points.

Anyway, the Scikit-learn package offers a couple of classes that can automatically work for you straight out of the box and signal all suspect cases:

- The `covariance.EllipticEnvelope` class fits a robust distribution estimation of your data, pointing out the outliers that might be contaminating your dataset because they are the extreme points in the general distribution of the data.
- The `svm.OneClassSVM` class is a support vector machine algorithm that can approximate the shape of your data and find out if any new instances provided should be considered as a novelty (it acts as a novelty detector because by default, it presumes that there is no outlier in the data). Anyway, by just modifying its parameters, it can also work on a dataset where outliers are present, providing an even more robust and reliable outlier detection system than `EllipticEnvelope`.

Both classes, based on different statistical and machine learning approaches, need to be known and applied during your modeling phase.

EllipticEnvelope

`EllipticEnvelope` is a function that tries to figure out the key parameters of your data's general distribution by assuming that your entire data is an expression of an underlying multivariate Gaussian distribution. That assumption cannot hold true for all datasets, yet when it does it proves an indeed effective method for spotting outliers. Simplifying as much as possible the complex estimations working behind the algorithm, we can say that it checks the distance of each observation with respect to a grand mean that takes into account all the variables in your dataset. For this reason, it is able to spot both univariate and multivariate outliers.

The only parameter that you have to take into account when using this function from the covariance module is the contamination parameter, which can take a value of up to 0.5. It provides information to the algorithm about the proportion of the outliers present in your dataset. Situations may vary from dataset to dataset. However, as a starting figure, we suggest a value from 0.01-0.02 since it is the percentage of observations that should fall over the absolute value 3 in the Z score distance from the mean in a standardized normal distribution. For this reason, we consider the default value of 0.1 to be too high.

Let's see this algorithm in action with the help of a synthetic distribution:

```
In: # Create an artificial distribution made of blobs
from sklearn.datasets import make_blobs
blobs = 1
blob = make_blobs(n_samples=100, n_features=2, centers=blobs,
cluster_std=1.5, shuffle=True, random_state=5)
# Robust Covariance Estimate
from sklearn.covariance import EllipticEnvelope
robust_covariance_est = EllipticEnvelope(contamination=.1).fit(blob[0])
detection = robust_covariance_est.predict(blob[0])
outliers = np.where(detection==-1)[0]
inliers = np.where(detection==1)[0]
# Draw the distribution and the detected outliers
from matplotlib import pyplot as plt
# Just the distribution
plt.scatter(blob[0][:,0],blob[0][:,1], c='blue', alpha=0.8,
s=60, marker='o', edgecolors='white')
plt.show()
# The distribution and the outliers
in_points = plt.scatter(blob[0][inliers,0],blob[0][inliers,1],
c='blue', alpha=0.8, s=60, marker='o', edgecolors='white')
out_points = plt.scatter(blob[0][outliers,0],blob[0][outliers,1],
c='red', alpha=0.8, s=60, marker='o', edgecolors='white')
plt.legend((in_points,out_points),('inliers','outliers'),
scatterpoints=1, loc='lower right')
plt.show()
```

Let's examine this code closely.

The make_blobs function creates a certain number of distributions into a bidimensional space for a total of 100 examples (the n_samples parameter). The number of distributions (parameter centers) is related to the user-defined variable blobs, which is initially set to 1.

After creating the artificial example data, running EllipticEnvelope with a contamination rate of 10 percent helps you find out the extreme values in the distribution. The model deploys first fit by using the .fit() method on the EllipticEnvelope class. Then, a prediction is obtained by using the .predict() method on the data that was used for the fit.

The results, corresponding to a vector of values 1 and -1 (with -1 being the mark for anomalous examples), can be displayed thanks to a couple of scatterplots using the plot function from the pyplot module in matplotlib.

The distinction between inliers and outliers is recorded in the variable's outliers and inliers, which contain the indexes of the examples.

Now, let's run the code a few more times after changing the number of blobs and examine the results when the blobs have a value of 1 and 4:

Out:

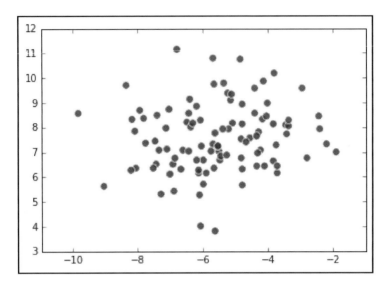

The distributions of data points after changing the number of blobs:

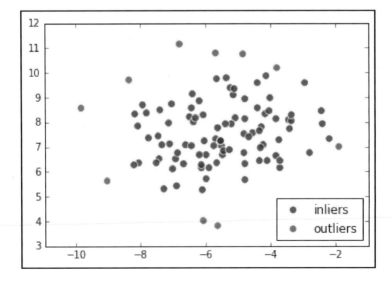

In the case of a unique underlying multivariate distribution (when the variable blobs = 1), the EllipticEnvelope algorithm has successfully located 10 percent of the observations on the fringe of the distribution itself and has consequently signaled all the suspect outliers.

Instead, when multiple distributions are present in the data as if there were two or more natural clusters, the algorithm, trying to fit a unique general distribution, tends to locate the potential outliers on just the most remote cluster, thus ignoring other areas of data that might be potentially affected by outlying cases.

This is not an unusual situation with real data, and it represents an important limitation of the EllipticEnvelope algorithm.

Now, let's get back to our initial Boston house price dataset for verification of some more data that is more realistic than our synthetic blobs. Here is the first part of the code that we can use for our experiment:

```
In: from sklearn.decomposition import PCA
# Normalized data relative to continuous variables
continuous_variables = [n for n in range(boston.data.shape[1])
if n!=3]
normalized_data = preprocessing.StandardScaler().fit_transform(boston.data
[:,continuous_variables])
# Just for visualization purposes pick the first 2 PCA components
pca = PCA(n_components=2)
Zscore_components = pca.fit_transform(normalized_data)
vtot = 'PCA Variance explained ' +
str(round(np.sum(pca.explained_variance_ratio_),3))
v1 = str(round(pca.explained_variance_ratio_[0],3))
v2 = str(round(pca.explained_variance_ratio_[1],3))
```

In this script, we will first standardize the data and then, just for subsequent visualization purposes, generate a reduction to two components by using PCA.

The two PCA components account for about 62 percent of the initial variance expressed by the 12 continuous variables available in the dataset (the summed value of the `.explained_variance_ratio_` variable that is internal to the fitted `PCA` class).

Although only two PCA components are sufficient for visualization purposes of this example, normally you'd get more than two components for this dataset since the target is to have enough to account for at least 95 percent of the total variance (as stated previously in the chapter).

We will continue with the script:

```
In: # Robust Covariance Estimate
robust_covariance_est = EllipticEnvelope(store_precision=False,
assume_centered = False, contamination=.05)
robust_covariance_est.fit(normalized_data)
detection = robust_covariance_est.predict(normalized_data)
outliers = np.where(detection==-1)
regular = np.where(detection==1)
In: # Draw the distribution and the detected outliers
from matplotlib import pyplot as plt
in_points = plt.scatter(Zscore_components[regular,0],Zscore_components
[regular,1], c='blue', alpha=0.8, s=60, marker='o', edgecolors='white')
out_points = plt.scatter(Zscore_components[outliers,0],Zscore_components
[outliers,1], c='red', alpha=0.8, s=60, marker='o', edgecolors='white')
plt.legend((in_points,out_points),('inliers','outliers'), scatterpoints=1,
loc='best')
plt.xlabel('1st component ('+v1+')')
plt.ylabel('2nd component ('+v2+')')
plt.xlim([-7,7])
plt.ylim([-6,6])
plt.title(vtot)
plt.show()
Out:
```

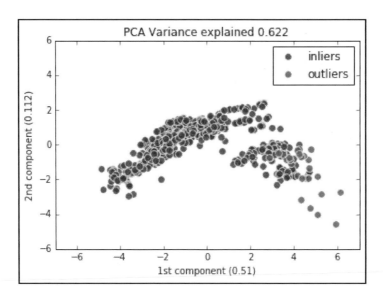

As in the previous example, assuming a low contamination that is equivalent to 0.05, the code based on `EllipticEnvelope` predicts the outliers and stores them in an array in the same way as it stores the inliers. Finally, there's the visualization (as mentioned before, we are going to discuss all the visualization methods in `Chapter 6`, *Visualization, Insights, and Results*).

Now, let's observe the result offered by the scatterplot we generated to visualize the first two `PCA` components of the data and mark the outlying observations. Concerning the general distribution of the data points in our example, as provided by the two components that account for about 62 percent of the variance in the data, it appears as if there are two distinct clusters of house prices in Boston, which correspond to the high-end and low-end units present in the market. Generally speaking, the presence of clusters in the data is a non-optimal situation for `EllipticEnvelope` estimations. In fact, according to what we've already noticed while experimenting using synthetic blobs, the algorithm has pointed out the outliers on just a cluster—the lesser one. Given such results, there is a strong reason to believe that we just received a biased, partial response and some further investigation will be required before deeming such points as outliers. The Scikit-learn package actually integrates the robust covariance estimation method, which is fundamentally a statistical approach, with another methodology that is well rooted in machine learning, the OneClassSVM class. Now, we will experiment with it.

 Before leaving this example, please note that to fit both PCA and EllipticEnvelope, we used an array named `normalized_data`, which contains just the standardized continuous dataset variables. Please always take into account in your projects that using non-standardized data and mixing binary or categorical data with continuous ones may induce errors and approximated estimations for the EllipticEnvelope algorithm.

OneClassSVM

As EllipticEnvelope fits a hypothetical Gaussian distribution, leveraging parametric and statistical assumption, OneClassSVM is a machine learning algorithm that learns from the data itself what the distribution of the features should be; and therefore it is applicable in a large variety of situations when you want to be able to catch all the outliers but also the unusual data examples.

It is great if you already have a clean dataset and have it fit by machine learning algorithms. Afterwards, OneClassSVM can be summoned to check if any new example fits in the historical distribution, and if it doesn't, it will signal a novel example, which might be both an error or some new, previously unseen situation.

Just think of data science situations as a machine learning classification algorithm trained to recognize posts and news on a Website and take online actions. OneClassSVM can easily spot a post that is different from the others present on the Website (spam, maybe?), whereas other algorithms will just try to fit the new example into the existing topic categorization.

However, OneClassSVM can also be used to spot existing outliers. If this specialized SVM class cannot fit some data, which is pointed out as being at the margins of the data distribution, then there is surely something fishy about those examples.

In order to have OneClassSVM work as an outlier detector, you need to work on its core parameters; it requires you to define the kernel, degree, gamma, and nu:

- **Kernel and degree**: These are interconnected. Usually, the values that we suggest based on our experience are the default ones; the type of kernel should be `rbf` and its degree should be 3. Such parameters will inform OneClassSVM to create a series of classification bubbles that span through three dimensions, allowing you to model even the most complex multidimensional distribution forms.
- **Gamma**: This is a parameter connected to the rbf kernel. We suggest that you keep it as low as possible. A good rule of thumb should be to assign it a minimum value that lies between the inverse of the number of cases and the variables. The role of Gamma in SVM will be explained further in `Chapter 4`, *Machine Learning*. Anyway, it will suffice for now to say that higher values of gamma tend to lead the algorithm to follow the data more to define the shape of the classification bubbles.
- **Nu**: This parameter determines whether we have to fit the exact distribution or if we try to obtain a certain degree of generalization by not adapting too much to the present data examples (a necessary choice if outliers are present). It can be easily determined with the help of the following formula:

nu_estimate = 0.95 * outliers_fraction + 0.05

- If the value of the outliers' fraction is very small, nu will be small and the SVM algorithm will try to fit the contour of the data points. On the other hand, if the fraction is high, so will be the parameter, forcing a smoother boundary of the inliers' distributions.

Let's immediately observe the performance of this algorithm on the problem that we faced before on the Boston house price dataset:

```
In: from sklearn.decomposition import PCA
from sklearn import preprocessing
from sklearn import svm
```

```
# Normalized data relative to continuous variables
continuous_variables = [n for n in range(boston.data.shape[1])
if n!=3]
normalized_data = preprocessing.StandardScaler().fit_transform(boston.data
[:,continuous_variables])
# Just for visualization purposes pick the first 5 PCA components
pca = PCA(n_components=5)
Zscore_components = pca.fit_transform(normalized_data)
vtot = 'PCA Variance explained ' +
str(round(np.sum(pca.explained_variance_ratio_),3))
# OneClassSVM fitting and estimates
outliers_fraction = 0.02 #
nu_estimate = 0.95 * outliers_fraction + 0.05
machine_learning = svm.OneClassSVM(kernel="rbf",
gamma=1.0/len(normalized_data), degree=3, nu=nu_estimate)
machine_learning.fit(normalized_data)
detection = machine_learning.predict(normalized_data)
outliers = np.where(detection==-1)
regular = np.where(detection==1)
```

We now visualize the results:

```
# Draw the distribution and the detected outliers
from matplotlib import pyplot as plt
for r in range(1,5):
 in_points = plt.scatter(Zscore_components[regular,0],
 Zscore_components[regular,r], c='blue', alpha=0.8, s=60,
 marker='o', edgecolors='white')
 out_points = plt.scatter(Zscore_components[outliers,0],
 Zscore_components[outliers,r], c='red', alpha=0.8, s=60,
 marker='o', edgecolors='white')
 plt.legend((in_points,out_points),('inliers','outliers'),
 scatterpoints=1, loc='best')
 plt.xlabel('Component
 1('+str(round(pca.explained_variance_ratio_[0],3))+')')
 plt.ylabel('Component'+str(r+1)+'('+str(round(pca.explained_variance_rati
 o_[r], 3))+')')
 plt.xlim([-7,7])
 plt.ylim([-6,6])
 plt.title(vtot)
 plt.show()
```

Compared to the code presented before, this snippet is different because the resulting PCA decomposition is made up of five components. The larger number explores more data dimensions. Another reason for increasing the number of PCA resulting component is because of our intention to use the transformed dataset with OneClassSVM.

The core parameters are calculated from the number of observations, as follows:

- *gamma=1.0/len(normalized_data)*
- *nu=nu_estimate*

In particular, nu depends on:

$$nu\_estimate = 0.95 * outliers\_fraction + 0.05$$

So, by changing `outliers_fraction` (from 0.02 to a larger value, such as 0.1), you require the algorithm to give more attention to possible anomalies when supposing a larger incidence of anomalous cases in your data.

Let's also observe the graphical output of PCA components from two to five and compare it with the principal component (51 percent of explained variance). The first graph of the series (comprising totally four scatterplots) is as follows:

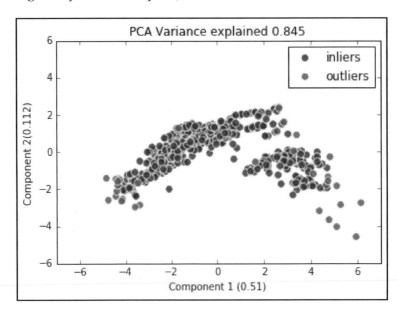

From our graphical exploration, it looks as if OneClassSVM modeled the distribution of house price data with a good fit and it helped spot a few extreme values on the borders of the distribution.

At this point, you can decide on one of the novelties and outlier detection approaches that we propose. You may even use both:

- To scrutinize the characteristics of the outliers in order to figure out a reason for their presence (a fact that could furthermore make you reflect on the generative processes underlying your data)
- To try to build some machine learning models both by using under-weighting for the outlying observations, or by just excluding them

In the end, in a pure data science approach, what will help you decide what to do next with any outlying observation is testing of the results of your decisions and consequent operations on data. How to test and experiment with hypotheses about your data is a topic that we are going to discuss with you in the upcoming sections.

Validation metrics

In order to evaluate the performance of the data science system that you have built and check how close you are to the objective that you have in mind, you need to use a function that scores the outcome. Typically, different scoring functions are used to deal with binary classification, multilabel classification, regression, or a clustering problem. Now, let's see the most popular functions for each of these tasks and how they are used by machine learning algorithms.

Learning how to choose the right score/error measure for your data science project is really a matter of experience. We found very helpful in our practice to consult (and participate) to the data science competitions held by Kaggle (https://www.kaggle.com/), a company devoted to organizing data challenges between data scientists from all over the World. By observing the various challenges and what score or error measure they try to optimize, you can surely get useful insights for your own problems. Kaggle's CTO, Ben Hammer, has even created a Python library of commonly used metrics in competitions which you can consult at https://github.com/benhamner/Metrics and install on your computer via pip install ml_metrics.

Multilabel classification

When your task is to predict more than a single label (for instance, What's the weather like today? Which flower is this? What's your job?), we call the problem as a multilabel classification. Multilabel classification is a very popular task, and many performance metrics exist to evaluate classifiers. Of course, you can use all these measures also in the case of a binary classification. Now, let's explain how it works using a simple real-world example:

```
In: from sklearn import datasets
iris = datasets.load_iris()
# No crossvalidation for this dummy notebook
from sklearn.cross_validation import train_test_split
X_train, X_test, Y_train, Y_test = train_test_split(iris.data,
iris.target, test_size=0.50, random_state=4)
# Use a very bad multiclass classifier
from sklearn.tree import DecisionTreeClassifier
classifier = DecisionTreeClassifier(max_depth=2)
classifier.fit(X_train, Y_train)
Y_pred = classifier.predict(X_test)
iris.target_names
Out: array(['setosa', 'versicolor', 'virginica'],
          dtype='<U10')
```

Now, let's take a look at the measures commonly used in multilabel classification:

- **Confusion matrix**: Before we describe the performance metrics for multilabel classification, let's take a look at Confusion matrix, a table that gives us an idea about what the misclassifications are for each class. Ideally, in a perfect classification, all the cells that are not on the diagonal should be 0s.

  In the following example, you will instead see that class 0 (setosa) is never misclassified, class 1 (versicolor) is misclassified twice as virginica, and class 2 (virginica) is misclassified twice as versicolor:

```
In: from sklearn import metrics
from sklearn.metrics import confusion_matrix
cm = confusion_matrix(Y_test, Y_pred)
print (cm)
Out: [[30  0  0]
      [ 0 19  3]
      [ 0  2 21]]
In: import matplotlib.pyplot as plt
img = plt.matshow(cm, cmap=plt.cm.autumn)
plt.colorbar(img, fraction=0.045)
for x in range(cm.shape[0]):
```

```
        for y in range(cm.shape[1]):
          plt.text(x, y, "%0.2f" % cm[x,y],
                  size=12, color='black', ha="center", va="center")
    plt.show()
    Out:
```

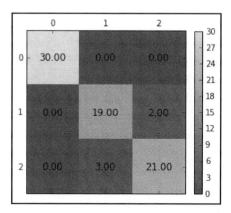

- **Accuracy**: Accuracy is the portion of the predicted labels that are exactly equal to the real ones. In other words, it's the percentage of overall correctly classified labels.

    ```
    In: print ("Accuracy:", metrics.accuracy_score(Y_test, Y_pred))
    Accuracy: 0.933333333333
    ```

- **Precision**: It is a measure that is taken from the information retrieval world. It counts the number of relevant results in the result set. Equivalently, in a classification task, it counts the number of correct labels in each set of classified labels. Then, results are averaged on all the labels:

    ```
    In: print ("Precision:", metrics.precision_score(Y_test,
    Y_pred))
    Precision: 0.933333333333
    ```

- **Recall**: It is another concept taken from information retrieval. It counts the number of relevant results in the result set, compared to all the relevant labels in the dataset. In classification tasks, that's the amount of correctly classified labels in the set divided by the total count of labels for that set. Finally, results are averaged as in the following:

    ```
    In: print ("Recall:", metrics.recall_score(Y_test, Y_pred))
    Recall: 0.933333333333
    ```

- **F1 Score**: It is the harmonic average of precision and recall, mostly used when dealing with unbalanced datasets in order to reveal if the classifier is performing well with all the classes:

```
In: print ("F1 score:", metrics.f1_score(Y_test, Y_pred))
F1 score: 0.933267359393
```

These are the most used measures in multilabel classification. A convenient function, `classification_report`, shows a report on these measures, which is very handy. Support is simply the number of observations with that label. It's pretty useful to understand whether a dataset is balanced (that is, whether it has the same share of examples for every class) or not:

```
In: from sklearn.metrics import classification_report
print (classification_report(Y_test, Y_pred,
target_names=iris.target_names))
Out:
```

	precision	recall	f1-score	support
setosa	1.00	1.00	1.00	30
versicolor	0.90	0.86	0.88	22
virginica	0.88	0.91	0.89	23
avg / total	0.93	0.93	0.93	75

In data science practice, Precision and Recall are used more extensively than Accuracy as most datasets in data problems tend to be unbalanced. To account for this imbalance, data scientists often present their results in terms of Precision, Recall, and F1-score. In addition, we have to notice how Accuracy, Precision, Recall, and F1 assume values in the [0.0, 1.0] range. Perfect classifiers achieve the score of 1.0 for all these measures (but beware of any perfect classification as of any too good to believe one, usually something wrong has happened; real-world data problems never have a perfect solution).

Binary classification

In addition to the error measures shown in the preceding section, in problems where you have only two output classes (for instance, if you have to guess the gender or predict whether the user will click/buy/like the item), there are some additional measures. The most used one, since it's very informative, is the area under **Receiver Operating Characteristics curve (ROC)** or **area under a curve (AUC)**.

The ROC curve is a graphical way to express how the performances of the classifier change over all the possible classification thresholds (that is, changes in the outcome when its parameters change). Specifically, the performances have a true positive (or hit) rate, and a false positive (or miss) rate. The first is the rate of the correct positive results, and the second is the rate of the incorrect ones. The area under that curve represents how well the classifier performs with respect to a random classifier (whose AUC is 0.50).

Here, we have a graphical example of a random classifier (dotted line) and a better one (solid line). You can see that the AUC of a random classifier is 0.5 (it is half of the square), and the other has a higher AUC (with its upper bound at 1.0):

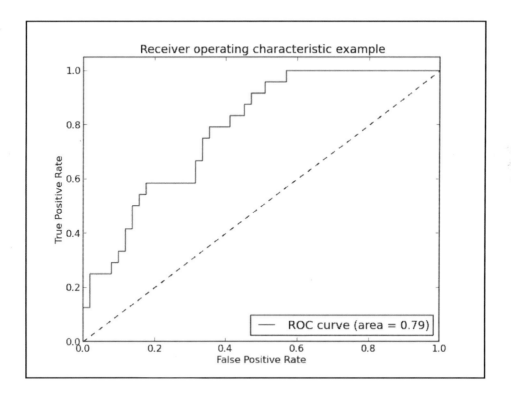

The function that is used to compute the AUC with Python is
`sklearn.metrics.roc_auc_score()`.

Regression

In tasks where you have to predict real numbers or regressions, many error measures are
derived from Euclidean algebra:

- **Mean absolute error or MAE**: This is the mean L1 norm of the difference vector
  between the predicted and real values:

  ```
  In: from sklearn.metrics import mean_absolute_error
  mean_absolute_error([1.0, 0.0, 0.0], [0.0, 0.0, -1.0])
  Out: 0.66666666666666663
  ```

- **Mean squared error or MSE**: This is the mean L2 norm of the difference vector
  between the predicted and real values:

  ```
  In: from sklearn.metrics import mean_squared_error
  mean_squared_error([-10.0, 0.0, 0.0], [0.0, 0.0, 0.0])
  Out: 33.333333333333336
  ```

- **R^2 score**: R^2 is also known as the Coefficient of Determination. In a nutshell, R^2
  determines how good a linear fit is that exists between the predictors and the
  target variable. It takes values between 0 and 1 (inclusive); the higher R^2 is, the
  better the model. It is a good score measure, yet it doesn't tell all of the story,
  especially if there are outliers in your data. There are even more intricacies about
  this metric that you can find in a reference book on Statistics. As a suggestion, use
  it, but accompany it with other score or error measurements. The function to use
  in this case is `sklearn.metrics.r2_score`.

Testing and validating

After loading our data, preprocessing it, creating new useful features, checking for outliers
and other inconsistent data points, and finally choosing the right metric, we are ready to
apply a machine learning algorithm.

A machine learning algorithm, by observing a series of examples and pairing them with their outcome, is able to extract a series of rules that can be successfully generalized to new examples by correctly guessing their resulting outcome. Such is the supervised learning approach, where it applies a series of highly specialized learning algorithms that we expect can correctly predict (and generalize) on any new data.

But how can we correctly apply the learning process in order to achieve the best model for prediction to be generally used with similar yet new data?

In data science, there are some best practices to be followed that can assure you the best results in future generalization of your model to any new data. Let's explain the practice by proceeding step by step, by first loading the dataset that we will be working on in the following example:

```
In: from sklearn.datasets import load_digits
digits = load_digits()
print (digits.DESCR)
X = digits.data
y = digits.target
```

The digit dataset contains images of handwritten numbers from zero to nine. The data format consists of a matrix of 8×8 images of this kind:

These digits are actually stored as a vector (resulting from the flattening of each 8×8 image) of 64 numeric values from 0 to 16, representing greyscale tonality for each pixel:

```
In: X[0]
Out: array([0., 0., 5., 13., 9., 1., 0., 0., ...])
```

We will also upload three different machine learning hypotheses (a hypotheses, in machine learning language, is an algorithm complete with all its parameters set ready for learning) using three different support vector machines for classification. They will be useful for our practical example:

```
In: from sklearn import svm
h1 = svm.LinearSVC(C=1.0)
h2 = svm.SVC(kernel='rbf', degree=3, gamma=0.001, C=1.0) # Radial basis SVC
h3 = svm.SVC(kernel='poly', degree=3, C=1.0) # 3rd degree polynomial SVC
```

As a first experiment, let's fit the linear SVM classifier to our data and verify the results:

```
In: h1.fit(X,y)
print (h1.score(X,y))
Out: 0.984974958264
```

The first method fits a model using the X array in order to predict correctly one of the 10 classes indicated by the y vector. After that, by calling the .score() method and specifying the same predictors (the X array), the method evaluates the performance in terms of mean accuracy with respect to the true values given by the y vector. The result is about 98.5 percent accurate in predicting the correct digit.

This number represents the in-sample performance, which is the performance of the learning algorithm. It is purely indicative, though it represents an upper bound of the performance (providing different examples, the average performance will always be inferior). In fact, every learning algorithm has a certain capability to memorize the data with which it has been trained. Therefore, the in-sample performance is partly due to the capability of the algorithm to learn some general inference from the data, and partly from its memorization capabilities. In extreme cases, if the model is overtrained or too much complex with respect to the available data, the memorized patterns prevail over the derived rules and the algorithm becomes unfit to predict correctly new observations (though it will be very good on the past ones). Such a problem is called overfitting. Since in machine learning we cannot separate these two concomitant effects, in order to have a proper estimate of the predictive performances of our hypothesis, we need to test it on some fresh data where there is no memorization effect.

Memorization happens because of the complexity of the algorithm. Complex algorithms own many coefficients, where information about the training data can be stored. Unfortunately, the memorization effect causes high variance in the estimation when predicting unseen examples since its predictive processes become random. Three solutions are possible.

Firstly, you can increase the number of examples so that it will become infeasible to store information about all the previously seen cases, but it may become more expensive to find all the necessary amount of data.

Secondly, you can use a simpler machine learning algorithm which is less prone to memorization, but at the cost of using a machine learning solution less capable of fitting the complexity of the rules underlying the data.

Thirdly, you can use regularization to penalize extremely complex models and force the algorithm to underweigh or even exclude a certain number of variables from the model, thus effectively reducing the number of coefficients in the model and its capacity to memorize data.

In many cases, fresh data is not available, if not at a certain cost. In such common case, a good approach would be to divide the initial data into a training set (usually 70-80 percent of the total data) and a test set (the remaining 20-30 percent). The split between the training and the test set should be completely random, taking into account any possible unbalanced class distribution:

```
In: In: chosen_random_state = 1
X_train, X_test, y_train, y_test = cross_validation.train_test_split(X, y,
test_size=0.30, ran-dom_state=chosen_random_state)
print ("(X train shape %s, X test shape %s, \ny train shape %s, y test
shape %s" \
% (X_train.shape, X_test.shape, y_train.shape, y_test.shape))
h1.fit(X_train,y_train)
print (h1.score(X_test,y_test))
# Returns the mean accuracy on the given test data and labels
Out:
    (X train shape (1257, 64), X test shape (540, 64),
    y train shape (1257,), y test shape (540,)
    0.953703703704
```

By executing the following code, the initial data is randomly split into two mutually exclusive sets by the `cross_validation.train_test_split()` function on the basis of the parameter `test_size` (which could be an integer indicating the exact number of examples for the test set or a float, indicating the percentage of the total data to be used for testing purposes). The split is governed by `random_state`, which assures that the operation is reproducible at different times and on different computers (even when you're using completely different operating systems).

The present average accuracy is 0.94. If you try to run the same cell again, using a different integer value for the `chosen_random_state` parameter, you will actually notice that the accuracy will change, hinting that the performance evaluation by a test set is not an absolute measure of performance and that it should be used with care. You have to be aware of its mutability given different test samples.

Actually, we can even get biased performance estimations from the test set. It could happen if we either choose (after various trials with `random_state`) a test set that can confirm our hypothesis, or start using the test set as a reference to take decisions in regard to the learning process (for example, selecting the best hypothesis that fits a certain test sample).

As with evaluating just the fit on the training data, working on a selected test set will make the resulting performance surely look great. Yet, the model you have built would not be replicating the same performances on a different test set (an overfitting problem again).

Therefore, when we have to choose between multiple hypotheses (a common experiment in data science) after fitting each of them onto the training data, we need a data sample that can be used to compare their performances, and it cannot be the test set (because of the reasons that we mentioned previously).

A correct approach is to use a validation set. We suggest that you split the initial data; 60 percent of the initial data can be reserved for the training set, 20 percent for the validation set, and 20 percent for the test set. Our initial code can be changed in order to consider this and it can be adapted to test all the three hypotheses:

```
In: chosen_random_state = 1
X_train, X_validation_test, y_train, y_validation_test =
cross_validation.train_test_split(X, y, test_size=.40,
random_state=chosen_random_state)
X_validation, X_test, y_validation, y_test =
cross_validation.train_test_split(X_validation_test,
y_validation_test, test_size=.50, random_state=chosen_random_state)
print ("X train shape, %s, X validation shape %s, X test shape %s,
\ny train shape %s, y validation shape %s, y test shape %s\n" % \
(X_train.shape, X_validation.shape, X_test.shape, y_train.shape,
y_validation.shape, y_test.shape))
```

```
for hypothesis in [h1, h2, h3]:
    hypothesis.fit(X_train,y_train)
    print ("%s -> validation mean accuracy = %0.3f" % (hypothesis,
    hypothesis.score(X_validation,y_validation)))
    h2.fit(X_train,y_train)
    print ("\n%s -> test mean accuracy = %0.3f" % (h2,
    h2.score(X_test,y_test)))
Out:
X train shape, (1078, 64), X validation shape (359, 64),
X test shape (360, 64),
y train shape (1078,), y validation shape (359,),
y test shape (360,)
LinearSVC(C=1.0, class_weight=None, dual=True, fit_intercept=True,
intercept_scaling=1, loss='squared_hinge', max_iter=1000,
multi_class='ovr', penalty='l2', random_state=None, tol=0.0001,
verbose=0) -> validation mean accuracy = 0.958
SVC(C=1.0, cache_size=200, class_weight=None, coef0=0.0,
decision_function_shape=None, degree=3, gamma=0.001, kernel='rbf',
max_iter=-1, probability=False, random_state=None, shrinking=True,
tol=0.001, verbose=False) -> validation mean accuracy = 0.992
SVC(C=1.0, cache_size=200, class_weight=None, coef0=0.0,
decision_function_shape=None, degree=3, gamma='auto',
kernel='poly', max_iter=-1, probability=False, random_state=None,
shrinking=True, tol=0.001, verbose=False) -> validation mean accuracy =
0.989
SVC(C=1.0, cache_size=200, class_weight=None, coef0=0.0,
decision_function_shape=None, degree=3, gamma=0.001, kernel='rbf',
max_iter=-1, probability=False, random_state=None, shrinking=True,
`tol=0.001, verbose=False) -> test mean accuracy = 0.978
```

As reported by the output, now the training set is made up of 1,078 cases (60 percent of the total cases). In order to divide the data in three parts—training, validation, and test—at first, the data is divided using the `cross_validation.train_test_split` function between the train set and a test/validation dataset. Then, the test/validation dataset is split into two parts using the same function. Each hypothesis, after being trained, is tested against the validation set. Obtaining an accuracy of 0.992, the SVC using a RBF kernel is the best model according to the validation set. Having decided to use this model, its performance is evaluated on the test set, resulting in an accuracy of 0.978 (which is a measure representative of the real performances of the model).

Since the test's accuracy is different from that of the validation one, is the chosen hypothesis really the best one? We suggest that you try to run the code in the cell multiple times (ideally, running the code at least 30 times should ensure statistical significance), each time changing the `chosen_random_state` value. In such a way, the same learning procedure will be validated with respect to different samples and you can be more confident of your expectations.

Cross-validation

If you have run the previous experiment, you may have realized that:

- Both the validation and test results vary, as their samples are different
- The chosen hypothesis is often the best one, but this is not always the case

Unfortunately, relying on the validation and testing phases of samples brings uncertainty along with a reduction of the learning examples dedicated to training (the fewer the examples, the more the variance of the estimates from the model).

A solution would be to use cross-validation, and Scikit-learn offers a complete module for cross-validation and performance evaluation (`sklearn.cross_validation`).

By resorting to cross-validation, you'll just need to separate your data into a training and test set, and you will be able to use the training data for both model optimization and model training.

How does cross-validation work? The idea is to divide your training data into a certain number of partitions (called folds) and train your model as many times as the number of partitions, keeping out a different partition every time from the training phase. After every model training, you will test the result on the fold that is left out and store it away. In the end, you will have as many results as folds, and you can calculate both the average and standard deviation on them.

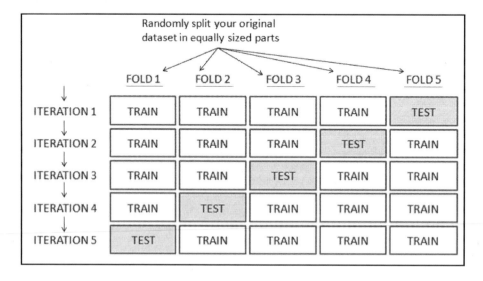

In the preceding graphical example, the chart depicts a dataset divided into five equally sized folds, which are differently used, depending on the iteration, as part of the train or test set during the machine learning process.

Ten folds is a quite common configuration in cross-validation that we recommend. Using fewer folds can be fine with biased estimators such as linear regression but it may penalize machine learning algorithms that are more complex. In some cases, you really need to use more folds to ensure that there is enough training data for the machine learning algorithm to generalize properly. That's happens quite commonly in medical datasets where there are not enough data points. On the other hand, if the number of examples at hand is not an issue, using more folds is more computationally intensive and it may require longer for the cross-validation to complete. Sometimes using five folds is a good compromise between accuracy of estimates and running times.

The standard deviation will provide a hint on how your model is influenced by the data that is provided for training (the variance of the model, actually), and the mean provides a fair estimate of its general performance. Using the mean of the cross-validation results of different models (different because of the model type, used selection of the training variables, or the model's hyperparameters), you can confidently choose the best performing hypothesis to be tested for general performance.

We strongly suggest that you use cross-validation just for optimization purposes and not for performance estimation (that is, to figure out what the error of the model might be on fresh data). Cross-validation just points out the best possible algorithm and parameter choice based on the best averaged result. Using it for performance estimation would mean using the best result found, a more optimistic estimation than it should be is. In order to report an unbiased estimation of your possible performance, you should prefer using a test set.

Let's execute an example in order to see cross-validation in action. At this point, we can review out the previous evaluation of three possible hypotheses for our digits dataset:

```
In: choosen_random_state = 1
cv_folds = 10 # Try 3, 5 or 20
eval_scoring='accuracy' # Try also f1
workers = -1 # this will use all your CPU power
X_train, X_test, y_train, y_test = cross_validation.train_test_split(X, y,
test_size=0.30, random_state=choosen_random_state)
for hypothesis in [h1, h2, h3]:
    scores = cross_validation.cross_val_score(hypothesis, X_train,
    y_train, cv=cv_folds, scoring= eval_scoring, n_jobs=workers)
    print ("%s -> cross validation accuracy: mean = %0.3f std =
    %0.3f" % (hypothesis, np.mean(scores), np.std(scores)))
Out:
LinearSVC(C=1.0, class_weight=None, dual=True, fit_intercept=True,
    intercept_scaling=1, loss='squared_hinge', max_iter=1000,
    multi_class='ovr', penalty='l2', random_state=None, tol=0.0001,
    verbose=0) -> cross validation accuracy: mean = 0.930 std =
    0.021
SVC(C=1.0, cache_size=200, class_weight=None, coef0=0.0,
    decision_function_shape=None, degree=3, gamma=0.001, kernel='rbf',
    max_iter=-1, probability=False, random_state=None, shrinking=True,
    tol=0.001, verbose=False) -> cross validation accuracy: mean =
    0.990 std = 0.007
SVC(C=1.0, cache_size=200, class_weight=None, coef0=0.0,
    decision_function_shape=None, degree=3, gamma='auto',
    kernel='poly', max_iter=-1, probability=False, random_state=None,
    shrinking=True, tol=0.001, verbose=False) -> cross validation
    accuracy: mean = 0.987 std = 0.010
```

The core of the script is the `cross_validation.cross_val_score` function. The function in our script receives the following parameters:

- A learning algorithm (`estimator`)
- A training set of predictors (`X`)
- A target variable (`y`)
- The number of cross-validation folds (`cv`)
- A scoring function (`scoring`)
- The number of CPUs to be used (`n_jobs`)

Given such input, the function wraps some other complex functions. It creates n-iterations, training a model of the n-cross-validation in-samples, testing the results, and storing scores derived at each iteration from the out-of-sample fold. In the end, the function reports a list of the recorded scores of this kind:

```
In: scores
Out: array([ 0.96899225, 0.96899225, 0.9921875, 0.98412698,
0.99206349, 1, 1., 0.984, 0.99186992, 0.98347107])
```

The main advantage of using `cross_val_score` resides in its simplicity of usage and in the fact that it automatically incorporates all the necessary steps for a correct cross-validation. For example, when deciding how to split the train sample into folds, if a y vector is provided, it keeps the same target class label's proportion in each fold as it was in the y initially provided.

Using cross-validation iterators

Though the `cross_val_score` function from the `cross_validation` module acts as a complete helper function for most of the cross-validation purposes, you may have the necessity to build up your own cross-validation process. In this case, the same `cross_validation` module guarantees a formidable selection of iterators.

Before examining the most useful ones, let's provide a clear overview about how they function by studying how one of the iterators, `cross_validation.KFold`, works.

`KFold` is quite simple in its functionality. If n-number of folds is given, it returns n iterations to the indexes of the training and validation sets for the testing of each fold.

Let's say that we have a training set made up of 100 examples and we would like to create a 10-fold cross-validation. First, let's set up our iterator:

```
In: kfolding = cross_validation.KFold(n=100, n_folds=10,
shuffle=True, random_state=1)
for train_idx, validation_idx in kfolding:
  print (train_idx, validation_idx)
Out: [ 0  1  2  3  4  5  6  7  8  9 10 11 12 13 14 15 16 18 19 20 21 22 23 24
25 26 27 28 29 30 31 32 34 35 37 38 39 40 41 42 43 44 45 46 47 48 49
50 51 52 53 54 55 56 57 58 59 60 61 62 63 64 66 67 68 70 71 72 73 74
75 76 77 78 79 83 85 86 87 88 89 90 91 92 94 95 96 97 98 99] [17 33
36 65 69 80 81 82 84 93] ...
```

By using the n parameter, we can instruct the iterator to perform the folding on 100 indexes. The n_folds specifies the number of folds. While the shuffle is set to `True`, it will randomly choose the fold components. Instead, if it is set to `false`, the folds will be created with respect to the order of the indexes (so, the first fold will be [0 1 2 3 4 5 6 7 8 9]).

As usual, the `random_state` parameter allows reproducibility of the folds generation.

During the iterator loop, the indexes for training and validation are provided with respect to your hypothesis for evaluation (let's figure out it works using h1, the linear SVC). You just have to select both X and y accordingly with the help of fancy indexing:

```
In: h1.fit(X[train_idx],y[train_idx])
h1.score(X[validation_idx],y[validation_idx])
Out: 0.90000000000000002
```

As you can see, a cross-validation iterator provides you with just the index functionality, and it is up to you when it comes to using indexes for your scoring evaluation on your hypothesis. This opens up opportunities for sophisticated operations of validation.

Among the other most useful iterators, the following are worth to be mentioned:

- `StratifiedKFold` works like `Kfold`, but it always returns folds with approximately the same class percentage as the training set. This leaves each fold balanced; therefore the learner is fitted on the correct proportion of classes. Instead of the number of cases, as an input parameter, it needs the target variable y. It is the iterator wrapped by default in the `cross_val_score` function as we have just seen in the preceding section.
- `LeaveOneOut` works like `Kfold`, but it returns as a validation set only one observation. Therefore, in the end, the number of folds will be equivalent to the number of examples in the training set. We recommend that you use this cross-validation approach only when the training set is heavily unbalanced (such as in fraud detection problems) or very small, especially if there are less than 100 observations and a k-fold validation would reduce the training set a lot.
- `LeavePOut` is similar in advantages and limitations to `LeaveOneOut`, but its validation set is made up of P cases. Therefore, the number of total folds will be the combination of P cases from all the available cases (which actually could be quite a large number as the size of your dataset grows).
- `LeaveOneLabelOut` provides a convenient way to cross-validate according to a scheme that you have prepared or computed in advance. In fact, it will act like `Kfolds` but for the fact that the folds will be already labeled and provided to the labels parameter.

- `LeavePLabelOut` is a variant of `LeaveOneLabelOut`. In this instance, the test folds are made of a number P of labels according to the scheme that you prepare in advance.

> To know more about the specific parameters required by each iterator, we suggest that you check out the Scikit-learn website: `http://scikit-learn.org/stable/modules/classes.html#module-sklearn.cross_validation`

As a matter of fact, cross-validation can also be used for prediction purposes. In fact, for specific data science projects, you may be required to build a model from your available data and then produce predictions on the very same data. As seen, using training predictions will lead to high variance estimates, given the model has been fitted on that very data and thus it has memorized much of its characteristics. The cross-validation process applied to prediction can came to the rescue:

Create a cross-validation iterator (preferably with a large number of k folds).

Iterate through the cross-validation and each time train your model with the k-1 training folds.

At each iteration, on the validation fold (which is an out-of-sample fold, actually), produce predictions and store them away, keeping track of their index. The best way for doing so is to have a prediction matrix which will be populated with predictions using fancy indexing.

Such an approach is commonly referred to as out-of-cross-validation fold prediction.

Sampling and bootstrapping

After illustrating iterators based on folds, p-out, and custom schemes, we'll continue our overview on cross-validation iterators and quote all the sampling-based ones.

The sampling schemes are different because they do not split the training set, but they sample it using different approaches: subsampling or bootstrap.

Subsampling is performed when you randomly select a part of the available data, obtaining a smaller dataset than the initial one.

Subsampling is very useful especially when you need to extensively test your hypothesis but you prefer not to obtain your validation from extremely small test samples (so, you can opt out of a leave-one-out approach or a KFold using a large number of folds). The following is an example of the same:

```
In: subsampling = cross_validation.ShuffleSplit(n=100, n_iter=10,
test_size=0.1, random_state=1)
for train_idx, validation_idx in subsampling:
  print (train_idx, validation_idx)
Out:
[92 39 56 52 51 32 31 44 78 10  2 73 97 62 19 35 94 27 46 38 67 99 54
95 88 40 48 59 23 34 86 53 77 15 83 41 45 91 26 98 43 55 24  4 58 49
21 87  3 74 30 66 70 42 47 89  8 60  0 90 57 22 61 63  7 96 13 68 85
14 29 28 11 18 20 50 25  6 71 76  1 16 64 79  5 75  9 72 12 37] [80
84 33 81 93 17 36 82 69 65]
. . .
```

Similar to the other iterators, `n_iter` will set the number of subsamples `test_size` the percentage (if a float is given) or the number of observations to be used as a test.

Bootstrap, as a resampling method, has been used since a long time to estimate the sampling distribution of statistics. Therefore, it is a proper method according to the evaluation of the out-of-sample performance of a machine learning hypothesis.

Bootstrap works randomly choosing observations and allowing repetitions, until a new dataset, which is of the same size as the original one, is built.

Unfortunately, since bootstrap works by sampling with replacement (that is, by allowing the repetition of the same observation), there are issues that arise due to the following:

- Cases that may appear both on the training and the test set (you just have to use out-of-bootstrap sample observations for test purposes)
- There is less variance and more bias than the cross-validation estimations due to non-distinct observations resulting from sampling with replacement

Scikit-learn's `cross_validation` module offered a bootstrap iterator. Anyway, the `Bootstrap` function has been deprecated as of version 0.15, and it will be removed in 0.17 because it implements a nonstandard way to perform cross-validation (it first separated the dataset in the train and test set and then bootstrapped each of them).

Although the function is useful (at least from our point of view as data science practitioners), we propose to you a simple replacement for Bootstrap that is suitable for cross-validating and which can be called by a for loop. It generates a sample bootstrap of the same size as the input data (the length of the indexes) and a list of the excluded indexes (out of the sample) that could be used for testing purposes:

```
In:
import random
def Bootstrap(n, n_iter=3, random_state=None):
    """
    Random sampling with replacement cross-validation generator.
    For each iter a sample bootstrap of the indexes [0, n) is
    generated and the function returns the obtained sample
    and a list of all the excluded indexes.
    """
    if random_state:
        random.seed(random_state)
    for j in range(n_iter):
        bs = [random.randint(0, n-1) for i in range(n)]
        out_bs = list({i for i in range(n)} - set(bs))
        yield bs, out_bs
boot = Bootstrap(n=100, n_iter=10, random_state=1)
for train_idx, validation_idx in boot:
    print (train_idx, validation_idx)
Out:
[37, 12, 72, 9, 75, 5, 79, 64, 16, 1, 76, 71, 6, 25, 50, 20, 18, 84,
11, 28, 29, 14, 50, 68, 87, 87, 94, 96, 86, 13, 9, 7, 63, 61, 22, 57,
1, 0, 60, 81, 8, 88, 13, 47, 72, 30, 71, 3, 70, 21, 49, 57, 3, 68,
24, 43, 76, 26, 52, 80, 41, 82, 15, 64, 68, 25, 98, 87, 7, 26, 25,
22, 9, 67, 23, 27, 37, 57, 83, 38, 8, 32, 34, 10, 23, 15, 87, 25, 71,
92, 74, 62, 46, 32, 88, 23, 55, 65, 77, 3] [2, 4, 17, 19, 31, 33, 35,
36, 39, 40, 42, 44, 45, 48, 51, 53, 54, 56, 58, 59, 66, 69, 73, 78,
85, 89, 90, 91, 93, 95, 97, 99]
...
```

The function performs subsampling and accepts the parameter n for the n_iter index to draw the bootstrap samples and the random_state index for reproducibility.

Hyperparameter optimization

A machine learning hypothesis is not simply determined by the learning algorithm but also by its hyperparameters (the parameters of the algorithm that have to be a priori fixed and which cannot be learned during the training process) and the selection of variables to be used to achieve the best learned parameters.

In this section, we will explore how to extend the cross-validation approach to find the best hyperparameters that are able to generalize to our test set. We will keep on using the handwritten digits dataset offered by the Scikit-learn package. Here's a useful reminder about how to load the dataset:

```
In: from sklearn.datasets import load_digits
digits = load_digits()
X, y = digits.data, digits.target
```

In addition, we will keep on using support vector machines as our learning algorithm:

```
In: from sklearn import svm
h = svm.SVC()
hp = svm.SVC(probability=True, random_state=1)
```

This time, we will work with two hypotheses. The first hypothesis is just the plain SVC that just outputs a label as a prediction. The second hypothesis is SVC enhanced by the computation of label probabilities (parameter `probability=True`) with the `random_state` fixed to the value 1 in order to guarantee reproducibility of the results. SVC outputting probabilities can be evaluated by all the loss metrics that require a probability and not a label prediction as a result, such as AUC.

After running the preceding code snippet, we are ready to import the `grid_search` module and set the list of hyperparameters that we want to test by cross-validation.

We are going to use the `GridSearchCV` function, which will automatically search for the best parameters according to a search schedule and score the results with respect to a predefined or custom scoring function:

```
In: from sklearn import grid_search
search_grid = [
  {'C': [1, 10, 100, 1000], 'kernel': ['linear']},
  {'C': [1, 10, 100, 1000], 'gamma': [0.001, 0.0001], 'kernel':
  ['rbf']},
]
scorer = 'accuracy'
```

Now we have imported the module, set the scorer variable using a string parameter (`'accuracy'`), and created a list made of two dictionaries.

The scorer is a string that we chose from a range of possible ones that you can find in the predefined values section of the Scikit-learn documentation, which can be viewed at `http:/ /scikit-learn.org/stable/modules/model_evaluation.html`.

Using predefined values just requires you to pick your evaluation metric from the list (there are some for classification and regression, and there are some for clustering) and use the string by plugging it directly, or by using a string variable, into the `GridSearchCV` function.

`GridSearchCV` also accepts a parameter called `param_grid`, which can be a dictionary containing, as keys, an indication of all the hyperparameters to be changed and, as values referring to the dictionary keys, lists of parameters to be tested. Therefore, if you want to test the performances of your hypothesis with respect to the hyperparameter C, you can create a dictionary like this:

```
{'C' : [1, 10, 100, 1000]}
```

Alternatively, according to your preference, you can use a specialized NumPy function to generate numbers that are evenly spaced on a log scale (as we have seen in the previous chapter):

```
{'C' :np.logspace(start=-2, stop=3, num=6, base=10.0)}
```

You can therefore enumerate all the possible parameters' values and test all their combinations. However, you can also stack different dictionaries, having each dictionary containing only a portion of the parameters that should be tested together. For example, when working with SVC, the kernel set to *linear* automatically excludes the gamma parameter. Combining it with the linear kernel would be in fact a waste of computational power since it would not have any effect on the learning process.

Now, let's proceed with the grid search, timing it (thanks to the `%timeit` command magic command) to know how much time it will take to complete the entire procedure:

```
In:
search_func = grid_search.GridSearchCV(estimator=h,
param_grid=search_grid, scoring=scorer, n_jobs=-1, iid=False,
refit=True, cv=10)
%timeit search_func.fit(X,y)
print (search_func.best_estimator_)
print (search_func.best_params_)
print (search_func.best_score_)
Out: 1 loops, best of 3: 9.56 s per loop
```

```
SVC(C=10, cache_size=200, class_weight=None, coef0=0.0, degree=3,
gamma=0.001, kernel='rbf', max_iter=-1, probability=False,
random_state=None, shrinking=True, tol=0.001, verbose=False)
{'kernel': 'rbf', 'C': 10, 'gamma': 0.001}
0.981081122784
```

It took about 10 seconds to complete the search on our computer. The search pointed out that the best solution is a SVC with `rbf` kernel, `C=10`, and `gamma=0.001` with a cross-validated mean accuracy of 0.981.

As for the `GridSearchCV` command, apart from our hypothesis (the estimator parameter), `param_grid`, and the scoring we just talked about, we decided to set other optional but useful parameters:

1. First, we will set `n_jobs=-1`. This forces the function to use all the processors available on the computer, we run the Jupyter cell.
2. We will then set `refit=True` so that the function fits the whole training set using the best estimator's parameters. Now, we just need to apply the `search_funct.predict()` method to fresh data in order to obtain new predictions.
3. The `cv` parameter is set to 10 folds (however, you can go for a smaller number, trading off speed with accuracy of testing).
4. The `iid` parameter is set to `False`. This parameter decides how to compute the error measure with respect to the classes. If the classes are balanced (as in this case), setting `iid` won't have much effect. However if they are unbalanced, by default, `iid=True` will make the classes with more examples weigh more on the computation of the global error. Instead, `iid=False` means that all the classes should be considered the same. Since we wanted SVC to recognize every handwritten number from 0 to 9, no matter how many examples were given for each of them, setting the `iid` parameter to `False` is the right choice. According to your data science project, you may decide that you actually prefer the default set to `True`.

Building custom scoring functions

For our experiment, we picked a predefined scorer function. For classification, there are five measures available (accuracy, AUC, precision, recall, F1 score), and for regression, there are three (R^2, mean absolute error, mean squared error). Though they are some of the most common measures, you may have to use a different measure. In our example, we find it useful to use a loss function in order to figure out if the right answer is still ranked high in probability, even when the classifier is wrong (thus considering if the right answer is the second or the third option of the algorithm). How do we manage that?

In the `sklearn.metrics` module, there's actually a `log_loss` function. All that we have to do is wrap it in a way that `GridSearchCV` might use it:

```
In: from sklearn.metrics import log_loss, make_scorer
Log_Loss = make_scorer(log_loss, greater_is_better=False,
needs_proba=True)
```

Here it is. Basically, a one-liner. We created another function (`Log_Loss`) by calling `make_scorer` to the `log_loss` error function from `sklearn.metrics`. We also want to point out that we want to minimize this measure (it is a loss, not a score) by setting `greater_is_better=False`. We will also specify that it works with probabilities, not predictions (so, set `needs_proba=True`). Since it works with probabilities, we will use the hp hypothesis, which was just defined in the preceding section, since SVC otherwise won't emit any probability for its predictions:

```
In: search_func = grid_search.GridSearchCV(estimator=hp,
param_grid=search_grid, scoring=Log_Loss, n_jobs=-1, iid=False,
refit=True, cv=3)
search_func.fit(X,y)
print (search_func.best_score_)
print (search_func.best_params_)
Out:
-0.16138394082
{'kernel': 'rbf', 'C': 1, 'gamma': 0.001}
```

Now, our hyperparameters are optimized for log loss, not for accuracy.

 A nice thing to remember-optimizing for the right function can bring much better results to your project. So, time spent working on the score function is always time well spent in data science.

At this point, let's imagine that you have a challenging task. Since it is easy to mistaken handwritten numbers 1 and 7, you have to optimize your algorithm to minimize its mistakes on these two numbers.

Ready? You can achieve this target by defining a new loss function:

```
In: import numpy as np
from sklearn.preprocessing import LabelBinarizer
def my_custom_log_loss_func(ground_truth, p_predictions,
penalty = list(), eps=1e-15):
    adj_p = np.clip(p_predictions, eps, 1 - eps)
    lb = LabelBinarizer()
    g = lb.fit_transform(ground_truth)
    if g.shape[1] == 1:
        g = np.append(1 - g, g, axis=1)
    if penalty:
        g[:,penalty] = g[:,penalty] * 2
    summation = np.sum(g * np.log(adj_p))
    return summation * (-1.0/len(ground_truth))
```

As a rule, the first parameter of your function should be the actual answer and the second should be the predictions or the predicted probabilities. You can also add parameters that have a default value or allow you to have their values fixed later on when you call the `make_scorer` function:

```
In: my_custom_scorer = make_scorer(my_custom_log_loss_func,
greater_is_better=False, needs_proba=True, penalty = [4,9])
```

In this case, we set the penalty on for highly confusable numbers 4 and 9 (however, you can change it or even leave it empty to check whether the resulting loss will be the same as that of the previous experiment with the `sklearn.metrics.log_loss` function).

Now, the new loss function computes the `log_loss` error as double when evaluating the results of the classes of numbers 4 and 9:

```
In:
from sklearn import grid_search
search_grid = [{'C': [1, 10, 100, 1000], 'kernel': ['linear']},
{'C': [1, 10, 100, 1000], 'gamma': [0.001, 0.0001], 'kernel':
['rbf']}]
search_func = grid_search.GridSearchCV(estimator=hp,
param_grid=search_grid, scoring=my_custom_scorer, n_jobs=1,
iid=False, cv=3)
search_func.fit(X,y)
print (search_func.best_score_)
print (search_func.best_params_)
Out:
-0.199610271298
{'kernel': 'rbf', 'C': 1, 'gamma': 0.001}
```

Note that for the last example, we set `n_jobs=1`. There's a technical reason behind the choice. If you are running this code on Windows (in any Unix or Mac OS system, it is actually fine), you may incur an error that may block your Jupyter notebook. All cross-validation functions (and many others) on the Scikit-learn package work by using multiprocessors, thanks to the Joblib package. Such a package requires all the functions to be run on multiple processors to be imported, and it cannot accept them being defined on the fly (they should be pickable). A possible workaround is saving the function into a file on the disk, such as `custom_measure.py`, and importing it using the `from custom_measure import Log_Loss` command.

Reducing the grid search runtime

The `GridSearchCV` function can really manage an extensive work for you by checking all combinations of parameters, as required by your grid specification. Anyway, when the data or grid search space is big, the procedure may take a long time to compute.

A potential remedy to this issue would be the following approach from the `grid_search` module offers `RandomizedSearchCV`, a procedure that randomly draws a sample of combinations and reports the best combination found.

This has some clear advantages:

- You can limit the number of computations.
- You can obtain a good result or, at worst, understand where to focus your efforts on in the grid search.
- `RandomizedSearchCV` has the same options as `GridSearchCV` but:
- An `n_iter` parameter, which is the number of random samples.
- A `param_distributions`, which has the same function as that of `param_grid`. However, it accepts only dictionaries and it works even better if you assign distributions as values, and not lists of discrete values. For instance, instead of `C: [1, 10, 100, 1000]`, you can assign a distribution such as `C:scipy.stats.expon(scale=100)`.

Let's test this function with our previous settings:

```
In: search_dict = {'kernel': ['linear','rbf'],'C': [1, 10, 100,
1000], 'gamma': [0.001, 0.0001]}
scorer = 'accuracy'
search_func = grid_search.RandomizedSearchCV(estimator=h,
param_distributions=search_dict, n_iter=7, scoring=scorer,
n_jobs=-1, iid=False, refit=True, cv=10)
%timeit search_func.fit(X,y)
print (search_func.best_estimator_)
print (search_func.best_params_)
print (search_func.best_score_)
Out:
1 loops, best of 3: 6.19 s per loop
SVC(C=1000, cache_size=200, class_weight=None, coef0=0.0, degree=3,
   gamma=0.001, kernel='rbf', max_iter=-1, probability=False,
   random_state=None, shrinking=True, tol=0.001, verbose=False)
{'kernel': 'rbf', 'C': 1000, 'gamma': 0.001}
0.981081122784
```

Using just half of the computations (7 draws against 14 trials with the exhaustive grid search), it found an equivalent solution. Let's also have a look at the combinations that have been tested:

```
In: search_func.grid_scores_
Out: [mean: 0.96108, std: 0.02191, params: {'kernel': 'linear', 'C':
1, 'gamma': 0.0001},
 mean: 0.98108, std: 0.01551, params: {'kernel': 'rbf', 'C': 1000,
'gamma': 0.001},
 mean: 0.97164, std: 0.02044, params: {'kernel': 'rbf', 'C': 100,
'gamma': 0.0001},
 mean: 0.96108, std: 0.02191, params: {'kernel': 'linear', 'C':
```

```
      1000,
     'gamma': 0.0001},
      mean: 0.96108, std: 0.02191, params: {'kernel': 'linear', 'C': 10,
     'gamma': 0.0001},
      mean: 0.96108, std: 0.02191, params: {'kernel': 'linear', 'C': 1,
     'gamma': 0.0001},
      mean: 0.96108, std: 0.02191, params: {'kernel': 'linear', 'C': 10,
     'gamma': 0.0001}]
```

Even without a complete overview of all combinations, a good sample can prompt you to look for just the RBF kernel and for certain C and gamma ranges, limiting a following grid search to a limited portion of the potential search space.

Resorting to optimization based on random processes may appear to rely on blind luck, but actually, it is a very efficient way to explore the hyperparameters' space, especially when it is a high-dimensional space. If properly arranged, random search does not sacrifice the completeness of exploration for its extent. In high dimensional hyperparameters' spaces, grid-search exploration tend to repeat testing too similar parameters' combinations, proving computationally highly inefficient in the case there are irrelevant parameters or parameters whose effects are very correlated.

Random Search has been devised by James Bergstra and Yoshua Bengio in order to make more efficient the search of optimal combinations of hyperparameters in deep learning. The original paper is a great source for further insight on the method: `http://www.jmlr.org/pa pers/volume13/bergstra12a/bergstra12a.pdf`

Statistical tests have demonstrated that for a randomized search to perform well, you should try from a minimum of 30 trials to a maximum of 60 (this rule of thumb is based on the assumption that the optimum covers from 5% to 10% of the hyperparameters' space and a 95% success rate is an acceptable one). Consequently, generally it makes sense to resort to random search if your grid search requires an analogue (so you can take advantage of random search properties) or a larger number of experiments (allowing you to save on computations).

Feature selection

With respect to the machine learning algorithm that you are going to use, irrelevant and redundant features may play a role in the lack of interpretability of the resulting model, long training times and, most importantly, overfitting and poor generalization.

Overfitting is related to the ratio of the number of observations and the variables available in your dataset. When the variables are many compared to the observations, your learning algorithm will have more chance of ending up with some local optimization or the fitting of some spurious noise due to the correlation between variables.

Apart from dimensionality reduction, which requires you to transform data, feature selection can be the solution to the aforementioned problems. It simplifies high dimensional structures by choosing the most predictive set of variables, that is, it picks the features that work well together, even if some of them are not such good predictors on an independent level.

The Scikit-learn package offers a wide range of feature selection methods:

- Selection based on the variance
- Univariate selection
- Recursive elimination
- Randomized Logistic Regression/stability selection
- L1-based feature selection
- Tree-based feature selection

Variance, univariate, and recursive elimination can be found in the `feature_selection` module. The others are a by-product of specific machine learning algorithms. Apart from tree-based selection (which will be mentioned in `Chapter 4`, *Machine Learning*), we are going to present all the methods and point out how they can help you improve your learning from the data.

Selection based on feature variance

This method is the simplest approach to feature selection, and it's often used as the baseline. Simply, it removes all the features which have small variance; typically, lower than the one set. By default, the VarianceThresholder object removes all the zero-variance features, but you can control it with the threshold parameter.

Let's create a small dataset composed by 10 observations and 5 features, 3 of them informative:

```
In: from sklearn.datasets import make_classification
X, y = make_classification(n_samples=10, n_features=5,
n_informative=3, n_redundant=0, random_state=101)
```

Now, let's measure their variance:

```
In: print ("Variance:", np.var(X, axis=0))
Out: Variance: [ 2.50852168  1.47239461  0.80912826  1.51763426
1.37205498]
```

The lower variance is associated with the third feature; therefore if we want to select the 4 beast feature, we should set the threshold of minimum variance to 1.0. Let's do that, and see what happens with the first observation of the dataset:

```
In: from sklearn.feature_selection import VarianceThreshold
X_selected = VarianceThreshold(threshold=1.0).fit_transform(X)
print ("Before:", X[0, :])
print ("After: ", X_selected[0, :])
Out:
Before: [ 1.26873317 -1.38447407  0.99257345  1.19224064
    -2.07706183]
After:  [ 1.26873317 -1.38447407  1.19224064 -2.07706183]
```

As expected, the third column is removed in the feature selection process, and all the output observations don't have it. Only the ones with variance greater than 1.0 have remained. Remember not to Z-normalize your dataset (with the StandardScaler, for example) before applying VarianceThresholder; otherwise all the features will have unitary variance.

Univariate selection

With the help of univariate selection, we intend to select single variables that are associated the most with your target variable according to a statistical test.

There are three available tests to base our selection on:

- The f_regression object uses an F-test and a p-value according to the ratio of explained variance against the unexplained one in a linear regression of the variable with the target. This is useful only for regression problems.
- The f_classif object is an Anova F test that can be used when dealing with classification problems.
- The Chi2 object is a chi-squared test, which is suitable when the target is a classification and the variables are count or binary data (they should be positive).

All the tests have a score and a p-value. Higher scores and p-values indicate that the variable is associated and consequently it is useful to the target. The tests do not take into account instances where the variable is a duplicate or is highly correlated to another variable. It is therefore mostly suited to rule out the not-so-useful variables than to highlight the most useful ones.

In order to automate the procedure, there are also some selection routines available:

- `SelectKBest`, based on the score of the test, takes the k best variables
- `SelectPercentile`, based on the score of the test, takes the top percentile of performing variables
- Based on the p-values of the tests, `SelectFpr` (false positive rate test), `SelectFdr` (false discovery rate test), and `SelectFwe` (family wise error rate procedure)

You can also create your own selection procedure with the `GenericUnivariateSelect` function using the `score_func` parameter, which takes predictors and the target and returns a score and a p-value based on your favorite statistical test.

The great advantage offered by these functions is that they present a series of methods to select the variables (fit) and later on automatically reduce (transform) all the sets to the best variables. In our example, we use the `.get_support()` method in order to get a Boolean indexing from both `Chi2` and `f_classif` tests on the top 25 percent predictive variables. We then decide on the variables selected by both the tests:

```
In:
X, y = make_classification(n_samples=800, n_features=100,
n_informative=25, n_redundant=0, random_state=101)
```

`make_classification` creates a dataset of 800 cases and 100 features. The important variables are a quarter of the total:

```
In: from sklearn.feature_selection import SelectPercentile
from sklearn.feature_selection import chi2, f_classif
from sklearn.preprocessing import Binarizer, scale
Xbin = Binarizer().fit_transform(scale(X))
# if you use chi2, input X must be non-negative: X must contain
booleans or frequencies
# hence the choice to binarize after the normalization if the
variable if above the average
Selector_chi2 = SelectPercentile(chi2, percentile=25).fit(Xbin, y)
Selector_f_classif = SelectPercentile(f_classif,
percentile=25).fit(X, y)
chi_scores = Selector_chi2.get_support()
```

```
f_classif_scores = Selector_f_classif.get_support()
selected = chi_scores & f_classif_scores # use the bitwise and operator
```

The final selected variable contains a Boolean vector, pointing out 21 predictive variables that have been made evident by both the tests.

> As a suggestion based on experience, by operating with different statistical tests and retaining a high percentage of your variables, you can usefully exploit univariate selection by ruling out less informative variables and thus simplify your set of predictors.

Recursive elimination

The problem with univariate selection is the likelihood of selecting a subset containing redundant information, whereas our interest is to get a minimum set that works with our predictor algorithm. Recursive elimination in this case could help provide the answer.

By running the script that follows, you'll find the reproduction of a problem that is quite challenging and which you may also often come across in datasets of different cases and variable sizes:

```
In: from sklearn.cross_validation import train_test_split
X, y = make_classification(n_samples=100, n_features=100,
n_informative=5, n_redundant=2, random_state=101)
X_train, X_test, y_train, y_test = train_test_split(X, y,
test_size=0.30, random_state=101)
In: from sklearn.linear_model import LogisticRegression
classifier = LogisticRegression(random_state=101)
classifier.fit(X_train, y_train)
print ('In-sample accuracy: %0.3f' % classifier.score(X_train,
y_train))
print ('Out-of-sample accuracy: %0.3f' % classifier.score(X_test,
y_test))
Out:
In-sample accuracy: 1.000
Out-of-sample accuracy: 0.667
```

We have a small dataset with quite a large number of variables. It is a problem of the p>n type, where p is the number of variables and n is the number of observations.

In such cases, there are surely some informative variables in the dataset, but the noise provided by the others may fool the learning algorithm while assigning the correct coefficients to the correct features. Keep in mind that this situation is not the best operative environment to do data science; therefore, expert mediocre results at its best.

This reflects in high (in our case, perfect) in-sample accuracy, which drops sharply when tested on an out-of-sample or using cross-validation.

In such a case, provided with a learning algorithm, instructions about the scoring/loss function and the cross-validation procedure, the RFECV class, starts fitting an initial model on all variables and calculates a score based on cross-validation. At this point, RFECV starts pruning the variables until it reaches a set of variables where the cross-validated score starts decreasing (whereas, by pruning, the score should have stayed stable or increased):

```
In:
from sklearn.feature_selection import RFECV
selector = RFECV(estimator=classifier, step=1, cv=10,
scoring='accuracy')
selector.fit(X_train, y_train)
print('Optimal number of features : %d' % selector.n_features_)
Out:
Optimal number of features : 4
```

In our example, from 100 variables, the RFECV ended up selecting just four of them. We can check the result on the test set after transforming both the training and test set in order to reflect the variable pruning:

```
In:
X_train_s = selector.transform(X_train)
X_test_s = selector.transform(X_test)
classifier.fit(X_train_s, y_train)
print ('Out-of-sample accuracy: %0.3f' % classifier.score(X_test_s,
y_test))
Out: Out-of-sample accuracy: 0.900
```

As a rule, when you notice a large discrepancy between the training results (based on cross-validation, not the in-sample score) and the out-of-sample results, recursive selection can help you achieve better performance from your learning algorithms by pointing out some of the most important variables.

Stability and L1-based selection

Though effective, recursive elimination is actually a step-by-step algorithm that bases its choices on sequences of single evaluations. While pruning, it opts for certain selections, potentially excluding many others. That's a good way to reduce a particularly challenging and time-consuming problem, such as an exhaustive search among possible sets, into a more manageable one. Anyway, there's another way to solve the problem using all the variables at hand conjointly. Some algorithms use regularization to limit the weight of the coefficients, thus preventing overfitting and the selection of the most relevant variables without losing predictive power. In particular, the regularization L1 (the lasso) is well-known for the creation of sparse selections of variables' coefficients since it pushes many variables to the 0 value according to the set strength of regularization.

An example will clarify the usage of the logistic regression classifier and the synthetic dataset that we used for recursive elimination.

By the way, `linear_model.Lasso` will work out the L1 regularization for regression, whereas `linear_model.LogisticRegression` and `svm.LinearSVC` will do it for the classification:

```
In:
from sklearn.svm import LinearSVC
classifier = LogisticRegression(C=0.1, penalty='l1',
random_state=101) # the smaller C the fewer features selected
classifier.fit(X_train, y_train)
print ('Out-of-sample accuracy: %0.3f' % classifier.score(X_test,
y_test))
Out:
Out-of-sample accuracy: 0.933
```

The out-of-sample accuracy is better than the previous one that was obtained by using the greedy approach. The secret is the `penalty='l1'` and the `C` value that was assigned when initializing the `LogisticRegression` class. Since `C` is the main ingredient of the L1-based selection, it is important to choose it correctly. This can be done by using grid-search and cross-validation, but there's an easier and an even more effective way to obtain variable selection through regularization: stability selection.

Stability selection successfully uses L1 regularization even under the default values (though you may change them in order to improve the results) because it verifies its results by subsampling, that is, by recalculating the regularization process a large number of times using a randomly chosen part of the training dataset.

The result excludes all the variables that often had their coefficient estimated to zero. Only if a variable has most of the time a non zero coefficient will the variable be considered stable to the dataset and feature set variations, and important to be included in the model (hence the name stability selection).

Let's test this by implementing the selection approach (by using the dataset that we used before):

```
In:
from sklearn.linear_model import RandomizedLogisticRegression
selector = RandomizedLogisticRegression(n_resampling=300,
random_state=101)
selector.fit(X_train, y_train)
print ('Variables selected: %i' % sum(selector.get_support()!=0))
X_train_s = selector.transform(X_train)
X_test_s = selector.transform(X_test)
classifier.fit(X_train_s, y_train)
print ('Out-of-sample accuracy: %0.3f' % classifier.score(X_test_s,
y_test))
Out:
Variables selected: 3
Out-of-sample accuracy: 0.933
```

Actually, we obtained results that were similar to that of the L1-based selection by just using the default parameters of the RandomizedLogisticRegression class.

The algorithm works fine. It is reliable and it works out of the box (there are no parameters to tweak unless you want to try lowering the C values in order to speed it up). We just suggest that you set the n_resampling parameter to a large number so that your computer can handle the stability selection in a reasonable amount of time.

If you want to resort to the same algorithm for a regression problem, you should use the RandomizedLasso class instead. Let's see now how to use it. First, we create a dataset adequate for a regression problem. For simplicity, we will use a 100-sample, 10-feature observation matrix; the number of informative features is 4.

Then, we can leave RandomizezLasso to figure out which are the most important features (the informative ones) by printing their score. Note that the score is a floating-point number:

```
In:
from sklearn.linear_model import RandomizedLasso
from sklearn.datasets import make_regression
X, y = make_regression(n_samples=100, n_features=10,
n_informative=4, random_state=101)
rlasso = RandomizedLasso()
```

```
rlasso.fit(X, y)
list(enumerate(rlasso.scores_))
Out:
  [(0, 1.0),
   (1, 0.0),
   (2, 1.0),
   (3, 0.0),
   (4, 0.0),
   (5, 1.0),
   (6, 0.0),
   (7, 0.0),
   (8, 1.0),
   (9, 0.0)]
```

As expected, the number of features with non-zero weights is 4. Select them, since they're the most informative to conduct any further analysis. That is, demonstrate the effectiveness of the method and that you can apply it safely in most feature selection situations in order to quickly have a working selection of useful features to be used in logistic or linear regression models as well as in other linear models.

Wrapping everything in a pipeline

As a concluding topic, we will discuss how to wrap together the operations of transformation and selection we have seen so far, into a single command, a pipeline that will take your data from source to your machine learning algorithm.

Wrapping all your data operations into a single command offers some advantages:

- Your code becomes clear and more logically constructed because pipelines force you to rely on functions for your operations (each step a function)
- You treat the test data in the same exact way as your train data without code repetitions or possibility of any mistake in the process
- You can easily grid-search the best parameters on all the data pipelines you devised, not just on the machine learning hyperparameters

We distinguish between two kinds of wrappers depending on the data flow you need to build: serial or parallel.

Serial processing means that your transformation steps are dependent one on the other, and consequently they have to be executed in a certain sequence. For serial processing, Scikit-learn offers the `Pipeline` class, to be found in the `pipeline` module.

Whereas, parallel processing implies that all your transformations just take origin from the same data and they can be easily executed by separate processes, whose results are to be gathered together at the end. Scikit-learn also has a class for parallel processing, `FeatureUnion`, which again is the `pipeline` module. The interesting aspect of `FeatureUnion` is that it can parallelize any serial pipeline too.

Combining features together and chaining transformations

The best way to figure out how `FeatureUnion` and `Pipeline` operate? Just recall how the Scikit-learn API works: first, a class is instantiated, then it is fitted to some data, and then the same data (or some different one) is transformed based on the previous fitting. Instead of doing so along your script, you just instruct a pipeline by providing tuples containing the name of the step and the command to be executed. According to the sequence, the operations will be executed by your Python's thread or distributed to different threads on multiple processors.

In our example, we try to replicate out previous example, building a logistic regression classifier by stability selection; we first add some unsupervised learning and feature creation on top of it. We start by setting up the problem by creating train and test datasets:

```
In:
import numpy as np
from sklearn.cross_validation import train_test_split
from sklearn.datasets import make_classification
from sklearn.linear_model import LogisticRegression
from sklearn.pipeline import Pipeline
from sklearn.pipeline import FeatureUnion
X, y = make_classification(n_samples=100, n_features=100, n_informative=5,
n_redundant=2, random_state=101)
X_train, X_test, y_train, y_test = train_test_split(X, y, test_size=0.30,
random_state=101)
classifier = LogisticRegression(C=0.1, penalty='l1', random_state=101)
```

After doing so, we instruct the parallel execution of a PCA, a KernelPCA and two custom transformers-one just passing the features as they are and the other one computing the inverse. You can expect each element in `transformer_list` to be fitted, the transformation applied, and all the results stacked together by column only when a `transform` method is executed (it is a lazy execution; defining FeatureUnion won't trigger any execution):

You will also find it useful to use the `make_pipeline` and `make_union` commands with the same results. In fact, they are commands that produce `FeatureUnion` and `Pipeline` classes ready set as an output. But they do not require you to name the steps since the naming will be done automatically by the function.

```
In:
from sklearn.decomposition import PCA
from sklearn.decomposition import KernelPCA
from sklearn.preprocessing import FunctionTransformer

def identity(x):
    return x

def inverse(x):
    return 1.0 / x

parallel = FeatureUnion(transformer_list=[
        ('pca', PCA()),
        ('kernelpca', KernelPCA()),
        ('inverse', FunctionTransformer(inverse)),
        ('original',FunctionTransformer(identity))], n_jobs=1)
```

Please notice that we have set `n_jobs` to 1, thus avoiding multiprocessing completely. That's because the `joblib` package, responsible for multi-core parallelism on Scikit-learn, is not working properly with custom-made functions on a Jupyter Notebook running on Windows. If you are working on Mac OS or Linux, you can safely set `n_jobs` to multiple workers or set all the multi-core resources on the problem (setting it to -1). Yet, when running on Windows, unless you are not using custom function but picking them from a package, or you are running your code in a script having set the __name__ variable to __main__, you will surely experience some problems. We already discussed this very same problem in more technical detail at the end of the Building custom scoring functions section in this chapter. Please also refer to our advice on that tip for more insights into the problem.

After having defined the parallel operations, we also set the rest of the pipeline ready:

```
In:
from sklearn.preprocessing import RobustScaler
from sklearn.linear_model import RandomizedLogisticRegression
from sklearn.feature_selection import RFECV
selector = RandomizedLogisticRegression(n_resampling=300, random_state=101,
n_jobs=1)
pipeline = Pipeline(steps=[('parallel_transformations', parallel),
                            ('random_selection', selector),
                            ('logistic_reg', classifier)])
```

Since one great advantage of having a complete pipeline of transformation and learning put together is the possibility to control all its parameters, we test a `grid_search` on the pipeline in order to find the best configuration of the hyperparameters:

```
In:
from sklearn import grid_search
search_dict = {'logistic_reg__C':[10,1,0.1],
 'logistic_reg__penalty':['l1','l2']}
search_func = grid_search.GridSearchCV(estimator=pipeline,
param_grid =search_dict, scoring='accuracy', n_jobs=1,
iid=False, refit=True, cv=10)
search_func.fit(X_train,y_train)
print (search_func.best_estimator_)
print (search_func.best_params_)
print (search_func.best_score_)
```

When defining your parameter grid search, you can refer to the different parts of the pipeline by writing its name, adding a couple of underscores and then the name of the parameters to tweak. For instance, acting on the `C` hyperparameter of the logistic regression requires you to address it as `'logistic_reg__C'`. If a parameter is nested in multiple pipelines, you just have to name them all, separated by double underscore, as if you were navigating into a disk directory.

Since double underscore is used to structure the hierarchy of pipeline's steps and hyperparameters, you cannot use it when naming the steps of your pipeline.

As a concluding step, we just use the resulting search for predictions on the test set. When this is done, Python will execute the complete pipeline, with the hyperparameters set by the grid search, and provide you the result. You do not anymore have to worry to replicate to the test set what you've done on the train set; a set of instructions in a pipeline will always assure consistence and reproducibility to your data munging operations:

```
In:
from sklearn.metrics import classification_report
print (classification_report(y_test, search_func.predict(X_test)))

Out:
```

	precision	recall	f1-score	support
0	0.94	0.94	0.94	17
1	0.92	0.92	0.92	13
avg / total	0.93	0.93	0.93	30

Building custom transformation functions

As you noticed, in our example we used a couple of custom transformation functions, identity and inverse, in order to have the original features along the transformed one and to make features inverse. Custom transformations help you to deal with the specific munging you have in mind for your problem and you will find them useful also just to select the features you want a certain transformation applied on (basically they can act as a filter).

You can create a custom transformation just by applying the FunctionTransformer function from sklearn.preprocessing, which turns any function into a Scikit-learn class with fit and transform methods. Yet, creating a transformation from scratch may help making things clear for you how it works.

You have to create a class. Let's see an example for filtering only certain columns, which you previously defined, from your dataset.

```
In:
class filtering():

    def __init__(self, columns):
        self.columns = columns
    def fit(self, X, y=None):
        return self

    def transform(self, X):
        if len(self.columns) == 0:
            return X
        else:
            return X[:,self.columns]
```

Using the __init__ method, you define the parameters to instantiate the class. In this case, you just record a list with the position of the columns you want to filter. Then you have to prepare both a fit and transform method for the class.

In the case of our example, the fit method just returns itself. Instead, in different situations it may be useful using the fit method in order to keep track of characteristics of the training set that you will later have to apply on the test set (for instance the mean and the variance of the features, or they maximum and minimum and so on).

The real operation that you want to achieve on data is executed in the transform method.

As you recall, since Scikit-learn operates internally using NumPy arrays, it is important to treat the data that you transform as a NumPy ndarray.

After defining the class, you can wrap it in a Pipeline or a FeatureUnion according to your needs. In our example, we just created a pipeline selecting the first five features of the training set and operating a PCA transformation on them:

```
In:
filtering([1,2,3]).transform(X_train)

Out:
array([[ 0.78503915,  0.84999568, -0.63974955],
       [-2.4481912 , -0.38522917, -0.14586868],
       [-0.6506899 ,  1.71846072, -1.14010846],
...
```

Summary

In this chapter, we extracted significant meanings from data by applying a number of advanced data operations-from EDA and feature creation to dimensionality reduction and outlier detection.

More importantly, we started developing, with the help of many examples, our data pipeline. This was achieved by encapsulating into a train/cross-validation/test setting our hypothesis that was expressed in terms of various activities-from data selection and transformation to the choice of learning algorithm and its best hyperparameters.

In the next chapter, we will delve into the principal machine learning algorithms offered by the Scikit-learn package, such as-among others-linear models, support vectors machines, ensembles of trees, and unsupervised techniques for clustering.

4

Machine Learning

After having illustrated all the data preparation steps in a data science project, we have finally arrived at the learning phase, where learning algorithms are applied. In order to introduce you to the most effective machine learning tools that are readily available in Scikit-learn and in other Python packages, we have prepared a brief introduction to all the major families of algorithms. We completed it with examples and tips on the hyper-parameters that guarantee the best possible results.

In this chapter, we will present the following topics:

- Linear and logistic regression
- Naive Bayes
- k-Nearest Neighbors (kNN)
- Support Vector Machines (SVM)
- Ensembles such as Random Forests, GBM, and XGBoost
- Stochastic, gradient-based classification and regression for big data
- Unsupervised clustering with K-means and DBSCAN
- Deep learning with Keras

Preparing tools and datasets

As introduced in the previous chapters, apart from the times when using special packages such as XGBoost for extreme gradient boosting and Keras for deep learning, the Python package for machine learning having the lion's share is Scikit-learn.

The motivations for using this open source package, developed at Inria, the French Institute for Research in Computer Science and Automation (https://www.inria.fr/en/), are multiple. It is worthwhile at this point to mention the most important reasons for using Scikit-learn for the success of your data science project:

- A consistent API (`fit`, `predict`, `transform`, and `partial_fit`) across models that naturally helps to correctly implement data science procedures working on data organized in NumPy arrays
- A complete selection of well-tested and scalable classical models for machine learning, offering many out-of-core implementations for learning from data that won't fit in your RAM memory
- A steady development with many new additions in the pipeline thanks to a group of top contributors (Andreas Mueller, Olivier Grisel, Fabian Pedregosa, Gael Varoquaux, Gilles Loupe, Peter Prettenhofer, and many others)
- Extensive documentation with many examples, to be consulted online or inline using the help command

Throughtout this chapter, we will apply Scikit-learn's machine learning algorithms to some example datasets. We will put aside the very instructive but too commonly used Iris and Boston datasets in order to demonstrate machine learning as applied to more real-life datasets. We have selected interesting examples from:

- The machine learning dataset repository (http://mldata.org/) hosted by Technische Universität Berlin
- The UCI Machine Learning Repository (http://archive.ics.uci.edu/ml/datasets.html)
- LIBSVM datasets (offered by Chih-Jen Lin from National Taiwan University)

In order to let you have such datasets, and so that do not have to rely on an Internet connect every time you want to test the examples, we advise you to download them and store them on your hard disk. Consequently, we have prepared some scripts for automatic downloading of the datasets that will be placed exactly in the directory in which you are working with Python, thus rendering data access easier:

```
import pickle
import urllib
from sklearn.datasets import fetch_mldata
from sklearn.datasets import load_svmlight_file
from sklearn.datasets import fetch_covtype
from sklearn.datasets import fetch_20newsgroups
In:
mnist = fetch_mldata("MNIST original")
```

```
pickle.dump(mnist, open( "mnist.pickle", "wb" ))
In:
target_page =
'http://www.csie.ntu.edu.tw/~cjlin/libsvmtools/datasets/binary/ijcnn1.bz2'
    with urllib.request.urlopen(target_page) as response:
        with open('ijcnn1.bz2','wb') as W:
            W.write(response.read())
In:
target_page =
'http://www.csie.ntu.edu.tw/~cjlin/libsvmtools/datasets/regression/cadata'
cadata = load_svmlight_file(urllib.request.urlopen(target_page))
pickle.dump(cadata, open( "cadata.pickle", "wb" ))
In:
covertype_dataset = fetch_covtype(random_state=101, shuffle=True)
pickle.dump(covertype_dataset, open( "covertype_dataset.pickle", "wb" ))
In:
newsgroups_dataset = fetch_20newsgroups(shuffle=True, remove=('headers',
'footers', 'quotes'), random_state=6)
pickle.dump(newsgroups_dataset, open( "newsgroups_dataset.pickle", "wb" ))
```

In case any part of the download procedure doesn't work for you, we will provide you a direct download for the datasets. After getting our compressed zip package, all you will have to do is unpack its data into the current working Python directory, which you can discover by running on your Python interface (a Jupyter notebook or any Python IDE) using this command:

```
In: import os
print ("Current directory is: "%s"" % (os.getcwd()))
```

Contrary to most of the book, the preceding scripts run only on Python3. If you really need to make them work with Python2, though this book is about Python3, you have to do some extra work and replace these words:

1. `import urlib` has to be substituted by `import urllib2`
2. `with urllib.request.urlopen(target_page) as response:` has to be removed and replaced with `response = urllib2.urlopen(target_page)`

Linear and logistic regression

Linear and logistic regressions are the two methods that can be used to linearly predict a target value or a target class, respectively. Let's start with an example of linear regression predicting a target value.

In this section, we will again use the Boston dataset, which contains 506 samples, 13 features (all real numbers), and a (real) numerical target (which renders it ideal for regression problems). We will divide our dataset into two sections by using a train/test split cross-validation to test our methodology (in the example, 80 percent of our dataset goes in training and 20 percent in test):

```
In: from sklearn.datasets import load_boston
boston = load_boston()
from sklearn.cross_validation import train_test_split
X_train, X_test, Y_train, Y_test = train_test_split(boston.data,
boston.target, test_size=0.2, random_state=0)
```

The dataset is now loaded and the train/test pairs have been created. In the next few steps, we're going to train and fit the regressor in the training set and predict the target variable in the test dataset. We are then going to measure the accuracy of the regression task by using the MAE score (as explained in Chapter 3, *The Data Pipeline*). As for the scoring function, we decided on the mean absolute error in order to penalize errors just proportionally to the size of the error itself (using the more common mean squared error would have emphasized larger errors more, since errors are squared):

```
In: from sklearn.linear_model import LinearRegression
regr = LinearRegression()
regr.fit(X_train, Y_train)
Y_pred = regr.predict(X_test)
from sklearn.metrics import mean_absolute_error
print ("MAE", mean_absolute_error(Y_test, Y_pred))
Out: MAE 3.84281058945
```

Great! We achieved our goal in the simplest possible way. Now, let's take a look at the time needed to train the system:

```
In: %timeit regr.fit(X_train, y_train)
Out: 1000 loops, best of 3: 381 µs per loop
```

That was really quick! The results, of course, are not all that great (if you see the comparison with another regressor based on Random Forest in the Jupyter notebook presented earlier in the book, in Chapter 1, *First Steps*). However, linear regression offers a very good trade-off between performance and speed of training and simplicity. Now, let's take a look under the hood of the algorithm. Why is it so fast but not that accurate? The answer is somewhat expected-this is so because it's a very simple linear method.

Let's briefly dig into a mathematical explanation of this technique. Let's name X(i) the *ith* sample (it is actually a row vector of numerical features) and Y(i) its target. The goal of linear regression is to find a good weight (column) vector W, which is best suited for approximating the target value when multiplied by the observation vector, that is, X(i) * W ≈ Y(i) (note that this is a dot product). W should be the same, and the best for every observation. Thus, solving the following equation becomes easy:

$$
\begin{bmatrix} X(0) \\ X(1) \\ \vdots \\ X(n) \end{bmatrix} * W = \begin{bmatrix} Y(0) \\ Y(1) \\ \vdots \\ Y(n) \end{bmatrix}
$$

W can be found easily with the help of a matrix inversion (or, more likely, a pseudo-inversion, which is a computationally efficient way) and a dot product. Here's the reason linear regression is so fast. Note that this is a simplistic explanation—the real method adds another virtual feature to compensate for the bias of the process. However, this does not change the complexity of the regression algorithm much.

We progress now to logistic regression. In spite of what the name suggests, it is a classifier and not a regressor. It must be used in classification problems where you are dealing with only two classes (binary classification). Typically, target labels are Boolean; that is, they have values as either True/False or 0/1 (indicating the presence or absence of the expected outcome). In our example, we keep on using the same dataset. The target is to guess whether a house value is over or under the average of a threshold value we are interested in. In essence, we moved from a regression problem to a binary classification one because now our target is to guess how likely an example is to be a part of a group. We start preparing the dataset by using the following commands:

```
In: import numpy as np
avg_price_house = np.average(boston.target)
high_priced_idx = (Y_train >= avg_price_house)
Y_train[high_priced_idx] = 1
Y_train[np.logical_not(high_priced_idx)] = 0
Y_train = Y_train.astype(np.int8)
high_priced_idx = (Y_test >= avg_price_house)
Y_test[high_priced_idx] = 1
Y_test[np.logical_not(high_priced_idx)] = 0
Y_test = Y_test.astype(np.int8)
```

Now, we will train and apply the classifier. To measure its performance, we will simply print the classification report:

```
In: from sklearn.linear_model import LogisticRegression
clf = LogisticRegression()
clf.fit(X_train, Y_train)
Y_pred = clf.predict(X_test)
from sklearn.metrics import classification_report
print (classification_report(Y_test, Y_pred))
Out:
             precision    recall  f1-score   support
          0       0.81      0.90      0.85        61
          1       0.82      0.68      0.75        41
avg / total       0.83      0.81      0.81       102
```

The output of this command can change on your machine depending on the optimization process of the LogisticRegression classifier (no seed has been set for replicability of the results).

The `precision` and `recall` values are over 80 percent. This is already a good result for a very simple method. The training speed is impressive, too. Thanks to Jupyter Notebook, we can have a comparison of the algorithm with a more advanced classifier in terms of performance and speed:

```
In: %timeit clf.fit(X_train, y_train)
100 loops, best of 3: 2.54 ms per loop
```

What's under the hood of a logistic regression? The simplest classifier a person could imagine (apart from a mean) is a linear regressor followed by a hard threshold:

$$y\_pred_i = sign(X_i * W)$$

Here, *sign(a)* = *+1* if *a* is greater or equal than zero, and 0 otherwise.

To smooth down the hardness of the threshold and predict the probability of belonging to a class, logistic regression resorts to the `logit` function. Its output is a (0 to 1] real number (0.0 and 1.0 are attainable only via rounding, otherwise the logit function just tends toward them), which indicates the probability that the observation belongs to class 1. Using a formula, that becomes:

$$Prob(y_i = +1 \mid X_i) = logistic(X_i \cdot W)$$

Here, $logistic(\alpha) = e^{\alpha} / (1 + e^{\alpha})$.

 Why the *logistic* function instead of some other function? Well, because it just works pretty well in most real cases. In the remaining cases, if you're not completely satisfied with its results, you may want to try some other nonlinear functions instead (there is limited variety of suitable ones, though).

Naive Bayes

Naive Bayes is a very common classifier used for probabilistic binary and multiclass classification. Given the feature vector, it leverages the Bayes rule to predict the probability of each class. It's often applied to text classification since it's very effective with large and fat data (that is, a data set with many features), characterized by a consistent a priori probability, handling effectively the curse of dimensionality issue.

There are three kinds of Naive Bayes classifiers; each of them has strong assumptions (hypotheses) about the features. If you're dealing with real/continuous data, the Gaussian Naive Bayes classifier assumes that features are generated from a Gaussian process (that is, they are normally distributed). Alternatively, if you're dealing with an event model where events can be modelled with a multinomial distribution (in such a case, features are counters or frequencies), you need to use the Multinomial Naive Bayes classifier. Finally, if all your features are independent and Boolean, and it is safe to assume that they're the outcome of a Bernullian process, you can use the Bernoulli Naive Bayes classifier.

Let's now try an example of the application of the Gaussian Naive Bayes classifier. Moreover, an example of text classification is given at the end of this chapter. You can test it working with a Naive Bayes by simply substituting the SGDClassifier of the example with a MultinomialNB.

In the following example, we're going to use the Iris dataset, assuming that the features are Gaussian ones:

```
In: from sklearn import datasets
iris = datasets.load_iris()
from sklearn.cross_validation import train_test_split
X_train, X_test, Y_train, Y_test = train_test_split(iris.data,
                    iris.target, test_size=0.2, random_state=0)
In: from sklearn.naive_bayes import GaussianNB
clf = GaussianNB()
clf.fit(X_train, Y_train)
```

```
Y_pred = clf.predict(X_test)
In: from sklearn.metrics import classification_report
print (classification_report(Y_test, Y_pred))
Out:
                precision    recall  f1-score   support
         0          1.00      1.00      1.00        11
         1          0.93      1.00      0.96        13
         2          1.00      0.83      0.91         6
avg / total          0.97      0.97      0.97        30
In: %timeit clf.fit(X_train, y_train)
Out: 1000 loops, best of 3: 338 µs per loop
```

The resulting model seems to have good performance and a high training speed, although we shouldn't forget that our dataset is also very small. Now, let's see how it works on another multiclass problem.

The aim of the classifier is to predict the probability that a feature vector belongs to the *Ck* class. In the example, there are three classes (setosa, versicolor, and virginica). So, we need to compute the membership probability of all classes; to make the explanation simple, let's name them *1, 2,* and *3*. Therefore, the goal of the Naive Bayes classifier for the *i*th observation is to compute the following:

$$Prob\big(Ck \mid X(i)\big)$$

Here, *X(i)* is the vector of the features (in the example, it is composed of four real numbers), whose components are [*X(i, 0), X(i, 1), X(i, 2), X(i, 3)*].

Using the Bayes' rule, it becomes:

$$Prob\big(Ck \mid X(i)\big) = \frac{Prob\big(Ck\big) \ Prob\big(X(i) \mid Ck\big)}{Prob\big(X(i)\big)}$$

We can describe the same formula, as follows: *The a-posteriori probability is the a-priori probability of the class multiplied by the likelihood and then divided by the evidence.*

From probability theory, we know that joint probability can be expressed as follows (simplifying the problem):

$$Prob\big(Ck, X(i,0),\ldots, X(i,n)\big) = Prob\big(X(i,0),\ldots, X(i,n) \mid Ck\big)$$

Then, the second factor of the multiplication can be rewritten as follows (conditional probability):

$$Prob\big(X(i,0)\,|\,Ck\big) \quad Prob\big(X(x,1),\ldots,X(i,n)\,|\,Ck,X(i,0)\big)$$

You can then use the conditional probability definition to express the second member of the multiplication. In the end, you'll have a very long multiplication:

$$Prob\big(Ck,X(i,0),\ldots,X(i,n)\big) =$$

$$\ldots$$

$$Prob(Ck) \quad Prob\big(X(i,0)\,|\,Ck\big) \quad Prob\big(X(i,1)\,|\,Ck,X(i,0)\big)\ldots$$

The naive assumption is that each feature is considered conditionally independent from the other features when related to each class. Thus, the probabilities can simply be multiplied. The formula for the same is as follows:

$$Prob\big(X(i,0)\,|\,Ck,X(:)\big) = Prob\big(X(i,0)\,|\,Ck\big)$$

Therefore, wrapping up the math, to select the best class, the following formula is used:

$$Y_{pred}(i) = \underset{k=0,1,2,3}{argmax} \ Prob(Ck) \prod_{k=0}^{n-1} Prob\big(X(i,k)\,|\,Ck\big)$$

That's a simplification, because the evidence probability (the denominator of the Bayes' rule) has been removed, since all the classes would have the same probability of the event.

From the previous formula, you can understand why the learning phase is so fast-it's just a counting of occurrences.

Note that, for this classifier, a corresponding regressor doesn't exist, but you can achieve modeling of a continuous target variable by binning it, that is, by transforming it into classes (for instance, low, average, and high values for our housing price problem).

K-Nearest Neighbors

K-Nearest Neighbors, or simply **kNN**, belongs to the class of instance-based learning, also known as lazy classifiers. It's one of the simplest classification methods because the classification is done by just looking at the K closest examples in the training set (in terms of Euclidean distance or some other kind of distance) in the case that we want to classify. Then, given the K similar examples, the most popular target (majority voting) is chosen as the classification label. Two parameters are mandatory for this algorithm: the neighborhood cardinality (K) and the measure to evaluate the similarity (although the Euclidean distance, or L2, is the most used and is the default parameter for most implementations).

Let's take a look at an example. We are going to use a large dataset, the MNIST handwritten digits. We will later explain why we decided to use this dataset for our example. We intend to use only a small portion of it (1000 samples) to keep the computational time reasonable and we will shuffle the observations in order to obtain better results (though, as a consequence, your final output may be slightly different from ours):

```
In: from sklearn.utils import shuffle
from sklearn.datasets import fetch_mldata
from sklearn.cross_validation import train_test_split
import pickle
mnist = pickle.load(open( "mnist.pickle", "rb" ))
mnist.data, mnist.target = shuffle(mnist.data, mnist.target)
# We reduce the dataset size, otherwise it'll take too much time
to run
mnist.data = mnist.data[:1000]
mnist.target = mnist.target[:1000]
X_train, X_test, y_train, y_test = train_test_split(mnist.data,
mnist.target, test_size=0.8, random_state=0)
In: from sklearn.neighbors import KNeighborsClassifier
# KNN: K=10, default measure of distance (euclidean)
clf = KNeighborsClassifier(3)
clf.fit(X_train, y_train)
y_pred = clf.predict(X_test)
In: from sklearn.metrics import classification_report
print (classification_report(y_test, y_pred))
Out:
          precision     recall   f1-score    support
    0.0       0.68        0.90       0.78         79
    1.0       0.66        1.00       0.79         95
    2.0       0.83        0.50       0.62         76
    3.0       0.59        0.64       0.61         85
    4.0       0.65        0.56       0.60         75
    5.0       0.76        0.55       0.64         80
    6.0       0.89        0.69       0.77         70
    7.0       0.76        0.83       0.79         76
```

8.0	0.91	0.56	0.69	77
9.0	0.61	0.75	0.67	87
avg / total	0.73	0.70	0.70	800

The performance is not so high on this dataset. However, please keep into consideration that the classifier has to work on ten different classes. Now, let's check the time the classifier needs for the training and predicting:

```
In: %timeit clf.fit(X_train, y_train)
Out: 1000 loops, best of 3: 1.66 ms per loop
In: %timeit clf.predict(X_test)
Out: 10 loops, best of 3: 177 ms per loop
```

The training speed is exceptional. Now, consider the algorithm. The training phase is just copying the data into some data structure the algorithm will later use and nothing else (that's the reason it is called a lazy learner). On the contrary, the prediction speed is connected to the number of samples you have in your training step and to the number of features composing it (that's actually the feature matrix number of elements). In all the other algorithms that we've seen, the prediction speed is independent of the number of training cases that we have in our dataset. In conclusion, we can say that kNN is great for small datasets, but it's definitely not the algorithm you would use when dealing with big data.

Just one last remark about this classification algorithm-you can also try the analogous regressor, `KNeighborsRegressor`, which works in the same way. Its algorithm is pretty much the same, except that the predicted value is the average of the K target values of the neighborhood.

Nonlinear algorithms

Support Vector Machine (SVM) is a powerful and advanced supervised learning technique for classification and regression that can automatically fit linear and nonlinear models.

SVM algorithms have quite a few advantages over other machine learning algorithms:

- They can handle the majority of supervised problems such as regression, classification, and anomaly detection (anyway, they are actually best at binary classification).
- Provide a good handling of noisy data and outliers. They tend to overfit less since they only work with some particular examples, the support vectors.

- Work fine with datasets presenting more features than examples, though, as other machine learning algorithms, also SVM would gain both from dimensionality reduction and feature selection.

As drawbacks, we have to mention these:

- They provide just estimates, but no probabilities unless you run some time-consuming and computationally intensive probability calibration by means of Platt scaling
- They scale super-linearly with the number of examples (so they cannot work with too large datasets)

Scikit-learn offers an implementation based on LIBSVM, a complete library of SVM classification and regression implementations, and LIBLINEAR, a scalable library for linear classification ideal of large datasets, especially any sparse text-based ones. Both libraries have been developed at the National Taiwan University, and both have been written in C++ with a C API to interface with other languages. Both libraries have been extensively tested (being free, they have been used in other open source machine learning toolkits) and have long since been proven to be both fast and reliable. The C API explains well two tricky needs for them to operate optimally under the Python Scikit-learn:

- LIBSVM, when operating, needs to reserve some memory for kernel operations. The `cache_size` parameter is used to set the size of the kernel cache, which is specified in megabytes. Though the default value is 200, it is advisable to raise it to 500 or 1000, depending on your available resources.
- They both expect C-ordered NumPy `ndarray` or SciPy `sparse.csr_matrix` (a row-optimized sparse matrix kind), preferably with float64 dtype. If the Python wrapper receives them under a different data structure, it will have to copy the data in a suitable format, slowing down the training process and consuming more RAM memory.

Nor LIBSVM nor LIBLINEAR offer an implementation capable of handling large datasets. SGDClassifier and SGDRegressor are the Scikit-learn classes that can produce a solution in a reasonable computational time even when data is too big to fit into memory. They are to be discussed in the following paragraph about handling big data.

SVM for classification

The implementations for SVM classification offered by Scikit-learn are:

Class	Purpose	Hyperparameters
sklearn.svm.SVC	The LIBSVM implementation for binary and multiclass linear and kernel classification	C, kernel, degree, and gamma
sklearn.svm.NuSVC	Same as above	nu, kernel, degree, and gamma
sklearn.svm.OneClassSVM	Unsupervised detection of outliers	nu, kernel, degree, and gamma
sklearn.svm.LinearSVC	Based on LIBLINEAR, it is a binary and multiclass linear classifier	Penalty, loss, and C

As an example of classification using SVM, we will use SVC with both a linear and a RBF kernel (**RBF** stands for **Radial Basis Function**, which is an effective nonlinear function). LinearSVC will instead be employed for a complex problem presenting a large number of observations (standard SVC won't perform well when working on more than 10,000 observations, due to the growing cubic complexity; LinearSVC can instead scale linearly).

For our first classification example, a binary one, we'll take on a dataset from the IJCNN'01 neural network competition. It is a time series of 50,000 samples produced by a physical system of a 10-cylinder internal combustion engine. Our target is binary: the normal engine firing or misfiring. We will use the dataset as retrieved from the LIBSVM website using the scripts at the beginning of the chapter. The data file is in the LIBSVM format and it is compressed by Bzip2. We operate on it using the load_svmlight_file function from Scikit-learn:

```
In: from sklearn.datasets import load_svmlight_file
X_train, y_train = load_svmlight_file('ijcnn1.bz2')
first_rows = 2500
X_train, y_train = X_train[:first_rows,:], y_train[:first_rows]
```

For exemplification purposes, we will limit the number of observations from 25,000 to 2,500. The number of available features is 22. Furthermore, we won't preprocess the data since it is already compatible with the SVM requirements, having already rescaled features in the range between 0 and 1:

```
In: import numpy as np
from sklearn.cross_validation import cross_val_score
from sklearn.svm import SVC
hypothesis = SVC(kernel='rbf', random_state=101)
scores = cross_val_score(hypothesis, X_train, y_train, cv=5,
scoring='accuracy')
print ("SVC with rbf kernel -> cross validation accuracy:
mean = %0.3f \
std = %0.3f" % (np.mean(scores), np.std(scores)))
Out: SVC with rbf kernel -> cross validation accuracy:
mean = 0.910   std = 0.001
```

In our example, we tested an SVC with an RBF kernel. All the other parameters were kept at the default values. You can try to modify `first_rows` to larger values (up to 25,000) and verify how well the algorithm scales up to an increase in the number of observations. Keeping track of the computation time, you will notice that the scaling is not linear; that is, the computation time will increase more than proportionally with the size of the data. Concerning the SVM scalability, it is interesting to see how such an algorithm behaves when faced with a multiclass problem and a large number of cases. The Covertype dataset, which we are going to use, features as examples a large number of 30×30 meter patches of forest in the US. The data pertaining to them is collected for the task of predicting the dominant species of tree of each patch (cover type). It is a multiclass classification problem (with seven `covertypes` to predict). Each sample has 54 features, and there are over 580,000 examples (but for performance reasons, we will work with just 25,000 of these cases). Moreover, the classes are unbalanced, having two kinds of trees with the most examples.

Here is the script that you can use to load the previously prepared dataset:

```
In:
import pickle
covertype_dataset = pickle.load(open("covertype_dataset.pickle",
"rb"))
covertype_X = covertype_dataset.data[:25000, :]
covertype_y = covertype_dataset.target[:25000] -1
```

Using this script, you can have an idea of the examples, features and targets to be predicted:

```
In: import numpy as np
covertypes = ['Spruce/Fir', 'Lodgepole Pine', 'Ponderosa Pine',
'Cottonwood/Willow', 'Aspen', 'Douglas-fir', 'Krummholz']
print ('original dataset:', covertype_dataset.data.shape)
print ('sub-sample:', covertype_X.shape)
print('target freq:', list(zip(covertypes,np.bincount(covertype_y))))
Out:
original dataset: (581012, 54)
sub-sample: (25000, 54)
target freq: [('Spruce/Fir', 9107), ('Lodgepole Pine', 12122), ('Ponderosa
Pine', 1583), ('Cottonwood/Willow', 120), ('Aspen', 412), ('Douglas-fir',
779), ('Krummholz', 877)]
```

Suppose we consider that, since we have seven classes, we will need to train seven different classifiers focused on predicting a single class against the others (one-vs-rest is the default behavior for `LinearSVC` in multi-class problems). We will then have 175,000 data points for each cross-validation test (so it has to be repeated three times if `cv=3`). This is quite a challenge for many algorithms, considering that there are 54 variables, but `LinearSVC` can demonstrate how to handle it in a reasonable amount of time:

```
In:
from sklearn.cross_validation import cross_val_score, StratifiedKFold
from sklearn.svm import LinearSVC
hypothesis = LinearSVC(dual=False, class_weight='balanced')
cv_strata = StratifiedKFold(covertype_y, n_folds=3, shuffle=True,
random_state=101)
scores = cross_val_score(hypothesis, covertype_X, covertype_y,
cv=cv_strata, scoring='accuracy')
print ("LinearSVC -> cross validation accuracy: mean = %0.3f \
std = %0.3f" % (np.mean(scores), np.std(scores)))
Out:
LinearSVC -> cross validation accuracy: mean = 0.645 std = 0.007
```

The resulting accuracy is 0.65, which is a good result. Yet, it surely leaves room for some further improvement. On the other hand, the problem seems to be a nonlinear one, though applying SVC with a nonlinear kernel would result into a very long training process as the number of observations is large. We will reprise this problem in the following examples by using other nonlinear algorithms in order to check whether we can improve the score obtained by `LinearSVC`.

SVM for regression

As for regression, the SVM algorithms presented by Scikit-learn are:

Class	Purpose	Hyperparameters
`sklearn.svm.SVR`	The LIBSVM implementation for regression	C, kernel, degree, gamma, and epsilon
`sklearn.svm.NuSVR`	Same as above	nu, C, kernel, degree, and gamma

To provide an example on regression, we decided on a dataset of real estate prices of houses in California (a slightly different problem than the previously seen Boston housing prices dataset):

```
In: import pickle
X_train, y_train = pickle.load(open( "cadata.pickle", "rb" ))
from sklearn.preprocessing import scale
first_rows = 2000
X_train = scale(X_train[:first_rows, :].toarray())
y_train = y_train[:first_rows]/10**4.0
```

The cases from the dataset are reduced to $2,000$ for performance reasons. The features have been scaled in order to avoid the influence of the different scale of the original variables. Also, the target variable is divided by $1,000$ in order to render it more readable in thousand dollar values:

```
In: import numpy as np
Out: SVR -> cross validation accuracy: mean = -4.618 std = 0.347
```

The chosen error is the mean absolute error, which is reported by the `sklearn` class as a negative number (but it is actually to be interpreted without a sign; the negative sign is just a computational trick used by Scikit-learn's internal functions).

Tuning SVM

Before we start working on the hyperparameters (which are typically a different set of parameters depending on the implementation), there are two aspects that are left to be clarified when working with an SVM algorithm.

The first is about the sensitivity of the SVM to variables of different scale, and large numbers. Similar to other learning algorithms based on linear combinations, having variables at different scales leads the algorithm to be dominated by features with the larger range or variance. Moreover, extremely high or low numbers may cause problems to the optimization process of the learning algorithms. It is advisable to scale all the data to limited intervals such as [0,+1], which is a necessary choice if you are working with sparse arrays. In fact, it is desirable to preserve zero entries. Otherwise, data will become dense, consuming more memory. You can also scale the data into the [-1,+1] interval. Alternatively, you can standardize them to zero mean and unit variance. You can use from the preprocessing module the `MinMaxScaler` and `StandardScaler` utility classes by first fitting them on the training data and then transforming both the train and test sets.

The second aspect is regarding unbalanced classes. The algorithm tends to favor the frequent classes. A solution, other than resampling or downsampling (reducing the majority class to the same number of the lesser one), is to weigh the C penalty parameter according to the frequency of the class (low values will penalize the class more, high values less). There are two ways to achieve this with respect to the different implementations; first there is the `class_weight` parameter in SVC (which can be set to the keyword `balanced` or provided with a dictionary containing specific values for each class). Then, there is also the `sample_weight` parameter in the `.fit()` method of SVC, NuSVC, SVR, NuSVR, and OneClassSVM (it requires a one-dimensional array as input, where each position refers to the weight of each training example).

Having dealt with scale and class balance, you can exhaustively search for optimal settings of the other parameters using `GridSearchCV` from the `grid_search` module in sklearn. Though SVM works fine with default parameters, they are often not optimal, and you need to test various value combinations using cross-validation in order to find the best ones.

According to their importance, you have to set the following parameters:

- C: The penalty value. Decreasing it makes the margin larger, thus ignoring more noise but also making the model more generalizable. A best value can normally be considered in the range `np.logspace(-3, 3, 7)`.
- `kernel`: The non-linearity workhorse for SVM can be set to linear, poly, rbf, sigmoid, or a custom kernel (for experts!). The most commonly used one is certainly `rbf`.

- degree: This works with kernel='poly', signaling the dimensionality of the polynomial expansion. Instead, it is ignored by other kernels. Usually, setting its value from 2 to 5 works the best.

- gamma: A coefficient for 'rbf', 'poly', and 'sigmoid'. High values tend to fit data in a better way but can lead to some overfitting. Intuitively, we can imagine gamma as the influence that a single example exercises on the model. Low values make the influence of each example felt quite far. Since many points have to be considered, the SVM curve will tend to take a shape less influenced by local points and the result will be a morbid contour curve. High values of gamma, instead, make the curve take into account more of how points are arranged locally. Many small bubbles explicating the influence exerted by local points will usually represent the results. The suggested grid search range for this hyperparameter is np.logspace(-3, 3, 7).

- nu: For regression and classification with nuSVR and nuSVC, this parameter approximates the training points that are not classified with confidence, that is, mis-classified points and correct points inside or on the margin. It should be in the range [0,1] since it is a proportion relative to your training set. In the end, it acts as C, with high proportions enlarging the margin.

- epsilon: This parameter specifies how much error SVR is going to accept by defining an epsilon large range where no penalty is associated with respect to the true value of the point. The suggested search range is np.insert(np.logspace(-4, 2, 7),0,[0]).

- penalty, loss, and dual: For LinearSVC, these parameters accept the ('l1','squared_hinge',False), ('l2','hinge',True), ('l2','squared_hinge',True), and ('l2','squared_hinge',False) combinations. The ('l2','hinge',True) combination is analogous to the SVC(kernel='linear') learner.

As an example, we will load the IJCNN'01 dataset again, and we will try to improve the initial accuracy of 0.91 by looking for better degree, C, and gamma values. In order to save time, we will use the RandomizedSearchCV class to increase the accuracy to 0.989 (cross-validation estimate):

```
In: from sklearn.svm import SVC
from sklearn.grid_search import RandomizedSearchCV
X_train, y_train = load_svmlight_file('ijcnn1.bz2')
first_rows = 2500
X_train, y_train = X_train[:first_rows,:], y_train[:first_rows]
hypothesis = SVC(kernel='rbf', random_state=101)
search_dict = {'C': [0.01, 0.1, 1, 10, 100],
'gamma': [0.1, 0.01, 0.001, 0.0001]}
search_func = RandomizedSearchCV(estimator=hypothesis,
```

```
param_distributions=search_dict, n_iter=10, scoring='accuracy',
n_jobs=-1, iid=True, refit=True, cv=5, random_state=101)
search_func.fit(X_train, y_train)
print ('Best parameters %s' % search_func.best_params_)
print ('Cross validation accuracy: mean = %0.3f' % search_func.best_score_)
Out: Best parameters {'C': 100, 'gamma': 0.1}
Cross validation accuracy: mean = 0.989
```

Ensemble strategies

Until now, we have seen single learning algorithms of growing complexity. Ensembles represent an effective alternative since they achieve better predictive accuracy by combining or chaining the results from models based on different data samples and algorithm settings. Ensemble strategies divide themselves into two branches. According to the method used, they assemble predictions together by:

- **Averaging algorithms**: These make predictions by averaging the results of various parallel estimators. The variations in the estimators provide further division into four families: pasting, bagging, subspaces, and patches.
- **Boosting algorithms**: These make predictions by using a weighted average of sequential aggregated estimators.

Before delving into some examples for both classification and regression, we will provide you with the necessary steps to reload the covertype dataset, a multi-class classification problem that we started exploring before when dealing with linear SVC:

```
In: import pickle
covertype_dataset = pickle.load(open( "covertype_dataset.pickle",
"rb" ))
print (covertype_dataset.DESCR)
covertype_X = covertype_dataset.data[:15000,:]
covertype_y = covertype_dataset.target[:15000]
covertypes = ['Spruce/Fir', 'Lodgepole Pine', 'Ponderosa Pine',
'Cottonwood/Willow', 'Aspen', 'Douglas-fir', 'Krummholz']
```

Pasting by random samples

Pasting is the first type of averaging ensembling we will discuss. In pasting, a certain number of estimators are built using small samples taken from the data (using sampling without replacement). Finally, the results are pooled and the estimate is obtained by averaging the results, in case of regression, or by taking the most voted class, when dealing with classification. Pasting is very useful when dealing with very large data (such as the case where it cannot fit into the memory) because it allows dealing with only those portions of data manageable by the available RAM and computational resources of your computer.

As a method, Leo Breiman, the creator of the RandomForest algorithm, devised this strategy for the first time. There are no specific algorithms in the Scikit-learn package that leverage pasting, though it is easily achievable by using the available bagging algorithms (BaggingClassifier or BaggingRegressor, the topic of the following paragraph) and setting their bootstrap parameter to False and max_features to 1.0.

Bagging with weak classifiers

Bagging works with samples in a way that is similar to that of pasting, but it allows replacement. Also theoretically elaborated by Leo Breiman, bagging is implemented in a specific Scikit-learn class for regression and one for classification. You just have to decide the algorithm that you'd like to use for the training; plug it into BaggingClassifier, or BaggingRegressor for regression problems; and set a sufficiently high number of estimators (and consequently a high number of samples):

```
In: import numpy as np
from sklearn.cross_validation import cross_val_score
from sklearn.ensemble import BaggingClassifier
from sklearn.neighbors import KNeighborsClassifier
hypothesis = BaggingClassifier(KNeighborsClassifier(n_neighbors=1),
max_samples=0.7, max_features=0.7, n_estimators=100)
scores = cross_val_score(hypothesis, covertype_X, covertype_y, cv=3,
scoring='accuracy', n_jobs=-1)
print ("BaggingClassifier -> cross validation accuracy: mean = %0.3f \
std = %0.3f" % (np.mean(scores), np.std(scores)))
Out: BaggingClassifier -> cross validation accuracy: mean = 0.795
std = 0.001
```

Weak predictors are good choices for the estimator to be used with bagging. A weak learner in classification or prediction is just an algorithm that performs poorly—just above the chance baseline with your data problem—because of its simplicity or high bias in estimation. Some good examples of this are Naive Bayes and K Nearest Neighbors. The advantage of using weak learners and ensembling them is that they can be trained more quickly than complex algorithms. Though weak in prediction, when combined, they usually achieve comparable or even better predictive performances than more sophisticated single algorithms.

Random subspaces and random patches

With random subspaces, estimators differentiate because of random subsets of the features. Again, such a solution is achievable by tuning the parameters of `BaggingClassifier` and `BaggingRegressor`, by setting `max_features` to a number less than 1.0, representing the percentage of features to be chosen randomly for each model of the ensemble.

Instead, in Random Patches, estimators are built on subsets of both samples and features.

Let's now examine, in a table, the different characteristics of pasting, bagging, random subspaces, and random patches as implemented using the `BaggingClassifier` and `BaggingRegressor` in Scikit-learn:

Ensembling	Purpose	Hyperparameters

Pasting	A number of models are built using subsamples (sampling without replacement of samples smaller than the original dataset)	`bootstrap=False`
		`max_samples <1.0`
		`max_features=1.0`

Bagging	A number of models is built using random selections of bootstrapped cases (sampling with replacement of the same size of the original sample)	`bootstrap=True`
		`max_samples = 1.0`
		`max_features=1.0`

Random Subspaces	As bagging, but also features are sampled when each model is selected	`bootstrap=True`
		`max_samples = 1.0`
		`max_features<1.0`

Random Patches	As bagging, but also features are sampled when each model is selected	`bootstrap=False`
		`max_samples <1.0`
		`max_features<1.0`

When `max_features` or `max_samples` have to be less than 1.0, they can be set at any value in the range [0,1) and you can test the best one by grid search. As per our experience, if you need to limit or speed up your search, the values that work best most frequently are between 0.7 and 0.9.

Random Forests and Extra-Trees

Leo Breiman and Adele Cutler originally devised the idea at the core of the Random Forests algorithms, and the name of the algorithm remains today a trademark of theirs (though the algorithm is open source). Random Forests are implemented in Scikit-learn as `RandomForestClassifier`/`RandomForestRegressor`.

Random Forests work in a similar way to bagging, also devised by Leo Breiman, but they operate only using binary split decision trees, which are left to grow to their extremes. Moreover, they sample the cases to be used in each of its models using bootstrapping. And as the tree is grown, at each split of a branch, the set of variables to be considered for the split is drawn randomly, too. In the end, that's the secret at the heart of the algorithm, because it ensembles trees that, due to different samples and considered variables at splits, are very different from each other. Being different, they are also uncorrelated. That's beneficial because when the results are ensembled, much variance is ruled out as in a mean the extreme values on both sides of a distribution, tend to balance each other. In other words, bagging algorithms guarantee a certain level of diversity in the predictions, allowing for developing rules that a single learner (like a decision tree) might never come across.

Extra-Trees, represented in Scikit-learn by the `ExtraTreesClassifier`/`ExtraTreesRegressor` class, are a more randomized kind of Random Forests that produce lower variance in the estimates, but at a price of greater bias of estimators. When it comes to CPU efficiency, Extra-Trees can deliver a considerable speed-up compared to Random Forests, so they can be ideal when you are working with large datasets in terms of both examples and features. The reason for the resulting higher bias but better speed is the way splits are built in an Extra-Trees. Whereas Random Forests carefully search the best values to assign to each branch from among the sampled features to be considered for splitting a branch of a tree, in Extra-Trees this is decided randomly. So there's no need for much computation, though the randomly chosen split may not be the most effective one (hence the bias).

Let's see how the two algorithms compare with the Covertype forest problem, both in terms of accuracy of the prediction and execution time. To do so, we will use the cell magic `%%time` in a Jupyter Notebook's cell in order to measure computational performance:

```
In:
import numpy as np
from sklearn.cross_validation import cross_val_score
from sklearn.ensemble import RandomForestClassifier
from sklearn.ensemble import ExtraTreesClassifier
In:
%%time
hypothesis = RandomForestClassifier(n_estimators=100,
random_state=101)
scores = cross_val_score(hypothesis, covertype_X, covertype_y,
cv=3, scoring='accuracy', n_jobs=-1)
print ("RandomForestClassifier -> cross validation accuracy:
mean = %0.3f \
std = %0.3f" % (np.mean(scores), np.std(scores)))
Out:
RandomForestClassifier -> cross validation accuracy: mean = 0.809
std = 0.009
Wall time: 7.01 s
In:
%%time
hypothesis = ExtraTreesClassifier(n_estimators=100, random_state=101)
scores = cross_val_score(hypothesis, covertype_X, covertype_y, cv=3,
scoring='accuracy', n_jobs=-1)
print ("ExtraTreesClassifier -> cross validation accuracy:
mean = %0.3f \
std = %0.3f" % (np.mean(scores), np.std(scores)))
Out: ExtraTreesClassifier -> cross validation accuracy:
mean = 0.821 std = 0.009
Wall time: 6.48 s
```

For both algorithms, the key hyperparameters that should be set are:

- `max_features`: This is the number of sampled features that are present at every split that can determine the performance of the algorithm. The lower the number, the speedier the performance will be, but with higher bias.
- `min_samples_leaf` : This allows you to determine the depth of the trees. Large numbers diminish the variance and increase the bias.
- `bootstrap` : This is a Boolean that allows bootstrapping
- `n_estimators` : This is the number of trees (remember that the more trees the better; but this comes at a computational cost that you have to take into account)

Both RandomForests and Extra-Trees are indeed parallel algorithms. Don't forget to set the appropriate number of n_jobs to speed up their execution. When classifying, they decide for the most voted class (majority voting); when regressing, they simply average the resulting values. As an example, we propose a regression example based on the California house prices dataset:

```
In: import pickle
from sklearn.preprocessing import scale
X_train, y_train = pickle.load(open( "cadata.pickle", "rb" ))
first_rows = 2000
In: import numpy as np
from sklearn.ensemble import RandomForestRegressor
X_train = scale(X_train[:first_rows, :].toarray())
y_train = y_train[:first_rows]/10**4.
hypothesis = RandomForestRegressor(n_estimators=300, random_state=101)
scores = cross_val_score(hypothesis, X_train, y_train, cv=3,
scoring='mean_absolute_error', n_jobs=-1)
print ("RandomForestClassifier -> cross validation accuracy:
mean = %0.3f \
std = %0.3f" % (np.mean(scores), np.std(scores)))
Out: RandomForestClassifier -> cross validation accuracy:
mean = -4.642 std = 0.514
```

Estimating probabilities from an ensemble

Random Forests offer a large range of advantages and they are deemed the first algorithm you should try on your data in order to figure out what kind of results can be obtained. This is because the Random Forests do not have too many hyperparameters to be fixed and they work perfectly fine out of the box. They can naturally work with multiclass problems. Moreover, Random Forests offer a way to estimate the importance of variables for your insight or feature selection, and they help in estimating the similarity between the examples, since similar cases should be ending up in the same terminal leaves of many trees of the ensemble.

However, in classification problems, the algorithm lacks the capability of predicting probabilities of an outcome (unless calibrated using the probability calibration offered in Scikit-learn by the CalibratedClassifierCV). In classification problems, often it does not suffice to predict a response label; we also need the probability associated with it (how likely it is to be true; that's a confidence of the prediction). This is particularly useful for multiclass problems since the right answer may be the second or the third most probable one (therefore, probability provides ranks of answers).

However, when Random Forests is required to estimate the probability of the response classes, the algorithm will just report the number of times an example has been classified into a class in the ensemble with respect to the number of all the trees in the ensemble itself. Such a ratio actually doesn't correspond to the correct probability, but it is a biased one (the predicted probability is just correlated to the true one; it doesn't represent it in a numerically correct way).

To help Random Forests-like other algorithms affected by a similar situation, such as Naive Bayes or linear SVM-to emit correct response probabilities, it has been introduced in Scikit-learn the wrapper `CalibratedClassifierCV` class.

`CalibrateClassifierCV` remaps the response of a machine learning algorithm to probabilities using two methods: Platt's scaling and Isotonic regression (the latter is a better performing non-parameter method under the condition that you have enough examples, that is, at least 1,000). Both approaches are, kind of, a second-level model aimed at just modeling a link between the original response of an algorithm and the expected probabilities. The results can be plotted by comparing the original probability distribution against the calibrated ones.

As an example, we refit the Covertype problem using `CalibratedClassifierCV`:

```
In:
import pandas as pd
import matplotlib.pyplot as plt
from sklearn.calibration import CalibratedClassifierCV, calibration_curve
hypothesis = RandomForestClassifier(n_estimators=100, random_state=101)
calibration = CalibratedClassifierCV(hypothesis, method='sigmoid', cv=5)
covertype_X = covertype_dataset.data[:15000,:]
covertype_y = covertype_dataset.target[:15000]
covertype_test_X = covertype_dataset.data[15000:25000,:]
covertype_test_y = covertype_dataset.target[15000:25000]
```

In order to evaluate the behavior of the calibration, we prepare a test set made of 10,000 examples that we do not use for training. Our calibration model will be based on Platt's model (`method='sigmoid'`) and use five cross-validation folds in order to tune the calibration:

```
In:
hypothesis.fit(covertype_X,covertype_y)
calibration.fit(covertype_X,covertype_y)
prob_raw = hypothesis.predict_proba(covertype_test_X)
prob_cal = calibration.predict_proba(covertype_test_X)
```

After fitting both the raw and the calibrated model, we estimate the probabilities, and we now plot them in a scatterplot in order to highlight the differences. After projecting the estimated probabilities for the ponderosa pine, it appears that the original Random Forests probabilities (actually percentages of votes) have been rescaled to resemble a logistic curve. Calibration, though not changing the accuracy of the model, helps you obtain probabilities that are more realistic:

```
In:
%matplotlib inline
tree_kind = covertypes.index('Ponderosa Pine')
probs =
pd.DataFrame(list(zip(prob_raw[:,tree_kind],prob_cal[:,tree_kind])),
columns=['raw','calibrted'])
plot = probs.plot(kind='scatter', x=0, y=1, s=64, c='blue',
edgecolors='white')
Out:
```

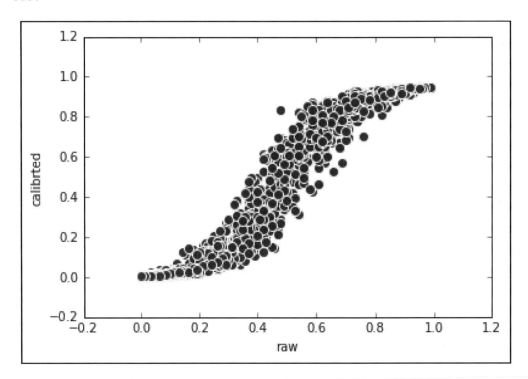

Sequences of models – AdaBoost

AdaBoost is a boosting algorithm based on the Gradient Descent optimization method. It fits a sequence of weak learners (originally stumps, that is, single-level decision trees) on reweighted versions of the data. Weights are assigned based on the predictability of the case. Cases that are more difficult are weighted more. The idea is that the trees first learn easy examples and then concentrate more on the difficult ones. In the end, the sequence of weak learners is weighted in order to maximize the overall performance:

```
In: import numpy as np
from sklearn.ensemble import AdaBoostClassifier
hypothesis = AdaBoostClassifier(n_estimators=300, random_state=101)
scores = cross_val_score(hypothesis, covertype_X, covertype_y, cv=3,
scoring='accuracy', n_jobs=-1)
print ("Adaboost -> cross validation accuracy: mean = %0.3f \
std = %0.3f" % (np.mean(scores), np.std(scores)))
Out: Adaboost -> cross validation accuracy: mean = 0.610 std = 0.014
```

Gradient tree boosting (GTB)

Gradient boosting is another improved version of boosting. Like AdaBoost, it is based on a gradient descent function. The algorithm has proven to be one of the most proficient ones from the ensemble though it is characterized by increased variance of estimates, more sensibility to noise in data (both problems could be attenuated by using sub-sampling), and significant computational costs due to nonparallel operations.

To demonstrate how GTB performs, we will again try checking if we can improve our predictive performance on the covertype dataset, which was already examined when illustrating linear SVM and ensemble algorithms:

```
In:
import pickle
covertype_dataset = pickle.load(open("covertype_dataset.pickle", "rb"))
covertype_X = covertype_dataset.data[:15000,:]
covertype_y = covertype_dataset.target[:15000] -1
covertype_val_X = covertype_dataset.data[15000:20000,:]
covertype_val_y = covertype_dataset.target[15000:20000] -1
covertype_test_X = covertype_dataset.data[20000:25000,:]
covertype_test_y = covertype_dataset.target[20000:25000] -1
```

After loading the data, the training sample size is limited to 15,000 observations in order to achieve reasonable training performance. We also extract a validation sample made of 5,000 examples and a test sample made of another 5,000 cases. We now proceed to train our model:

```
In: import numpy as np
from sklearn.cross_validation import cross_val_score, StratifiedKFold
from sklearn.ensemble import GradientBoostingClassifier
hypothesis = GradientBoostingClassifier(max_depth=5,
n_estimators=50, random_state=101)
hypothesis.fit(covertype_X, covertype_y)
In: from sklearn.metrics import accuracy_score
print ("GradientBoostingClassifier -> test accuracy:",
accuracy_score(covertype_test_y, hypothesis.predict(covertype_test_X)))
Out: GradientBoostingClassifier -> test accuracy: 0.8202
```

In order to obtain the best performance from `GradientBoostingClassifier` and `GradientBoostingRegression`, you have to tweak the following:

- `n_estimators`: Exceeding with estimators, this increases variance. If the estimators are not enough, the algorithm will suffer from high bias. The right number cannot be known a-priori and has to be found heuristically, by testing various configurations by cross-validation.
- `max_depth`: This increases the variance and complexity.
- `subsample`: This can effectively reduce variance.
- `learning_rate`: Smaller values can improve optimization in the training process, though that will require more estimators to converge and thus more computational time.
- `min_samples_leaf`: This can reduce the variance due to noisy data, reserving overfitting to rare cases.

XGBoost

XGBoost stands for eXtreme Gradient Boosting, an open source project that is not part of Scikit-learn, though recently it has been expanded by a Scikit-Learn wrapper interface that renders using models based on XGBoost more integrated into your data pipeline (http://xgboost.readthedocs.io/en/latest/python/python_api.html#module-xgboost.sklearn).

The XGBoost source code is available on GitHub, at `https://github.com /dmlc/XGBoost`; its documentation and some tutorials can be found at `http://xgboost.readthedocs.io/en/latest/`.

The XGBoost algorithm has gained recently gained momentum and popularity in data-science competitions such as Kaggle (`https://www.kaggle.com/`) and the KDD-cup 2015. As the authors (Tianqui Chen, Tong He, and Carlos Guestrin) report on papers they wrote on the algorithm, among 29 challenges held on Kaggle during 2015, 17 winning solutions used XGBoost as a standalone solution or as part of an ensemble of multiple different models.

In their paper, *XGBoost: A Scalable Tree Boosting System* (which can be found at `http://lear ningsys.org/papers/LearningSys_2015_paper_32.pdf`), the authors report that XGBoost was also used by every team that ended in the top 10 of the recent KDD-cup 2015.

Apart from the successful performances in both accuracy and computational efficiency, XGBoost is also a scalable solution under different points of view. XGBoost represents a new generation of GBM algorithms thanks to important tweaks to the initial tree boost GBM algorithm:

- A sparse-aware algorithm; it can leverage sparse matrices, saving both memory (no need for dense matrices) and computation time (zero values are handled in a special way).
- Approximate tree learning (weighted quantile sketch), which bears similar results but in much less time than the classical complete explorations of possible branch cuts.
- Parallel computing on a single machine (using multi-threading in the phase of the search for the best split) and similarly distributed computations on multiple ones.
- Out-of-core computations on a single machine leveraging a data storage solution called Column Block. This arranges data on a disk by columns, thus saving time by pulling data from the disk as the optimization algorithm (which works on column vectors) expects it.
- XGBoost can also deal with missing data in an effective way. Other tree ensembles based on standard decision trees require missing data first to be imputed using an off-scale value, such as a negative number, in order to develop an appropriate branching of the tree to deal with missing values.

XGBoost, instead, first fits all the non-missing values. After having created the branching for the variable, it decides which branch is better for the missing values to take in order to minimize the prediction error. Such an approach leads to both trees that are more compact and an effective imputation strategy leading to more predictive power.

From a practical point of view, XGBoost features mostly the same parameters as Scikit-learn's GBT. The key parameters are:

- `eta`: An equivalent of the learning rate in Scikit-learn's GTB. It impacts how fast the algorithm is learning and thus how many trees are necessary. Higher values help with better convergence of the learning process, but at the price of more training time and a larger number of trees.
- `gamma`: This acts as a stopping criteria in the tree development since it represents the minimum loss reduction required to make a further partition on a leaf node of the tree. Higher values make the learning more conservative.
- `min_child_weight`: These represent the minimum weight (examples) present on the leaf node of the tree. Higher values prevent overfitting and tree complexity.
- `max_depth`: The number of interactions in the trees.
- `subsample`: The fraction of examples from the training data to be used at each iteration.
- `colsample_bytree`: The fraction of features to be used at each iteration.
- `colsample_bylevel`: The fraction of features to be used at each branch splitting (as in Random Forests).

In our example of how to apply XGBoost, we first recall how to upload the Covertype dataset and divide it into train, validation, and test sets by partially slicing the initial NumPy array containing the complete dataset:

```
In:
from sklearn.datasets import load_svmlight_file
from sklearn.cross_validation import cross_val_score
from sklearn.cross_validation import StratifiedKFold
import pickle
covertype_dataset = pickle.load(open("covertype_dataset.pickle", "rb"))
covertype_dataset.target = covertype_dataset.target.astype(int)
covertype_X = covertype_dataset.data[:15000,:]
covertype_y = covertype_dataset.target[:15000] -1
covertype_val_X = covertype_dataset.data[15000:20000,:]
covertype_val_y = covertype_dataset.target[15000:20000] -1
covertype_test_X = covertype_dataset.data[20000:25000,:]
covertype_test_y = covertype_dataset.target[20000:25000] -1
```

After loading the data, we define the hyperparameters by first setting the objective (as `multi:softprob` but XGBoost offers other alternatives for regression, classification, multi-class and ranking) and then setting some of the preceding parameters.

When fitting the data, further indications can be given to the algorithm. In our case, we set `eval_metric` to accuracy for multi-class problems (`merror`), and provided an `eval_set` that is a validation set that XGBoost has to monitor during training by calculating the evaluation metric on it. If the training does not improve the evaluation metric for 25 rounds (as defined by `early_stopping_rounds`), then the training will stop before reaching the number of estimators (`n_estimators`) previously defined. This approach, called early-stop and derived from neural networks train, effectively helps avoid overfitting during the training phase:

For a complete list of both parameters and evaluation metrics, please see h ttps://github.com/dmlc/xgboost/blob/master/doc/parameter.md.

```
In: import xgboost as xgb
hypothesis = xgb.XGBClassifier(objective= "multi:softprob",
max_depth = 24, gamma=0.1, subsample = 0.90,
learning_rate=0.01, n_estimators = 500, nthread=-1)
hypothesis.fit(covertype_X, covertype_y, eval_set=[(covertype_val_X,
covertype_val_y)], eval_metric='merror', early_stopping_rounds=25,
verbose=False)
```

In order to obtain the predictions, we just use the same methods as Scikit-learn API: `predict` and `predict_proba`. Printing the accuracy reveals how the long fitting of the XGBoost algorithm actually brought about the best test result so far. Examination of the confusion matrix reveals that only the aspen tree type is difficult to be predicted:

```
In: from sklearn.metrics import accuracy_score, confusion_matrix
print ('test accuracy:', accuracy_score(covertype_test_y,
hypothesis.predict(covertype_test_X)))
print (confusion_matrix(covertype_test_y,
hypothesis.predict(covertype_test_X)))
Out:
test accuracy: 0.8454
[[1508  290    0    0    0    2   20]
 [ 224 2193   15    0    6   10    0]
 [   0   17  260    4    0   20    0]
 [   0    0    4   20    0    3    0]
 [   2   54    4    0   17    0    0]
 [   0   18   43    0    0   83    0]
 [  37    0    0    0    0    0  146]]
```

Dealing with big data

Big data puts data science projects under four points of view: **volume** (data quantity), **velocity**, **variety**, and **veracity** (is your data really representing what it should be or is it affected by some bias, distortion, or error?). The Scikit-learn package offers a range of classes and functions that will help you effectively work with data so large that it cannot entirely fit in the memory of a standard computer.

Before providing you with an overview of big data solutions, we have to create or import some datasets in order to give you a better idea of the scalability and performances of different algorithms. This will require about 1.5 gigabytes of your hard disk which will be let free after the experiment.

(Not big data in itself-nowadays it is hard to find computers with less than 4 GB of memory-yet not even a toy dataset, it should provide you some idea).

Creating some big datasets as examples

As a typical example of big data analysis, we will use some textual data from the Internet and we will take advantage of the available `fetch_20newsgroups`, which contains data of 11,314 posts, each one averaging about 206 words, which appeared in 20 different newsgroups:

```
In: import numpy as np
from sklearn.datasets import fetch_20newsgroups
newsgroups_dataset = fetch_20newsgroups(shuffle=True,
remove=('headers', 'footers', 'quotes'), random_state=6)
print 'Posts inside the data: %s' % np.shape(newsgroups_dataset.data)
print 'Average number of words for post: %0.0f' %
np.mean([len(text.split(' ')) for text in newsgroups_dataset.data])
Out: Posts inside the data: 11314
Average number of words for post: 206
```

Instead, to work out a generic classification example, we will create three synthetic datasets that contain from 100,000 to 10 million cases. You can create and use any of them according to your computer's resources. We will always refer to the largest one for our experiments:

```
In: from sklearn.datasets import make_classification
X,y = make_classification(n_samples=10**5, n_features=5,
n_informative=3, random_state=101)
D = np.c_[y,X]
np.savetxt('large_dataset_10__5.csv', D, delimiter=",")
# the saved file should be around 14,6 MB
del(D, X, y)
```

```
X,y = make_classification(n_samples=10**6, n_features=5,
n_informative=3, random_state=101)
D = np.c_[y,X]
np.savetxt('large_dataset_10__6.csv', D, delimiter=",")
# the saved file should be around 146 MB
del(D, X, y)
X,y = make_classification(n_samples=10**7, n_features=5,
n_informative=3, random_state=101)
D = np.c_[y,X]
np.savetxt('large_dataset_10__7.csv', D, delimiter=",")
the saved file should be around 1,46 GB
del(D, X, y)
```

After creating and using any of the datasets, you can remove them from the disk by the following command:

```
import os
os.remove('large_dataset_10__5.csv')
os.remove('large_dataset_10__6.csv')
os.remove('large_dataset_10__7.csv')
```

Scalability with volume

The trick to managing high volumes of data without loading too many megabytes (or gigabytes) of data into your memory is to incrementally update the parameters of your algorithm using only part of the examples at a time, repeating the update on the following data chunks until all the observations have been elaborated at least once by the machine learner.

This is possible in Scikit-learn thanks to the `.partial_fit()` method, which has been made available to a certain number of supervised and unsupervised algorithms. By using the `.partial_fit()` method and providing some basic information (for example, for classification, you should know beforehand the number of classes to be predicted), you can immediately start fitting your model even if you have a single case or a few observations.

This method is called `incremental learning`. The chunks of data that you incrementally fed into the learning algorithm are called batches. The critical points of incremental learning are as follows:

- Batch size
- Data preprocessing
- Number of passes with the same examples
- Validation and parameters fine tuning

Batch size generally depends on your available memory. The principle is that the larger the data chunks, the better, since the data sample will get more representatives of the data distributions as its size grows. In addition, data preprocessing is challenging. Incremental learning algorithms work well with data in the range of [-1,+1] or [0,+1] (for instance, Multinomial Bayes won't accept negative values). However, to scale into such a precise range, you need to know beforehand the range of each variable. Alternatively, you have to do one of these: pass all the data once, record the minimum and maximum values, or derive them from the first batch, trimming the following observations that exceed the initial maximum and minimum values.

 A more robust way to cope with this problem is to use a sigmoid normalization that bounds all of the range of possible values between 0 and 1.

The number of passes can become a problem. In fact, as you pass the same examples multiple times, you help the predictive coefficients converge to an optimum solution. If you pass too many of the same observations, the algorithm will tend to overfit; that is, it will adapt too much to the data repeated too many times. Some algorithms, such as the SGD family, are also very sensitive to the order that you propose the examples to be learned. Therefore, you have to either set their shuffle option (`shuffle=True`) or shuffle the file rows before the learning starts, keeping in mind that, for efficacy, the order of the rows proposed for the learning should be casual.

Validation is a stream of batches, which can be achieved in two ways:

- Validate in a progressive way; that is, test first how the model predicts newly arrived data chunks before passing them to training.
- Hold out some observations from every chunk. The latter is also the best way to reserve a sample for grid search or some other optimization.

In our example, we entrust the `SGDClassifier` with a log loss (analogous to a logistic regression) to learn how to predict a binary outcome given 10**7 observations:

```
In: from sklearn.linear_model import SGDClassifier
from sklearn.preprocessing import MinMaxScaler
import pandas as pd
streaming = pd.read_csv('large_dataset_10__7.csv',
                    header=None, chunksize=10000)
learner = SGDClassifier(loss='log')
minmax_scaler = MinMaxScaler(feature_range=(0, 1))
cumulative_accuracy = list()
for n,chunk in enumerate(streaming):
    if n == 0:
```

```
            minmax_scaler.fit(chunk.ix[:,1:].values)
        X = minmax_scaler.transform(chunk.ix[:,1:].values)
        X[X>1] = 1
        X[X<0] = 0
        y = chunk.ix[:,0]
        if n > 8 :
            cumulative_accuracy.append(learner.score(X,y))
        learner.partial_fit(X,y,classes=np.unique(y))
print ('Progressive validation mean accuracy \
%0.3f' % np.mean(cumulative_accuracy))
Out: Progressive validation mean accuracy 0.660
```

First, pandas `read_csv` allows us to iterate over the file by reading batches of 10,000 observations (the number can be increased or decreased according to your computing resources).

We use the `MinMaxScaler` in order to record the range of each variable on the first batch. For the following batches, we will use the rule that if it exceeds one of the limits of [0,+1], they are trimmed to the nearest limit. Otherwise, we can use the `partial_fit` method of the MinMaxScaler and learn the boundaries of the features as we learn with our model. The only caveat to be considered when using the `MinMaxScaler` though is attention to outliers, because they can compress the numeric transformation to a portion of the [0, +1] interval.

Eventually, starting from the tenth batch, we will record the accuracy of the learning algorithm on each newly received batch before using it to update the training. In the end, the accumulated accuracy scores are averaged, offering global performance estimation.

Keeping up with velocity

Various algorithms work using incremental learning. For classification, we will recall the following:

- `sklearn.naive_bayes.MultinomialNB`
- `sklearn.naive_bayes.BernoulliNB`
- `sklearn.linear_model.Perceptron`
- `sklearn.linear_model.SGDClassifier`
- `sklearn.linear_model.PassiveAggressiveClassifier`

For regression, we will recall the following:

- `sklearn.linear_model.SGDRegressor`
- `sklearn.linear_model.PassiveAggressiveRegressor`

As for velocity, they are all comparable in speed. You can try for yourself the following script:

```
In: from sklearn.naive_bayes import MultinomialNB
from sklearn.naive_bayes import BernoulliNB
from sklearn.linear_model import Perceptron
from sklearn.linear_model import SGDClassifier
from sklearn.linear_model import PassiveAggressiveClassifier
import pandas as pd
from datetime import datetime
classifiers  = {
'SGDClassifier hinge loss' : SGDClassifier(loss='hinge',
random_state=101),
'SGDClassifier log loss' : SGDClassifier(loss='log',
random_state=101),
'Perceptron' : Perceptron(random_state=101),
'BernoulliNB' : BernoulliNB(),
'PassiveAggressiveClassifier' :
PassiveAggressiveClassifier(random_state=101)
}
huge_dataset = 'large_dataset_10__6.csv'
for algorithm in classifiers:
    start = datetime.now()
    minmax_scaler = MinMaxScaler(feature_range=(0, 1))
    streaming = pd.read_csv(huge_dataset, header=None,
    chunksize=100)
    learner = classifiers[algorithm]
    cumulative_accuracy = list()
    for n,chunk in enumerate(streaming):
        y = chunk.ix[:,0]
        X = chunk.ix[:,1:]
        if n > 50 :
            cumulative_accuracy.append(learner.score(X,y))
        learner.partial_fit(X,y,classes=np.unique(y))
    elapsed_time = datetime.now() - start
    print (algorithm + ' : mean accuracy %0.3f in %s secs' \
% (np.mean(cumulative_accuracy),elapsed_time.total_seconds()))
Out: BernoulliNB : mean accuracy 0.734 in 41.101 secs
Perceptron : mean accuracy 0.616 in 37.479 secs
SGDClassifier hinge loss : mean accuracy 0.712 in 38.43 secs
SGDClassifier log loss : mean accuracy 0.716 in 39.618 secs
PassiveAggressiveClassifier : mean accuracy 0.625 in 40.622 secs
```

As a general note, remember that smaller batches are slower since that implies more disk access from a database or a file, which is always a bottleneck.

Dealing with variety

Variety is another typical characteristic of big data. This is especially true when we are dealing with textual data or very large categorical variables (for example, variables storing website names in programmatic advertising). As you learn from batches of examples and as you unfold categories or words, you will see that each one is an appropriate and exclusive variable. You may find it difficult to handle the challenge of variety and the unpredictability of large streams of data. Scikit-learn provides you with a simple and fast way to implement the hashing trick and completely forget the problem of defining in advance of a rigid variable structure.

The hashing trick uses hash functions and sparse matrices in order to save your time, resources, and hassle. The hash functions are functions that map in a deterministic way any input they receive. It doesn't matter if you feed them with numbers or strings, they will always provide you with an integer number in a certain range. Sparse matrices are, instead, arrays that record only values that are not zero, since their default value is zero for any combination of their row and column. Therefore, the hashing trick bounds every possible input; it doesn't matter if it was previously unseen to a certain range or position on a corresponding input sparse matrix, which is loaded with a value that is not 0.

Apart from the in-built hash function in Python, there are quite a few hashing algorithms available in packages such as hashlib (`https://docs.python.org/2/library/hashlib.html`). Interestingly, also the hash function heavily used by Scikit-learn in many functions and methods, the MurmurHash 32 (`https://en.wikipedia.org/wiki/MurmurHash`) is available for you to use. It can be found among the utilities for developers (`http://scikit-learn.org/stable/developers/utilities.html`); just import it and use it straight out of the box:

```
from sklearn.utils import murmurhash3_32
print (murmurhash3_32("something", seed=0, positive=True))
```

For instance, if your input is `Python`, a hashing command like `abs(hash('Python'))` can transform that into the integer number 539294296 and then assign the value of 1 to the cell at the 539294296 column index. The hash function is a very fast and convenient way to locate invariably the same column index given the same input. The use of only absolute values ensures that each index corresponds only to a column in our array (negative indexes just start from the last column, and hence, in Python, each column of an array can be expressed by both a positive and negative number).

The example that follows uses the `HashingVectorizer` class, a convenient class that automatically takes documents, separates the words, and transforms them, thanks to the hashing trick, into an input matrix. The script aims at learning why posts are published in 20 distinct newsgroups based on the words used in the existing posts in the newsgroups:

```
In: import pandas as pd
from sklearn.linear_model import SGDClassifier
from sklearn.feature_extraction.text import HashingVectorizer
def streaming():
    for response, item in zip(newsgroups_dataset.target,
    newsgroups_dataset.data): yield response, item
    hashing_trick = HashingVectorizer(stop_words='english',
    norm = 'l2', non_negative=True)
learner = SGDClassifier(random_state=101)
texts = list()
targets = list()
for n,(target, text) in enumerate(streaming()):
    texts.append(text)
    targets.append(target)
    if n % 1000 == 0 and n >0:
        learning_chunk = hashing_trick.transform(texts)
        if n > 1000:
            last_validation_score = learner.score(learning_chunk,
            targets),
        learner.partial_fit(learning_chunk, targets,
        classes=[k for k in range(20)])
        texts, targets = list(), list()
print ('Last validation score: %0.3f' % last_validation_score)
Out: Last validation score: 0.710
```

At this point, no matter what text you may input, the predictive algorithm will always answer by pointing out a class. In our case, it points out a `newsgroup` suitable for the post to appear on it. Let's try out this algorithm with a text taken from a classified ad:

```
In: New_text = ['A 2014 red Toyota Prius v Five with fewer than 14K miles.
Powered by a reliable 1.8L four cylinder hybrid engine that averages 44mpg
in the city and 40mpg on the highway.']
text_vector = hashing_trick.transform(New_text)
print (np.shape(text_vector), type(text_vector))
print ('Predicted newsgroup: %s' % \
newsgroups_dataset.target_names[learner.predict(text_vector)])
Out:
(1, 1048576) <class 'scipy.sparse.csr.csr_matrix'>
Predicted newsgroup: rec.autos
```

Naturally, you may change the `New_text` variable and discover where your text most likely to be displayed in a newsgroup. Note that the `HashingVectorizer` class has transformed the text into a `csr_matrix` (which is quite an efficient sparse matrix) in order to save memory, having a dataset of about one million columns.

An overview of Stochastic Gradient Descent (SGD)

We will complete this part of the chapter devoted to learning from big data with a quick overview of the SGD family, comprising SGDClassifier (for classification) and SGDRegressor (for regression).

Like other classifiers, they can be fit by using the `.fit()` method (passing the in-memory dataset to the learning algorithm row by row) or the previously seen `.partial_fit()` method based on batches. In the latter case, if you are classifying, you have to declare the predicted classes with the class parameter. It can accept a list containing all the class code that it should expect to meet during the training phase.

SGDClassifier can behave as a logistic regression when the loss parameter is set to `loss`. It transforms into a linear SVC if the loss is set to `hinge`. It can also take the form of other loss functions or even the loss functions working for regression.

SGDRegressor mimics a linear regression using the `squared_loss` loss parameter. Instead, the huber loss transforms the squared loss into a linear loss over a certain distance epsilon (another parameter to be fixed). It can also act as a linear SVR using the `epsilon_insensitive` loss function or the slightly different `squared_epsilon_insensitive` (which penalizes outliers more).

As in other situations with machine learning, performance of the different loss functions on your data science problem cannot be estimated a priori. Anyway, please take into account that if you are doing classification and you need an estimation of class probabilities, you will be limited in your choice to `log` or `modified_huber` only.

The key parameters that require tuning for this algorithm to work best with your data are:

- n_iter: The number of iterations over the data. As a rule of thumb, the more the passes, the better the optimization of the algorithm. However, there is a higher risk of overfitting if there are too many passes. Empirically, SGD tends to converge to a stable solution after having seen *10**6* examples. Given your examples, set your number of iterations accordingly.
- penalty: You have to choose l1, l2, or elasticnet, which are all different regularization strategies, in order to avoid overfitting because of overparametrization (using too many unnecessary parameters leads to the memorization of observations more than the learning of patterns). Briefly, l1 tends to reduce unhelpful coefficients to zero, l2 just attenuates them, and elasticnet is a mix of l1 and l2 strategies.
- alpha: This is a multiplier of the regularization term; the higher the alpha, the more the regularization. We advise you to find the best alpha value by performing a grid search ranging from *10**-7* to *10**-1*.
- l1_ratio: The l1 ratio is used for elastic net penalty. The suggested value or 0.15 will usually prove quite effective.
- learning_rate: This sets how much the coefficients are affected by every single example. Usually, it is optimal for classifiers and invscaling for regression. If you want to use invscaling for classification, you'll have to set eta0 and power_t (invscaling = eta0 / (t**power_t)). With invscaling, you can start with a lower learning rate, which is less than the optimal rate, though it will decrease slower.
- epsilon: This should be used if your loss is huber, epsilon_insensitive, or squared_epsilon_insensitive.
- shuffle: If this is True, the algorithm will shuffle the order of the training data in order to improve the generalization of the learning.

Approaching deep learning

Deep learning, along with neural networks, is an extension of the classical machine learning approach to solving a problem: instead of developing new learners, we can stack together some well-known ones to create an elaborate, but more powerful, learner. This is something similar to the bagging and boosting approach we've seen in the previous section, but with deep learning, this concept is pushed to the limits. Deep learning is nowadays one of the most popular methods of **Artificial Intelligence (AI)**, since it's very effective and general purpose.

The idea of neural networks came from the human central nervous system, where multiple nodes (or, *neurons)* able to process simple information are connected together to create a network capable to process complex information. In fact, neural networks are named so because they can learn autonomously and adaptively the weights of the model, and they're able to approximate any nonlinear function. In deep learning, the nodes are usually called units or neurons.

Let's see how a deep architecture is built and what its components are. We will start with a small deep architecture for a classification problem, composed of three layers.

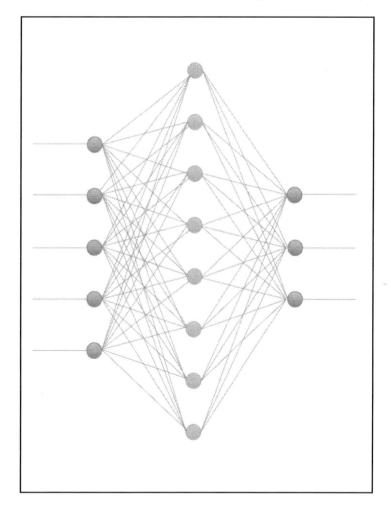

This network has the following characteristics:

- It has three layers. The left one (composed by blue units) is named input layer, the right one (purple units) is named output layer, and the central one (orange units) is the hidden layer. Generically in a neural network, there is always one input and one output layer, and zero or more hidden layers (when hidden layers are zero, the whole thing will turn into a logistic regression system).

- The input layer is composed of five units; that means that each observation vector is composed of five numerical features (that is, the observation matrix has five columns). Note that the features must be numeric and bounded in a bounded range of values (for better numeric convergence, ideally the range is 0 to +1, but -1 to +1 is also fine). Therefore, categorical features must be pre-processed in order to become numerical.

- The output layer is composed of three units; that means we want to differentiate among three output classes (that is, the task a three-class classification). In the case of a regression problem, there should be just one unit in this layer.

- The hidden layer is composed of eight units. Note that there's no rule about how many hidden layers should appear in the deep architecture and how many units each should have. These parameters are left to the scientist, and usually they are parameters of the optimization.

- Each connection has a weight associated with it. This is optimized during the learning algorithm.

Note that each unit of the input layer is connected to all the units of the next layer. There are neither connections between the units in the same layers, nor connections to units to two of the layers at a distance greater than 1.

In the example, the flow of information is passed forward, from the input to the output (passing eventually through the hidden layers); in literature, this network is referred to as *feed-forward neural network*.

How is it created the final prediction? Let's see, step by step, how it works. Starting from the top unit of the hidden layer, it performs a dot product between the output vector of the first layer (that is, the input observation vector) with the vector of weights of the connections between the first layer and the first unit of the hidden layer. The value is then transformed with the activation function of the unit (see later). This operation is repeated for all the units in the hidden layer. Finally, we can compute the feed-forward propagated values between the hidden layer and the output layer at the same way, producing the outputs of the network.

The process seems very easy, and it's composed of multiple embarrassingly parallel tasks. The last missing point of the explanation is the activation function: what is it and why is it needed? The activation function helps to make binary decisions more separable and it's a property (or an attribute) of each unit; ideally each unit can have a different activation function, although they're usually the grouped by layer.

Typical activation functions are the sigmoid, the hyperbolic tangent and the softmax (for classification problems), although one of the most popular is the rectified linear unit (or relu), whose output is the maximum between 0 and the input (where the input is the dot product between the previous layer output and the weights of the connections).

The activation function, as the number of units and the number of hidden layers, is a parameter of the deep network and should be optimized by the scientist to obtain the better performance.

Training a neural network is a hard operation, since there is a very high number (sometimes millions) of parameters to tune: the weights. The most common way to assign weights to the connections uses a similar approach as gradient descend, and it's named backpropagation, because it propagates back the errors from the output layer toward the input layer, updating each weight proportionally to the gradient of the error at that point in the network. Initially weights are assigned at random, but after a few steps, they should converge toward the optimal value.

This was a very short introduction to deep learning and neural networks; if you find the topic interesting and you want to dig more into it, we recommend these video series from Packt where you can find a better explanation and some nice tricks to master the learning process:

- *Deep Learning with Python [Video]* (https://www.packtpub.com/big-data-and-business-intelligence/deep-learning-python-video)
- *Deep Learning with TensorFlow [Video]* (https://www.packtpub.com/big-data-and-business-intelligence/deep-learning-tensorflow-video)

Let's now see something practical: how to solve a classification problem with neural networks. We will use Theano and Keras in this example, the first is a Python library for low level primitives, typically used in deep learning, able to take advantage of recent GPUs and numerical speedup to process efficiently multi-dimensional arrays; Keras is an advanced, fast and modular Python library for Neural Networks able to run on top of Theano (or TensorFlow).

Let see how they work together to simply train and test a neural network on a classification problem: the MNIST dataset. First at all, let's start the notebook with the necessary imports; you'll see from the output that when Keras is first imported it picks the backend module and, unsurprisingly, Theano is chosen in this case:

```
In: from keras.models import Sequential
from keras.layers import Dense, Dropout, Flatten
from keras.layers.convolutional import Convolution2D, MaxPooling2D
from keras.utils import np_utils
import numpy as np
Out:Using Theano backend.
```

Then loads the `mnist` dataset; we will use the Keras primitive to download it:

```
In: from keras.datasets import mnist
(X_train, y_train), (X_test, y_test) = mnist.load_data()
In: X_train.shape
Out: (60000, 28, 28)
```

The dataset is composed of 60 thousand grayscale images, each of them of 28 by 28 pixels. Now, we should preprocess the dataset, to make it in the right shape for Keras. Keras, when dealing with images, needs to have the number of channels in the size (in this case, it's one channel since it's a grayscale); also, it requires values in the range 0 to 1 of type `float32` (to optimize processing speed):

```
In: num_pixels = X_train.shape[1] * X_train.shape[2]
n_channels = 1
def preprocess(matrix):
return matrix.reshape(matrix.shape[0], \
                      n_channels, \
                      matrix.shape[1], \
                      matrix.shape[2]
                      ).astype('float32') / 255.
    In: X_train, X_test = preprocess(X_train), preprocess(X_test)
    In: X_train.shape, X_train.dtype, np.max(X_train)
    Out: ((60000, 1, 28, 28), dtype('float32'), 1.0)
```

Now, the outputs should be processed as well: it's a multi-class classification task (with 10 classes); therefore each class should have its own output column (one for each neuron in the output layer). Thanks to the helper function provided by Keras, we can achieve this goal quickly:

```
In: y_train = np_utils.to_categorical(y_train)
y_test = np_utils.to_categorical(y_test)
num_classes = y_train.shape[1]
y_train.shape
Out: (60000, 10)
```

Let's now create a simple model, let's say, the baseline one. We create a Sequential model (that is, the where each layer is stacked one after another). It first contains a flattening of the output (from a 28 x 28 one-channel image to a 784-dimension vector), then an input layer with 784 units, followed by an output layer of 10 neurons. For the first layer, we pick a *relu* activation, while for the second, a softmax (since it's a classification task). Finally, we instruct Keras to compile the model, using the categorical cross-entropy as optimization loss (that is, the multiclass logloss); the *adam* optimizer and compute the accuracy as the main metric of performance. We used the adam optimizer because it generically works well out-of-the-box. If you're not satisfied, or you want to optimize the network in a different way, please refer to the Keras documentation (http://keras.io/optimizers/) to see all the other optimizers available:

```
In: def baseline_model():
  # create model
  model = Sequential()
  model.add(Flatten(input_shape=(1, 28, 28)))
  model.add(Dense(num_pixels, init='normal', activation='relu'))
  model.add(Dense(num_classes, init='normal', activation='softmax'))
  # Compile model
  model.compile(loss='categorical_crossentropy', optimizer='adam',
  metrics=['accuracy'])
  return model
```

Then, in order to show a boost in the results, we build a more complex Sequential network (named `convolution_small`), containing the following:

1. A convolutional filter operating on 2D vectors (that is, images) which filters 2D window of data (of length 5 by 5), producing 32-D output vectors

2. A max-pooler, which subsample the image in a non-linear way, selecting the max for each 2 by 2 window

3. A dropout, which randomly sets 20% of the units to 0 (this step helps prevent overfitting)

4. The other steps are the same as in the baseline model

```
In: def convolution_small():
    # create model
    model = Sequential()
    model.add(Convolution2D(32, 5, 5, border_mode='valid',
    input_shape=(1, 28, 28), activation='relu'))
    model.add(MaxPooling2D(pool_size=(2, 2)))
    model.add(Dropout(0.2))
    model.add(Flatten())
    model.add(Dense(128, activation='relu'))
    model.add(Dense(num_classes, activation='softmax'))
    # Compile model
    model.compile(loss='categorical_crossentropy',
    optimizer='adam', metrics=['accuracy'])
    return model
```

Finally, to demonstrate the power of the neural network, we create another model, similar to the previous one but with twice as many layers of Convolution2D and MaxPooling2D:

```
In: def convolution_large():
    # create model
    model = Sequential()
    model.add(Convolution2D(30, 5, 5, border_mode='valid',
    input_shape=(1, 28, 28), activation='relu'))
    model.add(MaxPooling2D(pool_size=(2, 2)))
    model.add(Convolution2D(15, 3, 3, activation='relu'))
    model.add(MaxPooling2D(pool_size=(2, 2)))
    model.add(Dropout(0.2))
    model.add(Flatten())
    model.add(Dense(128, activation='relu'))
    model.add(Dense(50, activation='relu'))
    model.add(Dense(num_classes, activation='softmax'))
    # Compile model
    model.compile(loss='categorical_crossentropy',
    optimizer='adam', metrics=['accuracy'])
    return model
```

Let's test all of them, keeping an eye on the performance and on the timings to produce the results. We will test the algorithms on the same validation test, and each of them. The training phase is set to 10 passes:

```
In: np.random.seed(101)
models = [('baseline', baseline_model()),
          ('small', convolution_small()),
          ('large', convolution_large())]
for name, model in models:
    print("With model:", name)
    # Fit the model
    model.fit(X_train, y_train, validation_data=(X_test, y_test),
    nb_epoch=10, batch_size=100, verbose=2)
    # Final evaluation of the model
    scores = model.evaluate(X_test, y_test, verbose=0)
    print("Baseline Error: %.2f%%" % (100-scores[1]*100))
    print()
Out: With model: baseline
Train on 60000 samples, validate on 10000 samples
Epoch 1/10
3s - loss: 0.2332 - acc: 0.9313 - val_loss: 0.1113 - val_acc: 0.9670
Epoch 2/10
3s - loss: 0.0897 - acc: 0.9735 - val_loss: 0.0864 - val_acc: 0.9737
[...]
Epoch 10/10
2s - loss: 0.0102 - acc: 0.9970 - val_loss: 0.0724 - val_acc: 0.9796
Baseline Error: 2.04%
With model: small
Train on 60000 samples, validate on 10000 samples
Epoch 1/10
17s - loss: 0.1878 - acc: 0.9449 - val_loss: 0.0600 - val_acc:
0.9806
Epoch 2/10
16s - loss: 0.0631 - acc: 0.9808 - val_loss: 0.0424 - val_acc:
0.9850
[...]
Epoch 10/10
16s - loss: 0.0110 - acc: 0.9965 - val_loss: 0.0410 - val_acc:
0.9894
Baseline Error: 1.06%
With model: large
Train on 60000 samples, validate on 10000 samples
Epoch 1/10
26s - loss: 0.2920 - acc: 0.9087 - val_loss: 0.0738 - val_acc:
0.9749
Epoch 2/10
25s - loss: 0.0816 - acc: 0.9747 - val_loss: 0.0454 - val_acc:
0.9857
```

```
[...]
Epoch 10/10
27s - loss: 0.0253 - acc: 0.9921 - val_loss: 0.0253 - val_acc:
0.9919
Baseline Error: 0.81%
```

As expected, the deeper model (`convolution_large`) is the one with a lower error and, at the same time, the one taking more time at each step. On the contrary, the baseline model is quick but with a final lower accuracy.

A peek at Natural Language Processing (NLP)

This section is not strictly related to machine learning, but it contains some machine learning results in the area of Natural Language Processing. Python has many toolkits to process text data, but the most powerful and complete toolkit is **NLTK**, the Natural Language Tool Kit.

In the following sections, we'll explore its core functionalities. We will work on the English language; for other languages, you will first need to download the language corpora (note that sometimes languages have no free open source corpora for NLTK).

Refer to the official website of NLTK data, `http://www.nltk.org/nltk_data/`, to have access to corporas and lexical resources in many languages, ready to work with NLTK.

Word tokenization

Tokenization is the action of splitting text into words. Chunking whitespace seems very easy, but it's not, because text contains punctuation and contractions. Let's start with an example:

```
In: my_text = "The coolest job in the next 10 years will be statisticians.
People think I'm joking, but who would've guessed that computer engineers
would've been the coolest job of the 1990s?"
simple_tokens = my_text.split(' ')
print (simple_tokens)
Out: ['The', 'coolest', 'job', 'in', 'the', 'next', '10', 'years', 'will',
'be', 'statisticians.', 'People', 'think', "I'm", 'joking,', 'but', 'who',
"would've", 'guessed', 'that', 'computer', 'engineers', "would've", 'been',
'the', 'coolest', 'job', 'of', 'the', '1990s?']
```

Here, you can immediately see that something is wrong. The following tokens contain more than a word: `statisticians.` (with the final period), `I'm` (two words), `would've`, and `1990s?` (with the final question mark). Let's now see how NLTK performs better in this task (of course, under the hood, the algorithm is more complex than a simple whitespace chunker):

```
In: import nltk
nltk_tokens = nltk.word_tokenize(my_text)
print (nltk_tokens)
Out: ['The', 'coolest', 'job', 'in', 'the', 'next', '10', 'years', 'will',
'be', 'statisticians', '.', 'People', 'think', 'I', "'m", 'joking', ',',
'but', 'who', 'would', "'ve", 'guessed', 'that', 'computer', 'engineers',
'would', "'ve", 'been', 'the', 'coolest', 'job', 'of', 'the', '1990s',
'?']
```

While executing this or some other NLTK package calls, in case of an error saying "`Resource u'tokenizers/punkt/english.pickle' not found.`", just type `nltk.download()` on your console and select to either download everything or browse for the missing resource that triggered the warning.

Here, the quality is better, and each token is associated with a word in the text.

Note that `.`, `,`, and `?` are tokens, too.

There also exists a sentence tokenizer (see the `nltk.tokenize.punkt` module), but it's seldom used in data science.

Also, beyond the general-purpose English tokenizer, NLTK contains many other tokenizers to be used in different contexts. For example, if you're working on tweets, TweetTokenizer can be extremely useful to parse tweet-like documents. The most useful options are to remove handles, shorten consecutive characters and properly tokenize hashtags. Here's an example:

```
In:
from nltk.tokenize import TweetTokenizer
tt = TweetTokenizer(strip_handles=True, reduce_len=True)

tweet = '@mate: I looooooooove this city!!!!!!! #love #foreverhere'
tt.tokenize(tweet)
Out: [':', 'I', 'looove', 'this', 'city', '!', '!', '!', '#love',
'#foreverhere']
```

Stemming

Stemming is the action of reducing inflectional forms of words and taking the words to their core concepts. For example, the concept behind is, be, are, and am is the same. Similarly, the concept behind go and goes, as well as table and tables, is the same. The operation of deriving the root concept for each word is named stemming. In NLTK, you can choose the stemmer that you'd like to use (there are several ways to get the root part of words). We'll show you one of them, letting the others in Jupyter notebook associated with this part of the book:

```
In: from nltk.stem import *
stemmer = LancasterStemmer()
print ([stemmer.stem(word) for word in nltk_tokens])
Out: ['the', 'coolest', 'job', 'in', 'the', 'next', '10', 'year', 'wil',
'be', 'stat', '.', 'peopl', 'think', 'i', "'m", 'jok', ',', 'but', 'who',
'would', "'ve", 'guess', 'that', 'comput', 'engin', 'would', "'ve",
'been', 'the', 'coolest', 'job', 'of', 'the', '1990s', '?']
```

In the example, we used the Lancaster stemmer, which is one of the most powerful and recent algorithms. Checking the result, you will immediately see that it's all lowercased and statistician is associated with its root, stat. Good job!

Word tagging

Tagging, or POS-Tagging, is the association between a word (or a token) and its part-of-speech tag (POS-Tag). After tagging, you know what (and where) the verbs, adjectives, nouns, and so on, are in the sentence. Even in this case, NLTK makes this complex operation very easy:

```
In: import nltk
print (nltk.pos_tag(nltk_tokens))
Out: [('The', 'DT'), ('coolest', 'NN'), ('job', 'NN'), ('in', 'IN'),
('the', 'DT'), ('next', 'JJ'), ('10', 'CD'), ('years', 'NNS'), ('will',
'MD'), ('be', 'VB'), ('statisticians', 'NNS'), ('.', '.'), ('People',
'NNS'), ('think', 'VBP'), ('I', 'PRP'), ("'m", 'VBP'), ('joking', 'VBG'),
(',', ','), ('but', 'CC'), ('who', 'WP'), ('would', 'MD'), ("'ve", 'VB'),
('guessed', 'VBN'), ('that', 'IN'), ('computer', 'NN'), ('engineers',
'NNS'), ('would', 'MD'), ("'ve", 'VB'), ('been', 'VBN'), ('the', 'DT'),
('coolest', 'NN'), ('job', 'NN'), ('of', 'IN'), ('the', 'DT'), ('1990s',
'CD'), ('?', '.')]
```

Using the syntax of NLTK, you will realize that the `The` token represents a determiner (DT), `coolest` and `job` represent nouns (NN), `in` represents a conjunction, and so on. The association is really detailed; in the case of a verb, there are six possible tags, as follows:

- **take**: VB (verb, base form)
- **took**: VBD (verb, past tense)
- **taking**: VBG (verb, gerund)
- **taken**: VBN (verb, past participle)
- **take**: VBP (verb, singular present tense)
- **takes**: VBZ (verb, third-person singular present tense)

If you need a more detailed view of the sentence, you may want to use the parse tree tagger to understand its syntactic structure. This operation is rarely used in data science since it's great for sentence-by-sentence analysis.

Named Entity Recognition (NER)

The goal of NER is to recognize tokens associated with people, organizations, and locations. Let's use an example to explain it further:

```
In:
import nltk
text = "Elvis Aaron Presley was an American singer and actor. Born in
Tupelo, Mississippi, when Presley was 13 years old he and his family
relocated to Memphis, Tennessee."
chunks = nltk.ne_chunk(nltk.pos_tag(nltk.word_tokenize(text)))
print (chunks)
Out:
(S
(PERSON Elvis/NNP)
(PERSON Aaron/NNP Presley/NNP)
was/VBD
an/DT
(GPE American/JJ)
singer/NN
and/CC
actor/NN
./.
Born/NNP
in/IN
(GPE Tupelo/NNP)
,/,
(GPE Mississippi/NNP)
```

```
,/,
when/WRB
(PERSON Presley/NNP)
was/VBD
13/CD
years/NNS
old/JJ
he/PRP
and/CC
his/PRP$
family/NN
relocated/VBD
to/TO
(GPE Memphis/NNP)
,/,
(GPE Tennessee/NNP)
./.)
```

An extract of the Wikipedia page on Elvis is analyzed and NER-processed. A few entities that have been recognized by NER are:

- Elvis Aaron Presley: PERSON
- American: GPE (Geopolitical entity)
- Tupelo, Mississippi: GPE (Geopolitical entity)
- Memphis, Tennessee: GPE (Geopolitical entity)

Stopwords

Stopwords are the least informative pieces (or tokens) in text since they are the most common words (such as "the," "it," "is," "as," and "not"). Stopwords are often removed. And, exactly the way it happens in the feature selection phase, if you remove them, the processing takes less time and less memory; it is also sometimes more accurate. Removing stopwords decreases the overall entropy of the text, thereby making whatever signal is in there more apparent and easier to represent in features.

A list of English stopwords is available in Scikit-learn, too. For the stopwords in other languages, check out NLTK:

```
In:from sklearn.feature_extraction import text
stop_words = text.ENGLISH_STOP_WORDS
print (stop_words)
Out: frozenset(['all', 'six', 'less', 'being', 'indeed', 'over', 'move',
'anyway', 'four', 'not', 'own', 'through', 'yourselves', 'fify', 'where',
'mill', 'only', 'find', 'before', 'one', 'whose', 'system', 'how', ...
```

```
In: from nltk.corpus import stopwords
print(stopwords.words('english'))
Out: ['i', 'me', 'my', 'myself', 'we', 'our', 'ours', 'ourselves', 'you',
'your', 'yours', 'yourself', 'yourselves', 'he', 'him', 'his', 'himself',
'she', 'her', 'hers', 'herself', 'it', 'its', 'itself', 'they', 'them',
'their', 'theirs', 'themselves', 'what', 'which', 'who', 'whom', 'this',
'that', 'these', '...
In: print(stopwords.words('german'))
Out: ['aber', 'alle', 'allem', 'allen', 'aller', 'alles', 'als', 'also',
'am', 'an', 'ander', 'andere', 'anderem', 'anderen', 'anderer', 'anderes',
'anderm', 'andern', 'anderr', 'anders', 'auch', 'auf', 'au
```

A complete data science example – text classification

Now, here's a complete example that allows you to put each text in the right category. We will use the 20newsgroup dataset, which was already introduced in Chapter 1, *First Steps*. To make things more realistic and prevent the classifier from overfitting the data, we'll remove e-mail headers, footers (such as signatures), and quotes. In addition, in this case, the goal is to classify between two similar categories: sci.med and sci.space. We will use the accuracy measure to evaluate the classification:

```
In: import nltk
from sklearn.datasets import fetch_20newsgroups
from sklearn.feature_extraction.text import TfidfVectorizer
from sklearn.linear_model import SGDClassifier
from sklearn.metrics import accuracy_score
from sklearn.datasets import fetch_20newsgroups
import numpy as np
categories = ['sci.med', 'sci.space']
to_remove = ('headers', 'footers', 'quotes')
twenty_sci_news_train = fetch_20newsgroups(subset='train',
remove=to_remove, categories=categories)
twenty_sci_news_test = fetch_20newsgroups(subset='test', remove=to_remove,
categories=categories)
```

Let's start with the easiest approach to pre-process the textual data-using `Tfidf`. Remember that Tfidf is the multiplication of the frequency of the word within the document, by the inverse of its frequency across all the documents. High scores indicate that the word is used multiple times in the current document, but it's rare in the others (that is, it's a keyword of the document):

```
In: tf_vect = TfidfVectorizer()
X_train = tf_vect.fit_transform(twenty_sci_news_train.data)
X_test = tf_vect.transform(twenty_sci_news_test.data)
y_train = twenty_sci_news_train.target
y_test = twenty_sci_news_test.target
```

Now, let's use a linear classifier (`SGDClassifier`) to perform the classification task. One last thing to do is to print out the classification accuracy:

```
In: clf = SGDClassifier()
clf.fit(X_train, y_train)
y_pred = clf.predict(X_test)
print ("Accuracy=", accuracy_score(y_test, y_pred))
Out: Accuracy= 0.878481012658
```

An accuracy of 87.8 percent is a very good result. The entire program consists of less than 20 lines of code. Now, let's see if we can get something better. In this chapter, we've learned stopword removal, tokenization, and stemming. Let's see if we gain accuracy by using them:

```
In:
def clean_and_stem_text(text):
tokens = nltk.word_tokenize(text.lower())
clean_tokens = [word for word in tokens if word not in stop_words]
stem_tokens = [stemmer.stem(token) for token in clean_tokens]
return " ".join(stem_tokens)
cleaned_docs_train = [clean_and_stem_text(text) for text in
twenty_sci_news_train.data]
cleaned_docs_test = [clean_and_stem_text(text) for text in
twenty_sci_news_test.data]
```

The `clean_and_stem_text` function basically lowercases, tokenizes, stems, and reconstructs every document in the dataset. Finally, we will apply the same pre-processing (`Tfidf`) and classifier (`SGDClassifier`) that we used in the preceding example:

```
In: X1_train = tf_vect.fit_transform(cleaned_docs_train)
X1_test = tf_vect.transform(cleaned_docs_test)
clf.fit(X1_train, y_train)
y1_pred = clf.predict(X1_test)
print ("Accuracy=", accuracy_score(y_test, y1_pred))
Out: Accuracy= 0.893670886076
```

This processing requires more time, but we gained an accuracy of about 1.5 percent. An accurate tuning of the parameters of `Tfidf` and a cross-validated choice of the parameters of the classifier will eventually boost the accuracy to over 90 percent. So far, we're happy with this performance, but you can try to break that barrier.

An overview of unsupervised learning

In all the methods we've seen so far, every sample or observation has its own target label or value. In some other cases, the dataset is unlabeled and, in order to extract the structure of the data, you need an unsupervised approach. In this section, we're going to introduce two methods to perform clustering, as they are among the most used methods for unsupervised learning.

It is useful to keep in mind that often the terms "clustering" and "unsupervised learning" are considered synonymous, though actually unsupervised learning has a larger meaning.

The first method that we'll introduce, named K-means, is the most commonly used clustering algorithm despite its inevitable shortcomings. In signal processing, K-means is the equivalent of a vectorial quantization, that is, the selection of the best code word (from a given codebook) that better approximates the input observation (or a word).

You must provide the algorithm with the K parameter, which is the number of clusters. Sometimes, this might be a limitation because you first have to investigate which is the right K for the current dataset.

K-means iterates an EM (expectation/maximization) approach. During the first phase, it assigns each training point to the closest cluster centroid; during the second phase, it moves the cluster centroid to the center of mass of the points assigned to it (to reduce distortion). The initial placement of centroids is random. Consequently, you may need to run the algorithm several times so as not to find a local minimum.

That's all for the theory behind the algorithm; now, let's see it in practice. In this section, we're using two 2-dimensional dummy datasets that will explain what's going on better. Both datasets are composed of 2,000 samples so that you can also have an idea about the processing time.

Now, let's create the artificial datasets and then let's represent them by a plot:

```
In: %matplotlib inline
import numpy as np
import matplotlib.pyplot as plt
from sklearn import datasets
N_samples = 2000
dataset_1 = np.array(datasets.make_circles(n_samples=N_samples, noise=0.05,
factor=0.3)[0])
dataset_2 = np.array(datasets.make_blobs(n_samples=N_samples, centers=4,
cluster_std=0.4, random_state=0)[0])plt.scatter(dataset_1[:,0],
dataset_1[:,1], c=labels_1, alpha=0.8, s=64, edgecolors='white')
plt.show()
```

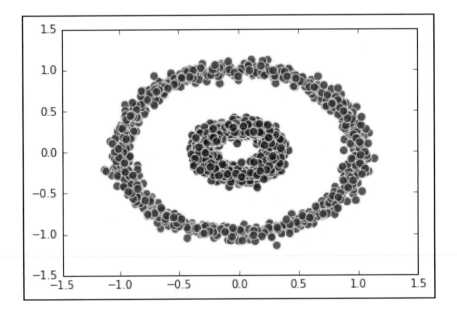

```
In: plt.scatter(dataset_2[:,0], dataset_2[:,1], alpha=0.8, s=64, c='blue',
edgecolors='white')
plt.show()
```

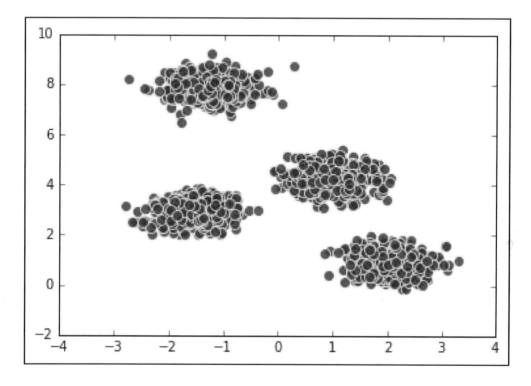

Now it's time to apply K-means. We will set K=2 in this case. Let's see the results:

```
In: from sklearn.cluster import KMeans
K_dataset_1 = 2
km_1 = KMeans(n_clusters=K_dataset_1)
labels_1 = km_1.fit(dataset_1).labels_
In: plt.scatter(dataset_1[:,0], dataset_1[:,1], c=labels_1, alpha=0.8,
s=64, edgecolors='white')
plt.scatter(km_1.cluster_centers_[:,0], km_1.cluster_centers_[:,1], s=200,
c=np.unique(labels_1), edgecolors='black')
plt.show()
```

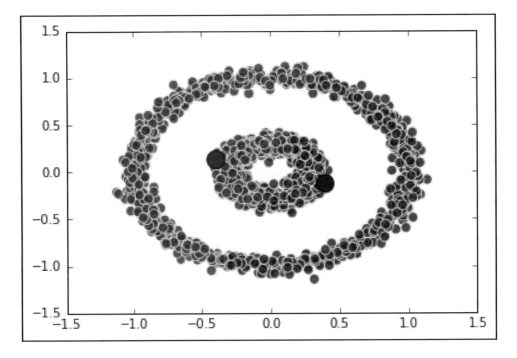

As you can see, K-means is not performing very well on this dataset, because it expects spherical-shaped data clusters. For this dataset, a Kernel-PCA should be applied before using K-means.

Now, let's see how it performs on a spherical-clustered data. In this case, based on our knowledge of the problem and the silhouette coefficient, we will set K=4:

```
In: K_dataset_2 = 4
km_2 = KMeans(n_clusters=K_dataset_2)
labels_2 = km_2.fit(dataset_2).labels_
In: plt.scatter(dataset_2[:,0], dataset_2[:,1], c=labels_2, alpha=0.8,
s=64, edgecolors='white')
plt.scatter(km_2.cluster_centers_[:,0], km_2.cluster_centers_[:,1],
marker='s', s=100, c=np.unique(labels_2), edgecolors='black')
plt.show()
```

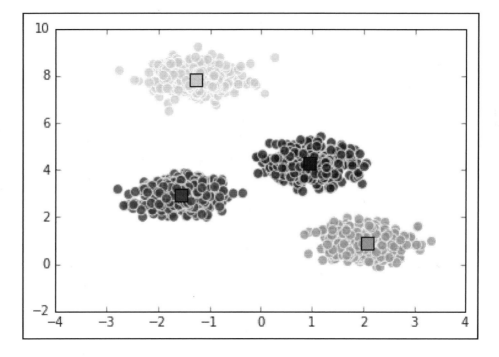

As expected, the plotted result is great. The centroids and clusters are exactly what we had in mind while looking at the unlabeled dataset.

> In real-world cases, you may consider using the Silhouette Coefficient to have an idea about how well-defined the clusters are. It is an evaluation metric of consistency within groups, applicable in various clustering results, and even class structures in supervised learning. You can read more about Silhouette Coefficient at
> http://scikit-learn.org/stable/modules/clustering.html#silhouett
> e-coefficient.

Now, we will introduce you to **DBSCAN**, a density-based clustering technique. It's a very simple technique. It selects a random point; if the point is in a dense area (that is, if it has more than N neighbors do), it starts growing the cluster, including all the neighbors and the neighbors of the neighbors, until it reaches a point where there are no more neighbors. If the point is not in a dense area, it is classified as noise. Then, another unlabeled point is selected randomly and the process starts over. This technique is great for non-spherical clusters but it works equally well with spherical ones. The input is just the neighborhood radius (the eps parameter, that is, the maximum distance between two points that are being considered neighbors), and the output is the cluster membership label for each point.

 Note that the points labeled -1 are classified as noise by DBSCAN.

Let's see an example on the dataset we had previously introduced:

```
In: from sklearn.cluster import DBSCAN
dbs_1 = DBSCAN(eps=0.25)
labels_1 = dbs_1.fit(dataset_1).labels_
In: plt.scatter(dataset_1[:,0], dataset_1[:,1], c=labels_1, alpha=0.8,
s=64, edgecolors='white')
plt.show()
```

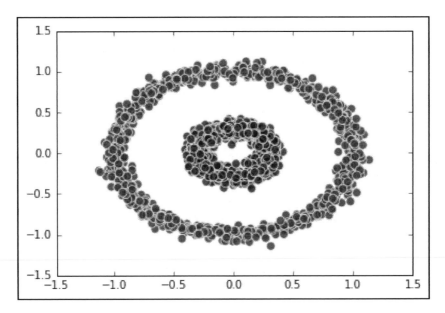

The result is perfect now. No points have been classified as noise (only the 0 and 1 labels appear in the label set).

```
In: np.unique(labels_1)
Out: array([0, 1])
```

Now, let's move on to the other dataset:

```
In: dbs_2 = DBSCAN(eps=0.5)
labels_2 = dbs_2.fit(dataset_2).labels_
In: plt.scatter(dataset_2[:,0], dataset_2[:,1], c=labels_2, alpha=0.8,
s=64, edgecolors='white')
plt.show()
In: np.unique(labels_2)
Out: array([-1, 0, 1, 2, 3])
```

It took some time to select the best settings for DBSCAN, and in this case, four clusters have been detected and a few points have been classified as noise (since the label set contains -1).

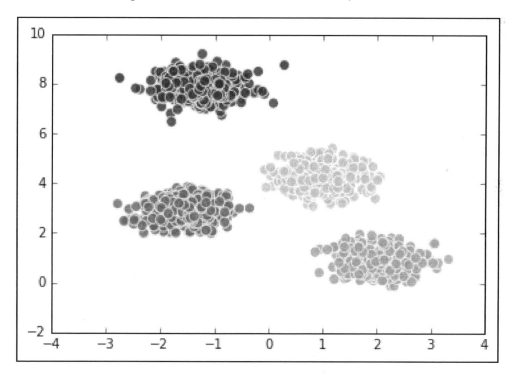

At the end of this section, a last important note is that in this essential introduction of K-means and DBSCAN, we have always used the Euclidean distance, as it is the default distance metric in these functions (though other distance metrics can also be used if you find them appropriate). When using this distance in real cases, remember that you have to normalize each feature (z-normalization) so that every feature contributes equally to the final distortion. If the dataset is not normalized, the features that have larger support will have more decision power on the output label, and that's something that we don't want.

For text, instead, a popular unsupervised algorithm that can be used to understand a common set of words in a collection of documents is Latent Dirichlet Allocation, or LDA.

 Note that another algorithm, the Linear Discriminant Analysis, also has the same acronym, but the two algorithms are completely unconnected.

LDA aims to extract sets of homogeneous words, or topics, out of a collection of documents. The math behind the algorithm is very advanced; here we will see just a practical notion of it.

Let's start with an example to explain why LDA is popular and why other unsupervised methods aren't good enough when dealing with text. K-means and DBSCAN, for example, provide a hard decision for each sample, putting each point in a disjoint partition. Documents, instead, often describe covering topics together (think about Shakespeare's books; they're a good mix of tragedy, romance, and adventure). On text documents, any hard decision would almost certainly be wrong. LDA, instead, provides as output a mixture of topics composing the document, along with an indication of how much the topic is represented in the document.

Let's use an example to explain how it works. We will train the algorithm on two categories, cars and medicine, of the 20-newsgroup dataset (we have already used the same dataset before in the chapter, in the early paragraph, Preparing tools and datasets):

```
In: import nltk
Import gensim
from sklearn.datasets import fetch_20newsgroups
def tokenize(text):
return [token.lower() for token in gensim.utils.simple_preprocess(text)
if token not in gensim.parsing.preprocessing.STOPWORDS]
text_dataset=fetch_20newsgroups(categories=['rec.autos','sci.med'],
random_state=101, remove=('headers', 'footers', 'quotes'))
documents = text_dataset.data
```

```
print("Document count:", len(documents))
Out: Document count: 1188
```

Each one of the 1,188 documents composing the dataset is a string. For example, the first document contains the follow text:

```
In: documents[0]
Out:
'\nI have a new doctor who gave me a prescription today for something
called \nSeptra DS.  He said it may cause GI problems and I have a
sensitive stomach \nto begin with.  Anybody ever taken this antibiotic.
Any good?  Suggestions \nfor avoiding an upset stomach?  Other tips?\n'
```

This document is definitely about medicine; nothing really important anyway for the algorithm. Now let's tokenize and create a dictionary of all the words included in the dataset. Mind that the tokenization operation also removes the stopwords and puts each word in lowercase:

```
In: processed_docs = [tokenize(doc) for doc in documents]
word_dic = gensim.corpora.Dictionary(processed_docs)
print("Num tokens:", len(word_dic))
Out:
Num tokens: 16161
```

In the dataset, there are just above 16 thousand distinct words. It's now time to filter too common words and too rare ones. In this step, we will keep the words appearing at least 10 times and in no more than 20% of the documents. At this point we have the **Bag Of Words** (or **BoW**) representation of each document; that is, each document is represented as a dictionary containing how many times each word appears in the text. The absolute position of each word in the text is lost, exactly as if you put all the words of the document in a bag. As a result, not all of the signal in the text is captured in the features based on this approach, but most of the times, it suffices to make an effective model:

```
In: word_dic.filter_extremes(no_below=10, no_above=0.2)
bow = [word_dic.doc2bow(doc) for doc in processed_docs]
```

Finally, here's the core class for LDA. In this example, we instruct LDA that in the dataset, there are just two topics. We also provide other parameters to make the algorithm converge (if not, you'll receive a Warning from the Python interpreter). Note that this algorithm works on many CPUs on your computer to speed up the process. If it doesn't work, please use the mono-process class, `gensim.models.ldamodel.LdaModel`, with the same parameters.

```
In: lda_model = gensim.models.LdaMulticore(bow, num_topics=2,
id2word=word_dic, passes=10, iterations=500)
```

Finally, after a couple of minutes, the model is trained. To see the association between words and topics, run the following code:

```
In: lda_model.print_topics(-1)
Out:
[(0,'0.011*edu + 0.008*com + 0.007*health + 0.007*medical + 0.007*new +
0.007*use + 0.006*people + 0.005*time + 0.005*years +
0.005*patients'),(1,'0.018*car + 0.008*good + 0.008*think + 0.008*cars +
0.007*msg + 0.006*time + 0.006*people + 0.006*water + 0.005*food +
0.005*engine')]
```

As you can see, the algorithm went through all the documents and learned that the main topics are cars and medicine. Note that the algorithm doesn't provide a short name for the topics, but their composition (the numbers are the weights of each word inside each topic, ranked from highest to lowest). Also note that some words appear in both topics; they are ambiguous words that can be used in both senses.

Finally, let's see how the algorithm works on an unseen document. To make things easier, let's create a sentence that contains both topics, for example, `"I've shown the doctor my new car. He loved its big wheels!"` Then, after having created a Bag-of-Words representation of this new document, LDA will produce two scores, one for each topic:

```
In: new_doc = "I've shown the doctor my new car. He loved its big wheels!"
bow_doc = word_dic.doc2bow(tokenize(new_doc))
for index, score in sorted(lda_model[bow_doc], key=lambda tup: -1*tup[1]):
print("Score: {}\t Topic: {}".format(score, lda_model.print_topic(index,
5)))
Out:
Score: 0.5047402389474193    Topic: 0.011*edu + 0.008*com + 0.007*health +
0.007*medical + 0.007*new
Score: 0.49525976105258074   Topic: 0.018*car + 0.008*good + 0.008*think +
0.008*cars + 0.007*msg
```

The scores for both the topics are around 0.5 and 0.5, meaning that the sentence contains a good balance of the subjects car and medicine. What we've shown here is just an example of two topics; but the same implementation, thanks to the performing library Gensim, can also allocate process the whole English Wikipedia in a matter of few hours.

A different approach from LDA is provided by the Word2Vec algorithm, a very recent model for embedding words in vectors. Compared to LDA, Word2Vec keeps track of the position of the words in a sentence, and this additional context helps to disambiguate some words better. Word2Vec is trained using a deep learning-like approach, but the implementation provided by the Gensim library makes it very easy to train and use. Note that while LDA aims to understand the topics in a document, Word2Vec works at the word level and tries to understand the semantic relationship between words in a low-dimensionality space (that is, creating an n-dimensional vector for each word). Let's see an example to make things clear.

We will use the movie review dataset to train the Word2Vec model. The training is done simply-simply passing the sentences composing the corpora to the Word2Vec constructor and, eventually, the number of workers that can work in parallel on the training task:

```
In: from gensim.models import Word2Vec
from nltk.corpus import movie_reviews
w2v = Word2Vec(movie_reviews.sents(), workers=4)
w2v.init_sims(replace=True)
```

The last line of code simply freezes the model, not allowing any additional updates. This also brings an additional and very welcome benefit: reducing the memory fingerprint of the object.

Visualizing vectors that represent the words may be complicated; therefore, let's see some similarities (that is, similar vectors in the low-dimensional subspace). Here we will ask the model to provide the top five most similar words (along with the similarity score) to the words "house" and "countryside." This is just an example; it's possible to retrieve similar words for all words contained in the input corpora:

```
In: w2v.most_similar('house', topn=5)
Out:
[('apartment', 0.8799251317977905),
('body', 0.8719735145568848),
('hotel', 0.8618944883346558),
('head', 0.848749041557312),
('boat', 0.8469674587249756)]
In: w2v.most_similar('countryside', topn=5)
Out:
[('motorcycle', 0.9531803131103516),
('marches', 0.9499938488006592),
('rural', 0.9467764496803284),
('shuttle', 0.9466159343719482),
('mining', 0.9461280107498169)]
```

How is Word2Vec able to do so? Simply with a similarity score in the low-dimensionality vector space. In fact, to see the vector representation of each word, do:

```
In: w2v['countryside']
Out:
array([-0.09412272,  0.07695948, -0.14981066,  0.04894404, -0.03712097,
       -0.17099065, -0.0379245 , -0.05336253,  0.06084964, -0.01273731,
       -0.03949985, -0.06456301, -0.03289359, -0.06889232,  0.02217194,
       [...]
```

The array is composed by 100 dimensions; you can increase or decrease it by setting the `size` parameter while training the model. 100 is the default value.

In the `most_similar` method we've previously used, you can also specify the negative words to use (that is, to subtract similar words). A classic example is finding a similar word of `woman` and `king` without `queen`. The top result is, unsurprisingly, *man*:

```
In: w2v.most_similar(positive=['woman', 'king'], negative=['queen'],
topn=3)
Out:
[('man', 0.8440324068069458),
('girl', 0.7671926021575928),
('child', 0.7635241746902466)]
```

The model, thanks to the vector representation, also provides the method to identify the non-matching words in a set of similar words; that is, what's the word that doesn't match the context (in this case, the context is the bedroom)?

```
In: w2v.doesnt_match(['bed', 'pillow', 'cake', 'mattress'])
Out: 'cake'
```

Finally, all the preceding methods are built on similarity scores. The model also provides the raw score of similarity between words; here's an example of the similarity score of `woman` and `girl` and `woman` and `boy`. The first similarity is higher, though the second is not zero, since both words are connected by the fact we're talking about persons:

```
In: w2v.similarity('woman', 'girl'), w2v.similarity('woman', 'boy')
Out:
(0.90198267746062233, 0.82372486297773828)
```

Summary

In this chapter, we introduced the essentials of machine learning. We started with some easy, but still quite effective, classifiers (linear and logistic regressors, Naive Bayes, and K-Nearest Neighbors). Then, we moved on to the more advanced ones (SVM). We explained how to compose weak classifiers together (ensembles, Random Forests, and Gradient Tree Boosting). Finally, we had a peek at the algorithms used in big data, clustering, and deep learning.

In the next chapter, you'll be introduced to graphs, which is an interesting deviation from the predictors/target flat matrices. It is quite a hot topic in data science now. Expect to delve into very complex and intricate networks!

5

Social Network Analysis

Social Network Analysis, usually referred to as **SNA**, models and studies the relationships in a group of social entities, which exist in the form of a network. An entity can be a person, a computer, or a web page, and a relation can be a like, link, or friendship (that is, a connection between entities).

In this chapter, you'll learn about the following:

- Graphs, since social networks are usually represented in this form
- Important algorithms that are used to gain insights from a graph
- How to load, dump, and sample large graphs

Introduction to graph theory

Basically, a graph is a data structure that's able to represent relations in a collection of objects. Under this paradigm, the objects are the graph's nodes and the relations are the graph's links (or edges). The graph is directed if the links have an orientation (conceptually, they're like the one-way streets of a city); otherwise, the graph is undirected. In the following table, examples of well-known graphs are provided:

Graph example	Type	Nodes	Edges
World Wide Web	Directed	Web pages	Links
Facebook	Undirected	People	Friendship
Twitter	Directed	People	Follower
IP network	Undirected	Hosts	Wires/connections
Navigation systems	Directed	Places/addresses	Streets

Wikipedia	Directed	Pages	Anchor links
Scientific literature	Directed	Papers	Citations
Markov chains	Directed	Status	Emission probability

All the preceding examples can be expressed as relations between nodes as in a traditional RDBMS, such as MySQL or Postgres. Now, to see the advantages of a graph data structure, try to think how complex the following query in SQL would be for a social network such as Facebook (think about a recommender system that helps you find people you may know):

```
Find all people who are friends of my friends, but not my friends
```

Compare the preceding query to the following query on a graph:

```
Get all friends connected to me having distance=2
```

Now, let's see how to create a graph or a social network with Python. The library that we're going to use extensively throughout the chapter is named NetworkX. It is capable of handling small to medium graphs and it is complete and powerful:

```
In: %matplotlib inline
import networkx as nx
import matplotlib.pyplot as plt
In: G = nx.Graph()
G.add_edge(1,2)
nx.draw_networkx(G)
plt.show()
```

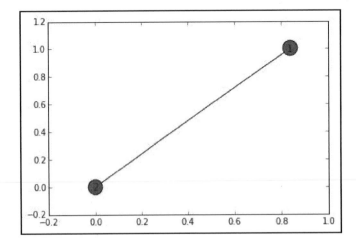

The command is self-explanatory. After the imports, we will first define a (NetworkX) graph object (by default, it's an undirected one). Then, we will add an edge (that is, a connection) between two nodes (since the nodes are not already in the graph, they're automatically created). Finally, we will plot the graph. The graph layout (the positions of the nodes) is automatically generated by the library.

With the .add_note() method, adding other nodes to the graph is pretty straightforward. For example, if you want to add nodes 3 and 4, you can simply use the following code:

```
In: G.add_nodes_from([3, 4])
```

The preceding code will add the two nodes. Since they're not linked to the other nodes, they'll be unconnected. Similarly, to add more edges to the graph, you can use the following code:

```
In: G.add_edge(3,4)
G.add_edges_from([(2, 3), (4, 1)])
nx.draw_networkx(G)
plt.show()
```

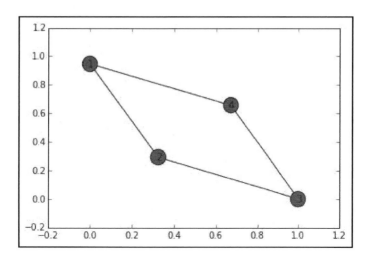

To obtain a collection of nodes in the graph, just use the .nodes() method. Similarly, .edges() gives you the list of edges as a list of connected nodes:

```
In: G.nodes()
Out: [1, 2, 3, 4]
In: G.edges()
Out: [(1, 2), (1, 4), (2, 3), (3, 4)]
```

There are several ways to represent and describe a graph. In the following section, we'll illustrate the most popular ones. At first, you can use an adjacency list. It lists the neighbors of every node; that is, `list[0]` contains the adjacency nodes of the first node, as in `G.nodes()`:

```
In: G.adjacency_list()
Out: [[2, 4], [1, 3], [2, 4], [1, 3]]
```

To make the description self-contained, you can represent the graph as a dictionary of lists. This is the most popular (and practical) way to describe a graph, due to its succinctness. Here, the nodes' names are the dictionary keys, and their values are the nodes' adjacency lists:

```
In: nx.to_dict_of_lists(G)
Out:
{1: [2, 4], 2: [1, 3], 3: [2, 4], 4: [1, 3]}
```

On the other hand, you can describe a graph as a **collection of edges**. In the output, the third element of each tuple is the attribute of the edge. In fact, every edge can have one or more attributes (such as its weight, its cardinality, and so on). Since we created a very simple graph, in the following example, we have no attributes:

```
In: nx.to_edgelist(G)
Out: [(1, 2, {}), (1, 4, {}), (2, 3, {}), (3, 4, {})]
```

Finally, a graph can be described as a NumPy matrix. If the matrix contains a 1 in the (i, j) position, it means that there is a link between the i and j nodes. Since the matrix usually contains very few ones (compared to the number of zeros), it's usually represented as a sparse (SciPy) matrix, a NumPy matrix, or a pandas DataFrame.

Please note that the matrix description is exhaustive. Therefore, undirected graphs are transformed to directed ones, and a link connecting (i, j) is transformed into two links, (i, j) and (j, i). This representation is often called an adjacency matrix or connection matrix.

Thus, a symmetric matrix is created, as in the following example:

```
In: nx.to_numpy_matrix(G)
Out:
matrix([[ 0.,  1.,  0.,  1.],
 [ 1.,  0.,  1.,  0.],
 [ 0.,  1.,  0.,  1.],
 [ 1.,  0.,  1.,  0.]])
In: print (nx.to_scipy_sparse_matrix(G))
Out:
(0, 1)  1
```

```
(0, 3)   1
(1, 0)   1
(1, 2)   1
(2, 1)   1
(2, 3)   1
(3, 0)   1
(3, 2)   1
In:  nx.to_spandas_dataframe(G)
Out:
```

	0	1	2	3	4	5	6	7	8	9
0	0.0	1.0	1.0	1.0	0.0	1.0	0.0	0.0	0.0	0.0
1	1.0	0.0	0.0	1.0	1.0	0.0	1.0	0.0	0.0	0.0
2	1.0	0.0	0.0	1.0	0.0	1.0	0.0	0.0	0.0	0.0
3	1.0	1.0	1.0	0.0	1.0	1.0	1.0	0.0	0.0	0.0
4	0.0	1.0	0.0	1.0	0.0	0.0	1.0	0.0	0.0	0.0
5	1.0	0.0	1.0	1.0	0.0	0.0	1.0	1.0	0.0	0.0
6	0.0	1.0	0.0	1.0	1.0	1.0	0.0	1.0	0.0	0.0
7	0.0	0.0	0.0	0.0	0.0	1.0	1.0	0.0	1.0	0.0
8	0.0	0.0	0.0	0.0	0.0	0.0	0.0	1.0	0.0	1.0
9	0.0	0.0	0.0	0.0	0.0	0.0	0.0	0.0	1.0	0.0

Of course, if you want to load a NetworkX graph, you can use the opposite functions (changing *to* to *from* in the function name), and you'll be able to load NetworkX graphs from a dictionary of lists; edge lists; and NumPy, SciPy and pandas structures.

An important measure of each node in a graph is its degree. In an undirected graph, the degree of a node represents the number of links the node has. For directed graphs, there are two types of degree: in-degree and out-degree. These respectively count the inbound and outbound links of the node.

Let's add a node (to unbalance the graph) and calculate the nodes' degrees, as follows:

```
In: G.add_edge(1,3)
nx.draw_networkx(G)
plt.show()
```

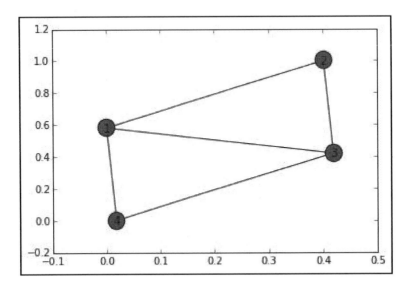

Graphs in this chapter can be different to the ones obtained on your local computer because graphical layout initialization is made with random parameters.

The degree of the nodes is displayed as follows:

```
In: G.degree()
Out: {1: 3, 2: 2, 3: 3, 4: 2}
```

For large graphs, this measure is impractical since the output dictionary has an item for every node. In such cases, a histogram of the nodes' degree is often used to approximate its distribution. In the following example, a random network with 10,000 nodes and a link probability of 1 percent is built. Then, the histogram of the node degree is extracted and shown as follows:

```
In: k = nx.fast_gnp_random_graph(10000, 0.01).degree()
plt.hist(list(k.values()))
```

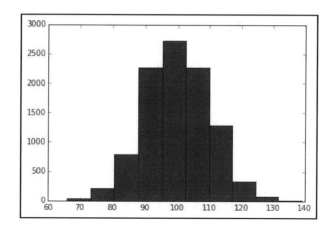

Graph algorithms

To get insights from graphs, many algorithms have been developed. In this chapter, we'll use a well-known graph in `NetworkX`, the `Krackhardt Kite` graph. It is a dummy graph containing 10 nodes, and it is typically used to proof graph algorithms. Krackhardt is the name of the creator of the structure, which has the shape of a kite. It's composed of two different zones. In the first zone (composed of nodes 0 to 6), the nodes are interlinked; in the other zone (nodes 7 to 9), they are connected as a chain:

```
In: G = nx.krackhardt_kite_graph()
nx.draw_networkx(G)
plt.show()
```

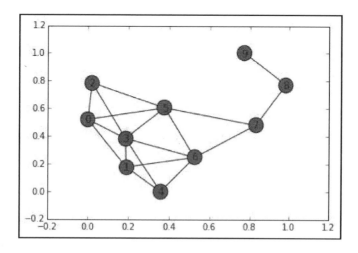

Let's start with connectivity. Two nodes of a graph are connected if there is at least a path (that is, a sequence of nodes) between them.

If at least a path exists, the shortest path between the two nodes is the one with the shortest collection of nodes you should pass (or traverse) to go from the source to the destination node.

 Note that in a directed graph, you must follow the link's directions.

In NetworkX, checking whether a path exists between two nodes, calculating the shortest route, and getting its length is very easy. For example, to check the connectivity and the path between nodes 1 and 9, you can use the following code:

```
In: print (nx.has_path(G, source=1, target=9))
print (nx.shortest_path(G, source=1, target=9))
print (nx.shortest_path_length(G, source=1, target=9))
Out:
True
[1, 6, 7, 8, 9]
4
```

This function just gives the shortest path from a node to another: what about if we want to see all the paths to reach node 9 from node 1? The algorithm proposed by Jin Yen provides the answer, and it's implemented in the function shortest_simple_paths in NetworkX. This function returns a generator of all the paths, from the shortest to the longest, between the node source and the target in the graph:

```
In: print (list(nx.shortest_simple_paths(G, source=1, target=9)))
Out:
[[1, 6, 7, 8, 9], [1, 0, 5, 7, 8, 9], [1, 6, 5, 7, 8, 9], [1, 3, 5,
7, 8, 9], [1, 4, 6, 7, 8, 9], [1, 3, 6, 7, 8, 9], [1, 0, 2, 5, 7, 8,
9], [...]
```

Finally, another handy function provided by NetworkX is the all_pairs_shortest_path, which returns a Python dictionary containing the shortest path between all the pairs of nodes in the network. For example, to see the shortest path from node 5, you just need to see what's inside key 5:

```
In: paths = nx.all_pairs_shortest_path(G)
paths[5]
Out: {0: [5, 0],
1: [5, 0, 1],
2: [5, 2],
```

```
3:  [5, 3],
4:  [5, 3, 4],
5:  [5],
6:  [5, 6],
7:  [5, 7],
8:  [5, 7, 8],
9:  [5, 7, 8, 9]}
```

As expected, the paths between 5 and all the other nodes start with 5 itself. Note also that this structure is a dictionary, therefore to obtain the shortest path between the node a and b it can just be called `paths[a][b]`. Use this function carefully on large networks; in fact, under the hood, it computes all the pairwise shortest paths, with a computational complexity of $O(N^2)$.

We will now talk about node centrality. It roughly represents the importance of the node inside the network. It gives an idea about how well the node connects to the network. There are multiple types of centrality. We will discuss the betweenness centrality, degree centrality, closeness centrality, harmonic centrality, and eigenvector centrality:

- **Betweenness centrality**: This type of centrality gives you an idea about the number of shortest paths in which the node is present. Nodes with high betweenness centrality are the core components of the network, and many shortest paths route through them. In the following example, NetworkX offers a straightforward way to compute the betweenness centrality of all the nodes:

```
In:  nx.betweenness_centrality(G)
Out:
{0:  0.023148148148148143,
 1:  0.023148148148148143,
 2:  0.0,
 3:  0.10185185185185183,
 4:  0.0,
 5:  0.23148148148148148,
 6:  0.23148148148148148,
 7:  0.38888888888888884,
 8:  0.222222222222222,
 9:  0.0}
```

As you can imagine, the highest betweenness centrality is achieved by node 7. It seems very important since it's the only node that connects elements 8 and 9 (it's their gateway to the network). On the contrary, nodes such as 9, 2, and 4 are on the extreme border of the network, and they are not present in any of the shortest paths of the network. Therefore, these nodes can be removed without affecting the connectivity of the network.

- **Degree centrality**: This type of centrality is simply the percentage of the vertexes that are incident upon a node. Note that in directed graphs, there are two degree centralities for every node: in-degree and out-degree centrality. Let's have a look at the following example:

```
In: nx.degree_centrality(G)
Out:
{0: 0.4444444444444444,
 1: 0.4444444444444444,
 2: 0.3333333333333333,
 3: 0.6666666666666666,
 4: 0.3333333333333333,
 5: 0.5555555555555556,
 6: 0.5555555555555556,
 7: 0.3333333333333333,
 8: 0.2222222222222222,
 9: 0.1111111111111111}
```

As expected, node 3 has the highest degree centrality since it's the node with the maximum number of links (it's connected to six other nodes). On the contrary, node 9 is the node with the lowest degree since it has only one edge.

- **Closeness centrality**: To compute this for every node, calculate the shortest path distance to all other nodes, average it, divide the average by the maximum distance, and take the inverse of that value. It results in a score between 0 (the greater average distance) and 1 (the lower average distance). In our example, for node 9, the shortest path distances are [1, 2, 3, 3, 4, 4, 4, 5, 5]. The average (3.44) is then divided by 5 (the maximum distance) and subtracted from 1, resulting in a closeness centrality score of 0.31. You can use the following code to compute the closeness centrality for all the nodes in the example graph:

```
In: nx.closeness_centrality(G)
Out:
{0: 0.5294117647058824,
 1: 0.5294117647058824,
 2: 0.5,
 3: 0.6,
 4: 0.5,
 5: 0.6428571428571429,
```

```
6: 0.6428571428571429,
7: 0.6,
8: 0.42857142857142855,
9: 0.310344827586069}
```

The nodes with high closeness centrality are 5, 6, and 3. In fact, they are the nodes that are present in the middle of the network, and on an average, they can reach all the other nodes with a few hops. The lowest score belongs to node 9. In fact, its average distance to reach all the other nodes is pretty high.

- **Harmonic centrality**: This measure is similar to closeness centrality, but instead of having the inverse of the sum of the reciprocal of the distances, it has the sum of the reciprocal of the distances. Doing so, it emphasizes the extremes distances. Let's see what the harmonic distances look like in our network:

```
In: nx.harmonic_centrality(G)
Out:
{0: 6.083333333333333,
1: 6.083333333333333,
2: 5.583333333333333,
3: 7.083333333333333,
4: 5.583333333333333,
5: 6.833333333333333,
6: 6.833333333333333,
7: 6.0,
8: 4.666666666666666,
9: 3.4166666666666665}
```

Node 3 is the one with the highest harmonic centrality, while 5 and 6 have a comparable but lower value. Again, those nodes are in the center of the network, and on an average, they can reach all the other nodes with few hops. In contrast, node 9 has the lowest harmonic centrality; in fact, it's the farthest from all the other nodes on an average.

- **Eigenvector centrality**: If the graph is directed, the nodes represent web pages and the edges represent page links. A slightly modified version is named pagerank. This metric, invented by Larry Page, is the core ranking algorithm of Google, as well as of Bing, and possibly other search engines. It gives to every node a measure of how important the node is from the point of view of a random surfer. Its name derives from the fact that if you think of the graph as a Markov Chain, the graph represents the eigenvector associated with the greatest eigenvalue. Therefore, from this point of view, this probabilistic measure represents the static distribution of the probability of visiting a node.

Let's have a look at the following example:

```
In: nx.eigenvector_centrality(G)
Out:
{0: 0.35220918419838565,
 1: 0.35220918419838565,
 2: 0.28583482369644964,
 3: 0.481020669200118,
 4: 0.28583482369644964,
 5: 0.3976909028137205,
 6: 0.3976909028137205,
 7: 0.19586101425312444,
 8: 0.04807425308073236,
 9: 0.011163556091491361}
```

In this example, nodes 3 and 9 respectively have the highest and the lowest scores according to the eigenvector centrality measure. Compared to the degree centrality, the eigenvalue centrality gives an idea about the static distribution of the surfers across the network because it considers, for each node, not only the directly connected neighbors (as in the degree centrality), but also the whole structure of the network. If the graph represented web pages and their connections, this makes them the most/least (probable) visited pages.

As a concluding topic, we'll introduce a clustering coefficient. In brief, it is the proportion of the node's neighbors that are also neighbors with each other (that is, the proportion of possible triplets or triangles that exists). Higher values indicate higher cliquishness. It's named this way because it represents the degree to which nodes tend to cluster together. Let's have a look at the following example:

```
In: nx.clustering(G)
Out:
{0: 0.6666666666666666,
 1: 0.6666666666666666,
 2: 1.0,
 3: 0.5333333333333333,
 4: 1.0,
 5: 0.5,
 6: 0.5,
 7: 0.3333333333333333,
 8: 0.0,
 9: 0.0}
```

Higher values are seen in the highly connected sections of the graph and lower values in the least connected areas.

Now, let's look at the way by which you can partition the network into multiple subnetworks of nodes. One of the most used algorithms is the Louvain method, which was specifically created to accurately detect communities in large graphs (with a million nodes). We will first introduce the modularity measure. It's a measure of the structure of the graph (it's not node-oriented), whose formal math definition is very long and complex and which is beyond the scope of this book (readers can find more information at `https://sites.google.com/site/findcommunities/`). It intuitively measures the quality of the division of a graph into communities, comparing the actual community linkage with a random one. The modularity score falls between -0.5 and +1.0; the higher the value, the better is the division (there is a dense intragroup connectivity and a sparse intergroup connectivity).

It's a two-step iterative algorithm: first a local optimization, then a global one, then the local again, and so on. In the first step, the algorithm locally maximizes the modularity of small communities. Then, it aggregates the nodes of the same community and hierarchically builds a graph whose nodes are the communities. The method repeats these two steps iteratively until the maximum global modularity score is reached.

To take a peek at this algorithm in a practical example, we first need to create a larger graph. Let's consider a random network with 100 nodes. In this example, we will build the graph with the `powerlaw` algorithm, which tries to maintain an approximate average clustering. For every new node added to the graph, an `m` number of random edges are also added to it and each of them has a probability of `p` to create a triangle. The source code is not included in `NetworkX`, but it's in a separate module named `community`. An implementation of this algorithm is shown in the following example:

```
In:
import community # Community module for community detection
and clustering
G = nx.powerlaw_cluster_graph(100, 1, .4, seed=101)
partition = community.best_partition(G)
for i in set(partition.values()):
  print ("Community", i)
  members = list_nodes = [nodes for nodes in partition.keys()
  if partition[nodes] == i]
  print (members)
values = [partition.get(node) for node in G.nodes()]
nx.draw_spring(G, cmap = plt.get_cmap('jet'), node_color = values,
node_size=30, with_labels=False)
plt.show()
print ("Modularity score:", community.modularity(partition, G))
```

```
Out:
Community 0
[0, 46, 50, 61, 73, 74, 75, 82, 86, 96]
Community 1
[1, 2, 9, 16, 20, 28, 29, 35, 57, 65, 78, 83, 89, 93]
[...]
```

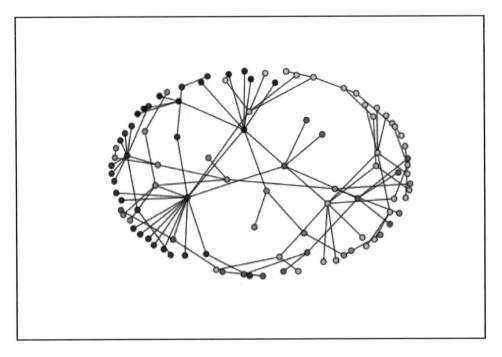

Modularity score: 0.7941026425874911

The first output of the program is the list of the communities detected in the graph (each community is a collection of nodes). In this case, the algorithm detected eight groups. We wanted to highlight that we didn't specify the number of output communities that we were looking for, but it was automatically decided by the algorithm. That's a desirable feature and is not shared with all the clustering algorithms (k-means, for example, needs the number of clusters as a parameter).

Then, we printed the graph, assigning a different color to each community. You can see that the colors are pretty homogeneous on the edge nodes.

Lastly, the algorithm returns the modularity score of the solution: 0.79 (that's a pretty high score).

The last algorithm in this short introduction to graphs relates to coloring, Coloring is a graphical way to assign labels to the nodes, in a way that neighbors (that is, nodes with a link) must have different labels (or colors). To explain why this algorithm is important, we will use a practical example. Telecommunication networks are composed by antennas at different frequency spread across the Earth. Think about each antenna as a node, and the frequency as a label of the node. If antennas are closer than a defined distance—let's say close enough to cause interference—they're connected with an edge. Can we find the lowest number of different frequencies to allocate (to minimize the price the company has to pay) and avoid interferences between close antennas (that is, by allocating different frequency to linked nodes)? The solution is given by the graph coloring algorithms.

In theory, the solution of such a class of algorithm is NP-hard, and it's almost impossible to find the optimal solution though there are many approximations to obtain sub-optimal solutions quickly. NetworkX implements a greedy approach to solve the coloring problem. What's returned by the function is a dictionary containing for each node (the key in the dictionary), the color (the value of the key in the dictionary). As an example, let's see the allocation of colors in our example graph, and then let's see it colored:

```
In: d = nx.coloring.greedy_color(G)
print(d)
nx.draw_networkx(G, node_color=[d[n] for n in sorted(d.keys())])
plt.show()
Out:{0: 2, 1: 1, 2: 3, 3: 0, 4: 3, 5: 1, 6: 2, 7: 0, 8: 1, 9: 0}
```

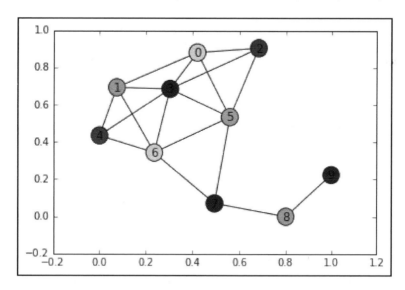

As expected, linked nodes have different colors. It seems that for this configuration of the network, four colors are needed. It it was a telecommunication network; it means four frequencies are needed to avoid interferences.

Graph loading, dumping, and sampling

Beyond NetworkX, graphs and networks can be generated and analyzed with other software. One of the best open source multi-platform software that can be used for their analysis is named Gephi. It's a visual tool and it doesn't require programming skills. It's freely available at http://gephi.github.io.

As in machine learning datasets, even graphs have standard formats for their storing, loading, and exchanging. In this way, you can create a graph with NetworkX, dump it to a file and then load and analyze it with Gephi.

One of the most frequently used formats is **Graph Modeling Language (GML)**. Now, let's see how to dump a graph to GML file:

```
In:
dump_file_base = "dumped_graph"
# Be sure the dump_file file doesn't exist
def remove_file(filename):
    import os
    if os.path.exists(filename):
        os.remove(filename)
In: G = nx.krackhardt_kite_graph()
In:
# GML format write and read
GML_file = dump_file_base + '.gml'
remove_file(GML_file)
nx.write_gml(G, GML_file)
G2 = nx.read_gml(GML_file)
assert(G.edges() == G2.edges())
```

In the preceding chunk of code, we first removed the dumped file, if it did exist in the first place. Then, we created a graph (the Kite), and after that, we dumped and loaded it. Finally, we compared the original and the loaded structure, asserting that they're equal.

Beyond GML, there are a variety of formats. Each of the formats has different features. Note that some of them remove information pertaining to the network (like edge / node attributes). Similar to the `write_gml` function and its equivalent `read_gml` are the following ones (the names are self-explanatory):

- The adjacency list (`read_adjlist` and `write_adjlist`)
- The multiline adjacency list (`read_multiline_adjlist` and `write_multiline_adjlist`)
- The edge list (`read_edgelist` and `write_edgelist`)
- GEXF (`read_gexf` and `write_gexf`)
- Pickle (`read_gpickle` and `write_gpickle`)
- GraphML (`read_graphml` and `write_graphml`)
- LEDA (`read_leda` and `parse_leda`)
- YAML (`read_yaml` and `write_yaml`)
- Pajek (`read_pajek` and `write_pajek`)
- GIS Shapefile (`read_shp` and `write_shp`)
- JSON (load/loads and dump/dumps provides JSON serialization)

The last topic of this chapter is sampling. Why sample a graph? We sample graphs because working with large graphs is sometimes impractical (remember that in the best case, the processing time is proportional to the graph size). Therefore, it's better to sample it, create an algorithm by working on the small-scale scenario, and then test it on the full-scale problem. There are several ways to sample a graph. Here, we're going to introduce the three most frequently used techniques.

In the first technique, which is known as node sampling, a limited subset of nodes, along with their links, forms the sampled set. In the second technique, which is known as link sampling, a subset of links forms the sampled set. Both these methods are simple and fast, but they might potentially create a different structure of the network. The third method is named snowball sampling. The initial node, all its neighbors, and the neighbors of the neighbors (expanding the selection this way until we reach the *maximum traversal depth* parameter) form the sampled set. In other words, the selection is like a rolling snowball.

 Note that you can also subsample the traversed links. In other words, each link has a probability of p that has to be followed and selected in the output set.

The last sampling method is not a part of NetworkX, but you can find an implementation for the same in the snowball_sampling.py file.

In this example, we will subsample the LiveJournal network by starting with the person with an alberto ID and then expanding recursively twice (in the first example) and three times (in the second example). In the latter instance, every link is followed by a probability of 20 percent, thus decreasing the retrieval time. Here is an example that demonstrates the same:

```
In:
import snowball_sampling
my_social_network = nx.Graph()
snowball_sampling.snowball_sampling(my_social_network, 2, 'alberto')
nx.draw(my_social_network)
plt.show()
Out:
Reaching depth 0
 new nodes to investigate: ['alberto']
Reaching depth 1
 new nodes to investigate: ['its_kerrie_duhh', 'ph8th',
 'nightraven', 'melisssa', 'mischa', 'deifiedsoul',
 'cookita', '_____eric_', 'seraph76', 'msliebling',
 'hermes3x3', 'eldebate', 'adriannevandal', 'clymore']
```

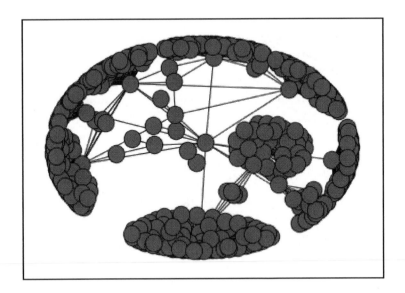

```
In: my_sampled_social_network = nx.Graph()
snowball_sampling.snowball_sampling(my_sampled_social_network,
3, 'alberto', sampling_rate=0.2)
nx.draw(my_sampled_social_network)
plt.show()
Out:
Reaching depth 0
 new nodes to investigate: ['alberto']
Reaching depth 1
 new nodes to investigate: ['its_kerrie_duhh', 'ph8th',
 'nightraven', 'melisssa', 'mischa', 'deifiedsoul',
 'cookita', '_____eric_', 'seraph76', 'msliebling',
 'hermes3x3', 'eldebate', 'adriannevandal', 'clymore']
Reaching depth 2
 new nodes to investigate: ['torcboy', 'flower899', 'inbredhatred',
 'cubnurse', 'motleyprose', 'djbloodrose', 'skullosvibe',
 'necro_man', 'jagbear', 'eeyoredung', 'bearsbearsbears',
 'djmrswhite', 'moonboynm', 'vianegativa', 'blktalon',
 'chironae', 'grimmdolly', 'morpheusnaptime', 'handelwithcare',
 'robdeluxe', 'popebuck1', 'leafshimmer', 'herbe', 'jeffla',
 'rhyno1975', 'needleboy', 'penaranda', 'maigremeg', 'stargirlms',
 'paladincub21', 'rawsound', 'moroccomole', 'heidilikesyou',
 'arshermetica', 'leashdog', 'apollonmk', 'greekcub', 'drubear',
 'gregorbehr', 'trickytoro']
```

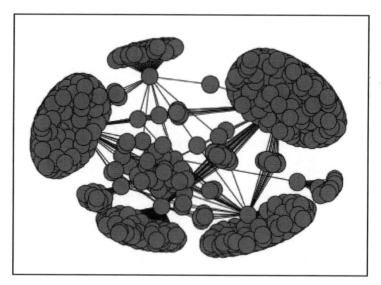

Summary

In this chapter, we learned what a social network is, discussing its creation and modification, representation, and some of the important measures of the social network and its nodes. Finally, we discussed the loading and saving of large graphs and ways to deal with the same.

With this chapter, all the essential data science algorithms have been presented; machine learning techniques were discussed in `Chapter 4`, *Machine Learning*, and social network analysis methods in the current one.

In the next chapter, which is the concluding one, we are going to introduce you to the basics of visualization with Matplotlib, how to operate EDA with pandas and achieve beautiful visualizations with Seaborn and Bokeh, and how to set up a web server to provide information on demand.

6
Visualization, Insights, and Results

Finally, yet importantly, we are going to illustrate how to create visualizations with Python to enrich your data science project. Visualization plays an important role in helping you communicate the results and insights derived from data and the learning process.

In this chapter, you will learn how to:

- Use the basic pyplot functions from the matplotlib package
- Leverage pandas DataFrame for Explorative Data Analysis (EDA)
- Create beautiful and interactive charts with Seaborn and Bokeh
- Visualize the machine learning and optimization processes we discussed in Chapter 3, *The Data Pipeline*, and Chapter 4, *Machine Learning*
- Understand and visually communicate the importance of variables and their relationship with the target outcome
- Set up a prediction server that uses HTTP to accept and provide predictions as-a-service.

Introducing the basics of matplotlib

Visualization is a fundamental aspect of data science, allowing data scientists to better and more effectively communicate their findings to the organization they operate in, to both data experts and non-experts. Providing the nuts and bolts of the principles behind communicating information and crafting engagingly beautiful visualizations is beyond the scope of our book, but we can recommend resources.

For basic visualization rules, you can visit
`http://lifehacker.com/5909501/how-to-choose-the-best-chart-for-your-data`. We also recommend the books of Prof. Edward Tufte on analytic design and visualization.

We can instead provide a fast and to-the-point series of essential recipes that can get you started on visualization using Python and which you can refer to whenever you need to create a specific graphic chart. Consider all the snippets of code as your visualization building blocks; you can arrange them with different configurations and features just by using the large choice of parameters that we are going to present to you.

matplotlib is a Python package for plotting graphics. Created by John Hunter, it has been developed in order to address a lack of integration between Python and external software with graphical capabilities, such as MATLAB or gnuplot. Greatly influenced by MATLAB's way of operating and functions, matplotlib presents a quite similar syntax. In particular, the `matplotlib.pyplot` module, perfectly compatible with MATLAB, will be the core of our essential introduction to all the indispensable graphical tools to represent your data and analysis. MATLAB is indeed a standard for visualization in the data analysis and scientific community due to its recognized capabilities when it comes to exploratory analysis, mainly due to its smooth and easy to use plotting functions.

Each pyplot command makes a change on an initially instantiated figure. Once you set a figure, all additional commands will operate on it. Thus, it is easy to incrementally improve and enrich your graphic representation. In order for you to take advantage of the code and be able to personalize it to your needs, all the following examples are presented together with commented building blocks so that you can later draft your basic representation and then look through this chapter for specific parameters among the examples in order to improve your chart as planned.

With the `pyplot.figure()` command, you can initialize a new visualization, though it's enough to call a plotting command to automatically start it. Instead, by using `pyplot.show()`, you close the figure that you were operating on and you can open and operate on new figures.

Before starting with a few visualization examples, let's import the necessary packages in order to run all the examples:

```
In: import numpy as np
import matplotlib.pyplot as plt
import matplotlib as mpl
```

In this way, we can always refer to pyplot, the MATLAB-like module, as `plt` and access the complete matplotlib functionality set with the help of `mpl`.

If you are using a Jupyter notebook, use this line: `%matplotlib inline`. After writing the command in a cell of the notebook and running it, you can have your plots drawn directly on the notebook itself, instead of having the graphics presented in a separated window (by default, the GUI backend of matplotlib is the TkAgg backend). If you prefer a different backend such as Qt (https://www.qt.io/), which is often distributed with Python scientific distributions, you just have to run this line magic instead: `%matplotlib qt`

Curve plotting

Our first problem will require you to draw a function with pyplot. Drawing a function is quite straightforward; you just have to get a series of *x* coordinates and map them to the *y* axis by using the function that you want to plot. Since the mapping results are stored away into two vectors, the `plot` function will deal with the curve representation. The precision of the representation will be greater if the mapped points are enough (50 points is a good sampling number):

```
In: import numpy as np
import matplotlib.pyplot as plt
x = np.linspace(0, 5, 50)
y_cos = np.cos(x)
y_sin = np.sin(x)
```

Using the NumPy `linspace()` function, we will create a series of 50 equally distanced numbers ranging from zero to five. We can use them to map our *y* to the cosine and sine functions:

```
In: plt.figure() # initialize a figure
plt.plot(x,y_cos) # plot series of coordinates as a line
plt.plot(x,y_sin)
plt.xlabel('x') # adds label to x axis
plt.ylabel('y') # adds label to y axis
plt.title('title') # adds a title
plt.show() # close a figure
```

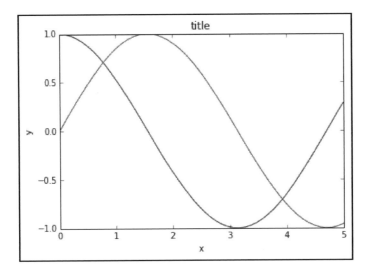

The `pyplot.plot` command can plot more curves in a sequence, with each curve taking a different color according to an internal color schema, which can be customized by explicating the favoured color sequence. To do so, you have to manipulate the list containing the sequence of colors that matplotlib uses:

```
In: list(mpl.rcParams['axes.prop_cycle'])
```

```
Out:
[{'color': 'b'},
 {'color': 'g'},
 {'color': 'r'},
 {'color': 'c'},
 {'color': 'm'},
 {'color': 'y'},
 {'color': 'k'}]
```

The hack can be done by using the cycler function and feeding it with a list of string names referring to the colors you want to use in sequence:

```
In: mpl.rcParams['axes.prop_cycle'] = mpl.cycler('color', ['blue', 'red',
'green'])
```

Moreover, the `plot` command, if not given any other information, will assume that you are going to plot a line. Therefore, it will link all the provided points in a curve. If you add a new parameter such as `'.'`, that is, `plt.plot(x,y_cos,'.')`, you signal that you instead want to plot a series of separated points (the string for a line is `'-'`, but we will soon show another example).

In this way, if you've customized `rcParams['axes.prop_cycle']` as proposed previously, the next graph will first have a blue curve, then the second will be red, and the third green. Then, the color loop will restart. We leave this decision to you. All the examples in this chapter will just follow the standard color sequence, but you are free to experiment with better color settings.

Note that you can also set the title of the graph and label the axis with the title, `xlabel`, and `ylabel` from pyplot.

Using panels

Our second example will show you how to create multiple graphic panels and plot a representation on each of them. We will also try to personalize the drawn curves by using different colors, sizes, and styles. Here is the example:

```
In: import matplotlib.pyplot as plt
In: plt.subplot(1,2,1) # defines 1 row 2 column panel, activates
figure 1
plt.plot(x,y_cos,'r--')
plt.title('cos') # adds a title
plt.subplot(1,2,2) # defines 1 row 2 column panel, activates
figure 2
plt.plot(x,y_sin,'b-')
plt.title('sin')
plt.show()
```

The plot displays the cosine and sine curves on two distinct graphic panels:

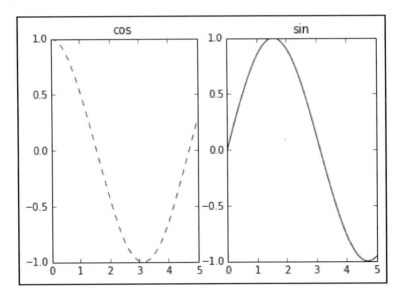

The subplot command accepts the `subplot(nrows, ncols, plot_number)` parameter form. Therefore, when instantiated, it reserves a certain amount of space for the representation based on the `nrows` and `ncols` parameters and the number of plots on the `plot_number` area (starting from the area 1 on the left).

You can also accompany the `plot` command coordinates with another string parameter, which is useful to define a color and the type of the represented curve. The strings work by combining the codes that you can find on the following links:

- `http://matplotlib.org/api/lines_api.html#matplotlib.lines.Line2D.set_l inestyle` will present the different line styles.
- `http://matplotlib.org/api/colors_api.html` offers a complete overview of the basic built-in colors. The page also points out that you can either use the `color` parameter together with the HTML names or hex strings for colors, or define the color you desire by using an RGB tuple, where each value of the tuple lies in the range [0,1]. For instance, a valid parameter is `color = (0.1,0.9,0.9)`, which will create a color made of 10% red, 90% green, and 90% blue.
- `http://matplotlib.org/api/markers_api.html` lists all the possible marker styles you can adopt for your points.

Scatterplots for relationships in data

Scatterplots plot two variables as points on a plane, and they can help you figure out the relationship between the two variables. They are also quite effective if you want to represent groups and clusters. In our example, we will create three data clusters and represent them in a scatterplot with different shapes and colors:

```
In: from sklearn.datasets import make_blobs
import matplotlib.pyplot as plt
D = make_blobs(n_samples=100, n_features=2, centers=3,
random_state=7)
groups = D[1]
coordinates = D[0]
```

Since we have to plot three different groups, we will have to use three distinct `plot` commands. Each command specifies a different color and shape (the `'ys'`, `'m*'`, `'rD'` strings, where the first letter is the colour and the second is the marker). Please also note that each plot instance is marked by a `label` parameter, which is used to assign a name to the group that has to be reported later in a legend:

```
In: plt.plot(coordinates[groups==0,0], coordinates[groups==0,1],
'ys', label='group 0') # yellow square
plt.plot(coordinates[groups==1,0], coordinates[groups==1,1], 'm*',
label='group 1') # magenta stars
plt.plot(coordinates[groups==2,0], coordinates[groups==2,1], 'rD',
label='group 2') # red diamonds
plt.ylim(-2,10) # redefines the limits of y axis
plt.yticks([10,6,2,-2]) # redefines y axis ticks
plt.xticks([-15,-5,5,-15]) # redefines x axis ticks
plt.grid() # adds a grid
plt.annotate('Squares', (-12,2.5)) # prints text at coordinates
plt.annotate('Stars', (0,6))
plt.annotate('Diamonds', (10,3))
plt.legend(loc='lower left', numpoints= 1) # places a legend of
labelled items
plt.show()
```

The resulting plot will be a scatterplot of the three groups with their respective labels:

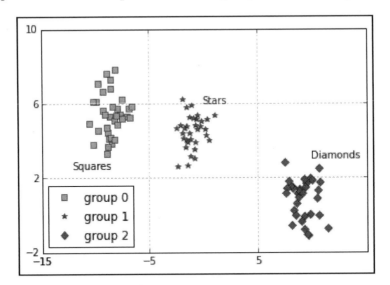

We have also added a legend (pyplot.legend), fixed a limit for both the axes (pyplot.xlim and pyplot ylim), and precisely explicated the ticks (plt.xticks and plt.yticks) that had to be put on them by specifying a list of values. Therefore, the grid (pyplot.grid) divides the plot exactly into nine quadrants and allows you to have a better idea of where the groups are positioned. We finally printed some text pointing out the group names (pyplot.annotate).

Histograms

Histograms can effectively represent the distribution of a variable. Here, we will visualize two normal distributions, both characterized by unit standard deviation, one having a mean of 0 and the other a mean of 3.0:

```
In: import numpy as np
import matplotlib.pyplot as plt
x = np.random.normal(loc=0.0, scale=1.0, size=500)
z = np.random.normal(loc=3.0, scale=1.0, size=500)
plt.hist(np.column_stack((x,z)), bins=20, histtype='bar',
color = ['c','b'], stacked=True)
plt.grid()
plt.show()
```

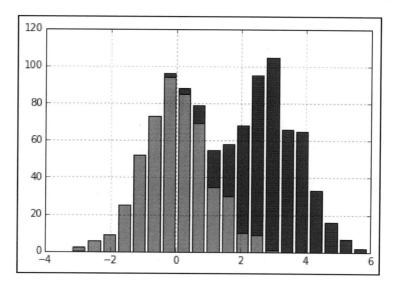

There are a few ways to personalize this kind of plot and obtain further insights about the analyzed distributions. First, by changing the number of bins, you will change how the distributions are discretized (discretization is the process that transforms continuous functions or series of values into a reduced, countable set of numbers: `https://en.wikiped ia.org/wiki/Discretization`). Generally, 10 to 20 bins offer a good understanding of the distribution, though it really depends on the size of the dataset as well as the distribution. For instance, the Freedman-Diaconis rule prescribes that the optimal number of bins in a histogram, in order to meaningfully visualize your data, depends on the bin's width, to be calculated using the **interquartile range (IQR)** and the number of observations:

$$h = 2 * IQR * n^{-1/3}$$

Having calculated h, which is the bin width, the number of bins is computed by dividing the difference between the maximum and the minimum value by h:

$$bins = (max - min) / h$$

We can also change the type of visualization from bars to steps by changing the parameters from *histtype='bar'* to *histtype='step'*. By changing the `stacked` Boolean parameter to `False`, the curves won't stack into a unique bar in the parts that overlap, but you will clearly see the separate bars of each one.

Bar graphs

Bar graphs are useful for comparing quantities in different categories. They can be arranged either horizontally or vertically to present the mean estimate and error bands. They can be used to present various statistics of your predictors and how they relate to the target variable.

In our example, we will present the mean and standard deviation for the four variables of the Iris dataset:

```
In: from sklearn.datasets import load_iris
import numpy as np
import matplotlib.pyplot as plt
iris = load_iris()
average = np.mean(iris.data, axis=0)
std     = np.std(iris.data, axis=0)
range_  = range(np.shape(iris.data)[1])
```

In our representation, we will prepare two subplots—one with horizontal bars (`plt.barh`), and the other with vertical bars (`plt.bar`). The standard error is represented by an error bar, and according to the graph orientation we can use the `xerr` parameter for horizontal bars and `yerr` for vertical ones:

```
In: plt.subplot(1,2,1) # defines 1 row, 2 columns panel, activates figure 1
plt.title('Horizontal bars') plt.barh(range_,average, color="r", xerr=std,
alpha=0.4, align="center") plt.yticks(range_, iris.feature_names)
plt.subplot(1,2,2) # defines 1 row 2 column panel, activates figure 2
plt.title('Vertical bars') plt.bar(range_,average, color="b", yerr=std,
alpha=0.4, align="center") plt.xticks(range_, range_) plt.show()
```

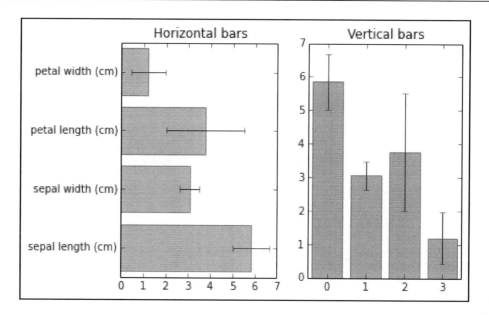

It is important to note the use of the `plt.xticks` command (and of `plt.yticks` for the ordinate axis). The first parameter informs the command about the number of ticks that have to be placed on the axis, and the second one explicates the labels that have to be put on the ticks.

Another interesting parameter to notice is `alpha`, which has been used to set the transparency level of the bar. The `alpha` parameter is a float number ranging from 0.0, fully transparent, to 1.0, which causes the colour to be shown in different levels of opaqueness.

Image visualization

The last possible visualization that we explore using matplotlib has to do with images. Resorting to `plt.imgshow` is useful when you are working with image data. Let's take as an example the Olivetti dataset, an open source set of images of 40 people who provided 10 images of themselves at different times (and with different expressions, a fact that makes it more challenging for testing face recognition algorithms). The images from this dataset are provided as feature vectors of pixel intensities. Therefore, it is important to reshape the vectors in order to make them resemble a matrix of pixels. Setting the interpolation to `'nearest'` helps smooth the picture:

```
In: from sklearn.datasets import fetch_olivetti_faces
import numpy as np
import matplotlib.pyplot as plt
dataset = fetch_olivetti_faces(shuffle=True, random_state=5)
photo = 1
for k in range(6):
    plt.subplot(2,3,k+1)
    plt.imshow(dataset.data[k].reshape(64,64), cmap=plt.cm.gray,
      interpolation='nearest')
    plt.title('subject '+str(dataset.target[k]))
    plt.axis('off')
plt.show()
```

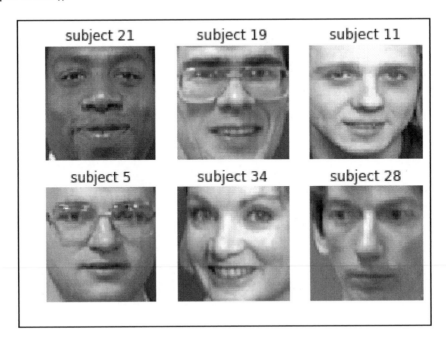

We can also visualize handwritten digits or letters. In our example, we will plot the first nine digits from the Scikit-learn handwritten digit dataset and set the extent of both the axes (by using the `extent` parameter and providing a list of minimum and maximum values) to align the grid to the pixels:

```
In: from sklearn.datasets import load_digits
digits = load_digits()
for number in range(1,10):
    plt.subplot(3, 3, number)
    plt.imshow(digits.images[number],cmap='binary',
               interpolation='none', extent=[0,8,0,8])
    plt.grid()
plt.show()
```

A simple close-up on a single number can be obtained by printing only one image:

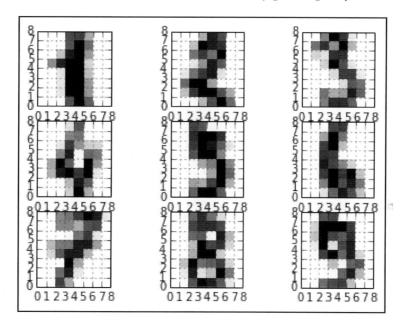

```
In: plt.imshow(digits.images[0],cmap='binary',interpolation='none',
extent=[0,8,0,8])
# Extent defines the images max and min of the horizontal and
vertical values
plt.grid()
plt.show()
```

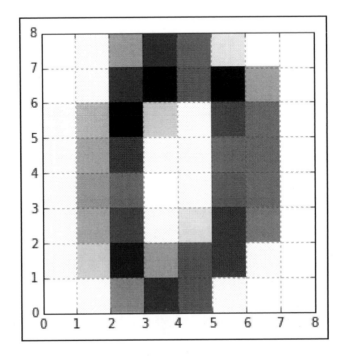

Selected graphical examples with pandas

Using appropriately set hyper-parameters, many machine learning algorithms can optimally learn how to map your data with respect to your target outcome. Yet their predictive performance can be improved further by fixing hidden and subtle problems in data. It is not simply a matter of detecting any missing or outlying case. Sometimes, it is a question of whether there are any groups or unusual distributions in the data (for instance, multimodal distributions). Clearly drafted data plots can explicate the relationship between variables and they can lead to the creation of new and better features in order to predict with increased accuracy your target variable.

The practice we have just described is called **Explorative Data Analysis (EDA)**, and it can bring effective results if it is done according to the following:

- It should be fast, allowing you to explore, develop new ideas and test them, and restart with a new exploration and fresh ideas
- It should be based on graphical representations in order to better describe data as a whole, no matter how high its dimensionality is

pandas DataFrame offers many EDA tools that can help you in your explorations. However, first you have to transform your data into a DataFrame:

```
In: import pandas as pd
print ('Your pandas version is: %s' % pd.__version__)
from sklearn.datasets import load_iris
iris = load_iris()
iris_df = pd.DataFrame(iris.data, columns=iris.feature_names)
groups = list(iris.target)
iris_df['groups'] = pd.Series([iris.target_names[k] for k in
groups])
Out: Your pandas version is: 0.18.1
```

Check your pandas version. We tested this code under version 0.18.1, and it should also hold for later releases.

We will be using the `iris_df` DataFrame for all the examples presented in the following paragraphs.

pandas actually relies on matplotlib functions for its visualizations. It simply provides a convenient wrapper around the otherwise complex plotting instructions. This offers advantages in terms of speed and simplicity, which are the core values of any EDA process. Instead, if your purpose is to best communicate your findings by using beautiful visualization, you may notice that it is not so easy to customize the pandas graphical outputs. Therefore, when creating specific graphic outputs is paramount, it is better to start working directly from scratch using matplotlib instructions.

Boxplots and histograms

Distributions should always be the first aspect to be inspected in your data. Boxplots draft the key figures in the distribution and help you spot outliers. Just use the `boxplot` method on your DataFrame for a quick overview:

```
In: boxplots = iris_df.boxplot(return_type='axes')
```

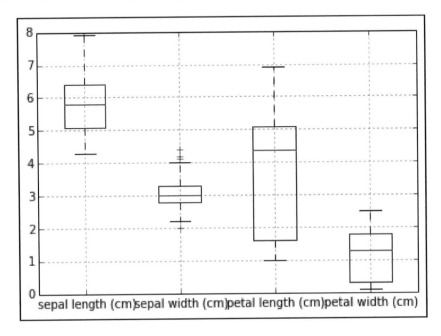

If you already have groups in your data (from categorical variables, or derived from unsupervised learning), just point out the variable you need data to be represented in the boxplot and specify that you need to have it separated by the groups (use the by parameter followed by the string name of the grouping variable):

```
In: boxplots = iris_df.boxplot(column='sepal length (cm)',
by='groups', return_type='axes')
```

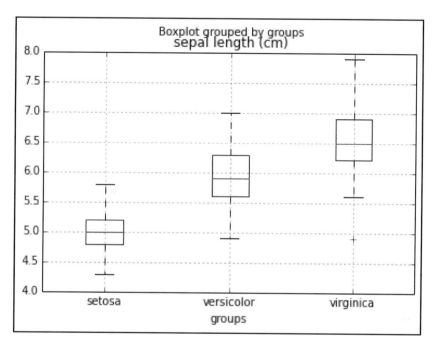

In this way, you can quickly know whether the variable is a good discriminator of the group differences. Anyway, Boxplots cannot provide you with a complete view of distributions as histograms and density plots. For instance, by using histograms and density plots, you can figure out whether there are distribution peaks or valleys:

```
In: densityplot = iris_df.plot(kind='density')
```

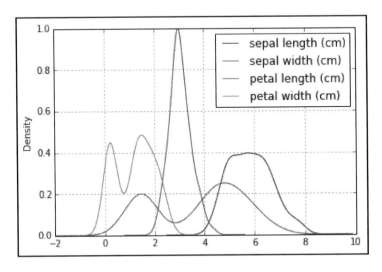

```
single_distribution = iris_df['petal width (cm)'
].plot(kind='hist', alpha=0.5)
```

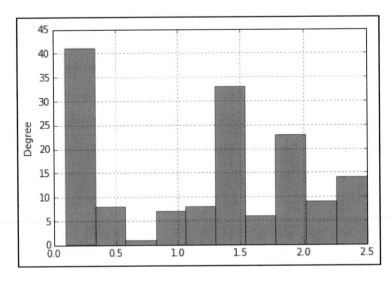

You can obtain both histograms and density plots by using the plot method. This method allows you to represent the whole dataset, specific groups of variables (you just have to provide a list of the string names and do some fancy indexing), or even single variables.

Scatterplots

Scatterplots can be used to effectively understand whether the variables are in a nonlinear relationship, and you can get an idea about their best possible transformations to achieve linearization. If you are using an algorithm based on linear combinations, such as linear or logistic regression, figuring out how to render their relationship more linearly will help you achieve better predictive power:

```
In: colors_palette = {0: 'red', 1: 'yellow', 2:'blue'}
colors = [colors_palette[c] for c in groups]
simple_scatterplot = iris_df.plot(kind='scatter', x=0, y=1,
c=colors)
```

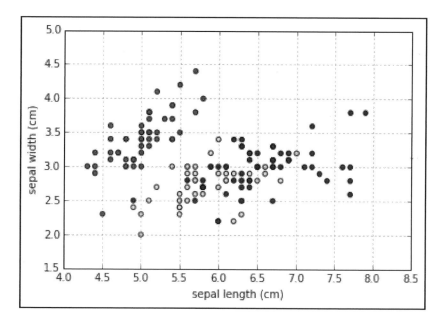

Scatterplots can be turned into hexagonal binning plots. In addition, they help you effectively visualize the point densities, where the point naturally more aggregate together, thus revealing clusters hidden in your data. For achieving such results, you may use some of the variables originally present in the dataset or the dimensions obtained by a PCA or by another dimensionality reduction algorithm:

```
In: hexbin = iris_df.plot(kind='hexbin', x=0, y=1, gridsize=10)
```

The gridsize parameter indicates how many data points the chart will summarize in a single grid. A larger number will create large grid cells, whereas a smaller one will create small cells.

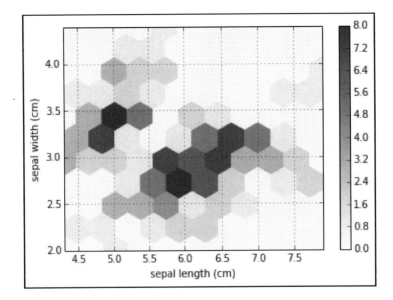

Scatterplots are bivariate. Consequently, you'll require a single plot for every variable combination. If your variables are fewer in number (otherwise, the visualization will be cluttered), a quick solution is to use the pandas command to draw a matrix of scatterplots automatically (using the kernel density estimation, 'kde', in order to plot the distribution of each feature on the diagonal of the chart):

```
In: from pandas.tools.plotting import scatter_matrix
colors_palette = {0: "red", 1: "green", 2: "blue"}
colors = [colors_palette[c] for c in groups]
matrix_of_scatterplots = scatter_matrix(iris_df, alpha=0.2,
figsize=(6, 6), color=colors, diagonal='kde')
```

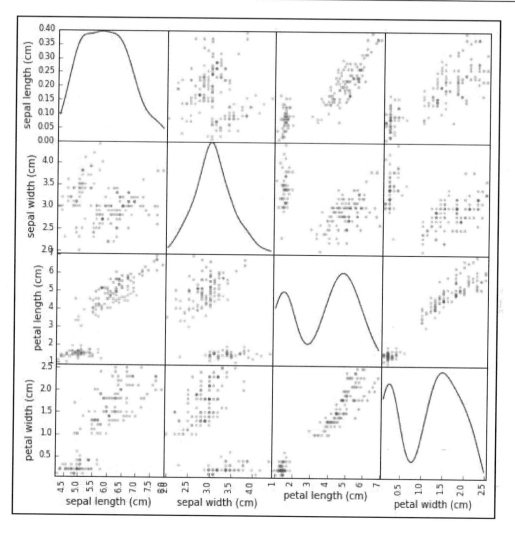

A few parameters can control various aspects of the scatterplot matrix. The `alpha` parameter controls the amount of transparency, and `figsize` provides the width and height of the matrix in inches. Finally, `color` accepts a list indicating the color of each point in the plot, thus allowing the depiction of different groups in data. In addition, by selecting `'kde'` or `'hist'` on your `diagonal` parameter, you can opt to represent density curves or histograms of each variable on the diagonal of the scatter matrix.

Parallel coordinates

The scatterplot matrix can inform you about the conjoint distributions of your features. It helps you locate groups in data and verify if they are distinguishable. Parallel coordinates are another kind of plot that is helpful in providing you with a hint about the most group-discriminating variables present in your data. By plotting all the observations as parallel lines with respect to all the possible variables (arbitrarily aligned on the abscissa), parallel coordinates will help you spot whether there are streams of observations grouped as your classes and understand the variables that best separate the streams (the most useful predictor variables). Naturally, in order for the chart to be meaningful, the features in the plot should have the same scale (otherwise, normalize them) as is the case in the Iris dataset:

```
In: from pandas.tools.plotting import parallel_coordinates
pll = parallel_coordinates(iris_df, 'groups')
```

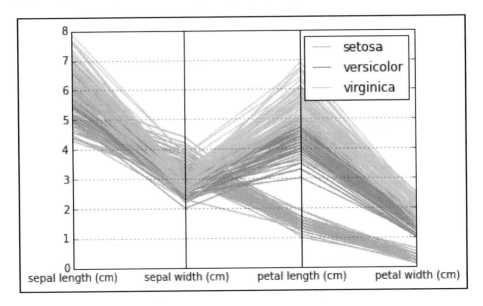

`parallel_coordinates` is a pandas function that, in order to work properly, just needs as parameters the data DataFrame and the string name of the variable containing the groups whose separability you want to test. For this reason, you should have the group variable available in your dataset. However, don't forget to remove it after you finish exploring by using the `DataFrame.drop('variable name', axis=1, inplace=True)` method.

Wrapping up matplotlib's commands

As we have seen in the previous paragraph, pandas can speed up exploring data visually since it wraps up into single commands what would have required an entire code snippet using Matplotlib. The idea behind this is that unless you need to tailor and configure a special visualization, using a wrapper can allow you to create standard graphics faster.

Apart from pandas, other packages assemble low-level instructions from matplotlib into more user-friendly commands for specific representations and uses:

- Seaborn is package that extends your visualization capabilities by providing you with a set of statistical plots useful for finding out trends and discriminating groups.
- ggplot is a port of a popular R library, ggplot2 (`http://ggplot2.org/`), based on the visualization grammar proposed in Leland Wilkinson's book, Grammar of Graphics. The R library is continuously developed and it offers much functionality, the Python porting (`http://ggplot.yhathq.com/`) features the basics (`http://ggplot.yhathq.com/docs/index.html`) and its complete development is still under way (`https://github.com/yhat/ggplot`).
- MPLD3 (`http://mpld3.github.io/`) leverages the JavaScript library for graphic manipulation, D3.js, in order to easily transform any matplotlib output into HTML code, which can be rendered using a browser and a tool such as a Jupyter notebook or within an Internet website.
- Bokeh is an interactive visualization package that leverages JavaScript and browser-rendered outputs. It is a great replacement for D3.js since you just need Python in order to leverage the capabilities of JavaScript to represent quickly your data in an interactive way.

In the following pages, we will introduce both Seaborn and Bokeh, providing some building blocks for leveraging their visualizations in your data science projects.

Introducing Seaborn

Created by Michael Waskom and hosted on the Stanford University website (`http://stanf ord.edu/~mwaskom/software/seaborn`), Seaborn is a library that wraps up the low-level matplotlib with the entire pyData stack, allowing integrating charts with data structures from Numpy and pandas and with statistical routines from Scipy and statmodels. All that is achieved with particular attention to aesthetics, thanks to built-in themes, and to color palettes, especially devised to reveal patterns in data.

If you don't have Seaborn presently installed on your system (the Anaconda distributions provides it by default, for instance), you can easily get it both by pip and conda (but remember that the conda version may lag behind the pip version taken directly from PyPI):

```
pip install seaborn
conda install seaborn
```

In these examples, we have used version 0.7.0 of the Seaborn package.

You can upload the package and set Seaborn as the default matplotlib style by:

```
In: import seaborn as sns
sns.set()
```

This is enough to turn all your matplotlib-based representations into more visually appealing charts:

```
In: x = np.linspace(0, 5, 50)
y_cos = np.cos(x)
y_sin = np.sin(x)
plt.figure()
plt.plot(x,y_cos)
plt.plot(x,y_sin)
plt.xlabel('x')
plt.ylabel('y')
plt.title('sin/cos functions')
plt.show()
Out:
```

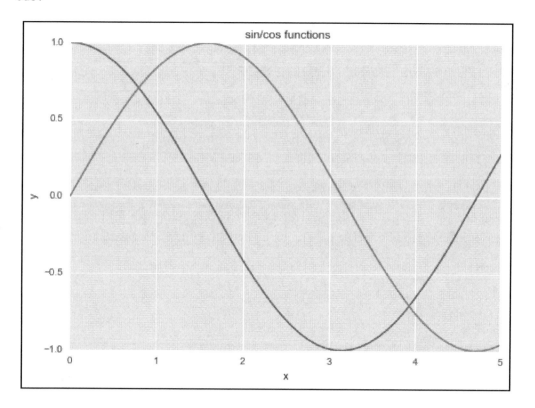

You can obtain interesting results from any of the previously seen charts, even the ones generated using graphical methods in pandas (after all, pandas also relies on matplotlib for creating its explorative plots).

There are five preset themes in seaborn: `darkgrid`, `whitegrid`, `dark`, `white`, and `ticks`, with `darkgrid` being the default one. You can easily try each one by using the set_style command and the name of your preferred theme and then running your plot commands:

```
In: sns.set_style('whitegrid')
```

All you have to do is just decide which theme best helps you convey information on your chart. You can limit a style to a single representation enclosing it:

```
In: with sns.axes_style('whitegrid'):
# Your plot commands here
```

Other stylish changes may involve the spines, which are the chart borders. Using the despine command, you can easily remove the top and right borders:

```
In: sns.despine()
```

Moreover, you can remove the left border using the `left=True` parameter, offset the axis using the `offset` parameter, and trim it (using `trim=True`). All these operations were otherwise not so accessible via matplotlib commands alone.

Another useful control that Seaborn allows you regards the scale of the chart. A certain chart scale (involving different lines thickness, font size, and so on) is called a context, and the available contexts are self-explanatory-paper, notebook, talk, and poster are all possible options. For instance, if your chart has to be displayed on an MS PowerPoint presentation, just run the following command before creating the graphics:

```
In: sns.set_context("talk")
```

Let's see an example of these effects on our initial sin/cos chart:

```
In: sns.set_context("talk")
with sns.axes_style('whitegrid'):
plt.figure()
plt.plot(x,y_cos)
plt.plot(x,y_sin)
plt.show()
sns.set()
Out:
```

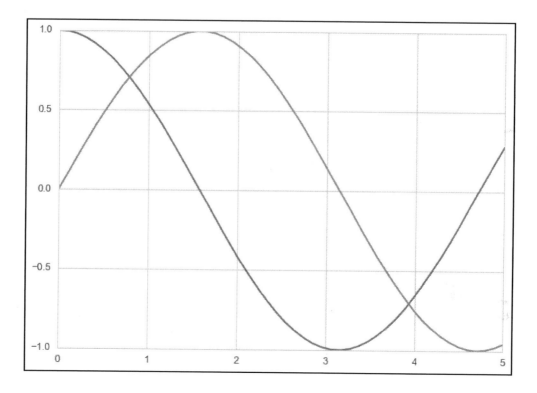

Also, choosing the right color cycle or set may help your graphical representation shine. For this, Seaborn offers the `color_palette()` command, which won't just tell you the current palette's RBG values (if run with no parameters); it will also accept the name of any palette offered by Seaborn or any matplotlib colormap. It even accepts custom lists of colors provided by you in any matplotlib format (RGB tuples, hex color codes, or HTML color names) in order to create your own palette:

```
In: current_palette = sns.color_palette()
print (current_palette)
sns.palplot(current_palette)
Out:
```

```
[(0.2980392156862745, 0.4470588235294118, 0.6901960784313725), (0.3333333333333333, 0.6588235294117647, 0.4078431372549019
6), (0.7686274509803922, 0.3058823529411765, 0.3215686274509804), (0.5058823529411764, 0.4470588235294118, 0.69803921568627
45), (0.8, 0.7254901960784313, 0.4549019607843137), (0.39215686274509803, 0.7098039215686275, 0.803921568627451)]
```

There are a few palettes available, as mentioned. First, all the Seaborn palettes are:

- deep
- muted
- bright
- pastel
- dark
- colorblind

You also have to add `hls`, `husl`, and all the matplotlib colormaps, which can be reversed by appending `_r` to their name, or made darker by appending `_d`.

 Both the names and examples of matplotlib colormaps can be found at this web page:
http://matplotlib.org/examples/color/colormaps_reference.html.

The `hls` colour space is an automatic transformation in the RGB scale of values, which may or may not work for your representations, since colours have different intensities (for instance, yellow and green colours are perceived as brighter whereas blue is perceived as darker).

As an alternative to `hsl`, you can use the `husl` palette, which is friendlier for the human eye, as explained by http://www.husl-colors.org/.

Finally, you can just create a personalized palette using the Color Brewer tool, which can be both found online (`http://colorbrewer2.org/`) or required in an app from your Jupyter Notebook. In a notebook cell, using the `choose_colorbrewer_palette` command will make an interactive tool appear. To get everything working, it is essential that you specify as a parameter `data_type`, a string explicating the nature of your palette related to the data you intend to represent:

- 'sequential' if you want to represent continuity
- 'diverging' to represent contrasts
- 'qualitative' when you just want to discriminate between different classes

Let's see how to create a custom sequential palette and use it:

```
In: your_palette = sns.choose_colorbrewer_palette('sequential')
Out:
```

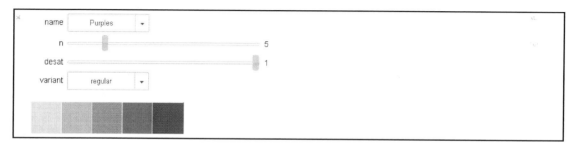

```
In: print (your_palette)
Out:
[(0.91109573770971852, 0.90574395025477683, 0.94832756940056306),
 (0.7764706015586853, 0.77908498048782349, 0.88235294818878174),
 (0.61776242186041452, 0.60213766261643054, 0.78345253116944269),
 (0.47320263584454858, 0.43267974257469177, 0.69934642314910889),
 (0.35681661753093497, 0.20525952297098493, 0.58569783322951374)]
```

When you are done with your choice, you can just call `sns.set_palette(your_palette)` and have the colours used when drawing all your charts.

If you need just to operate on a chart with some specific colours, using a `with` statement and nesting the chart snippet under it will suffice, as we saw previously for themes. Instead, if you definitely need to set a certain palette for all your plotting, use `set_palette`.

The colour palette is made up of six colours, helping you distinguish at least six trends or classes. If you need to distinguish more, you simply can operate with the `hls` palette and point out the number of colours you need to cycle:

```
In: new_palette=sns.color_palette('hls', 10)
sns.palplot(new_palette)
Out:
```

Finally, closing our paragraph about themes and colors, since Seaborn is another smarter way to use functions offered by matplotlib, remember that the resulting charts can be modified further using any basic command coming from matplotlib itself. Or they can be further transformed by packages such as MPLD3 or Bokeh into JavaScript.

Enhancing your EDA capabilities

Seaborn doesn't just make your charts more beautiful and easier to control in their aspects, it also provides you with new tools for EDA to help you discover distributions and relationships between variables.

Before proceeding, let's reload the package and have both the Iris and Boston datasets ready in pandas DataFrame format:

```
In:
import seaborn as sns
sns.set()

from sklearn.datasets import load_iris
iris = load_iris()
X_iris, y_iris = iris.data, iris.target
features_iris = [a[:-5].replace(' ','_') for a in iris.feature_names]
target_labels = {j: flower for j, flower in enumerate(iris.target_names)}
df_iris = pd.DataFrame(X_iris, columns=features_iris)
df_iris['target'] = [target_labels[y] for y in y_iris]

from sklearn.datasets import load_boston
boston = load_boston()
X_boston, y_boston = boston.data, boston.target
features_boston = np.array(['V'+'_'.join([str(b), a]) for a,b in
zip(boston.feature_names,range(len(boston.feature_names)))])
```

```
df_boston = pd.DataFrame(X_boston, columns=features_boston)
df_boston['target'] = y_boston
df_boston['target_level'] = pd.qcut(y_boston, 3)
```

As for as the Iris dataset, the target variable has been converted into descriptive text of the Iris species. For the Boston dataset, the continuous target variable, the median value of owner-occupied homes, has been divided into three equal parts, representing lower, median and high prices (using the pandas function qcut).

Seaborn can first help your data exploration with figuring out how discretely valued or categorical variables are related to numeric ones. This is achieved using the factorplot function.

```
In:
with sns.axes_style("ticks"):
    sns.factorplot(data=df_boston, x='V8_RAD', y="target")
```

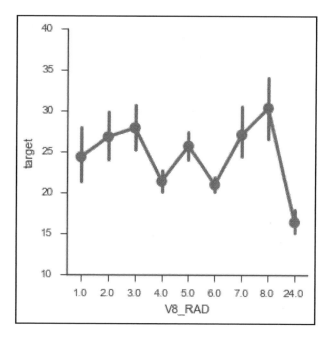

In our example, in the Boston dataset, the index of accessibility to radial highways, which is discretely valued, it is compared with the target in order to check both the functional form of its relationships and the associated variance at each level.

If instead the comparison is between numeric variables, Seaborn offers an enhanced scatterplot incorporating a regression fitted curve trend, which can point you towards possible data transformations when the relationship is not linear:

```
In:
with sns.axes_style("whitegrid"):
    sns.regplot(data=df_boston, x='V12_LSTAT', y="target", order=3)
```

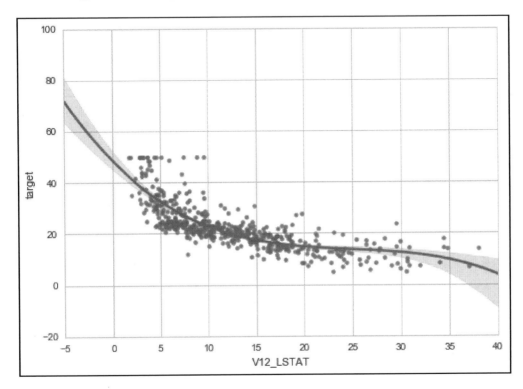

`regplot` in Seaborn can visualize regression plots of any order (we have displayed a second-degree polynomial fit). Using standard linear regression, robust regression and even logistic regression is one of the inspected features is a binary one.

Where it is necessary to consider distributions too, jointplot will provide additional plots on the side of the scatterplot:

```
In:
with sns.axes_style("whitegrid"):
    sns.jointplot("V4_NOX", "V7_DIS", data=df_boston, kind='reg',
    order=3)
```

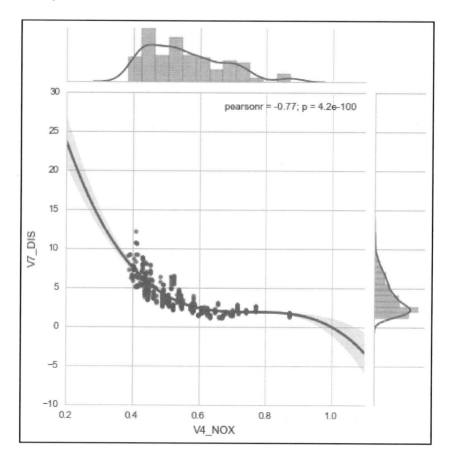

Ideal for representing bivariate relationships by acting on the `kind` parameter, `jointplot` can also represent simple scatterplots or densities (`kind='scatter'` or `kind='kde'`).

When the purpose is to discover what discriminates classes, FacetGrid can arrange different plots in a comparable way and help you understand where there are differences. For instance, we can inspect the scatterplot of Iris species in order to figure out if they occupy different parts of the feature state:

```
In: with sns.axes_style("darkgrid"):
        chart = sns.FacetGrid(df_iris, col="target_level")
        chart.map(plt.scatter, "sepal_length", "petal_length")
```

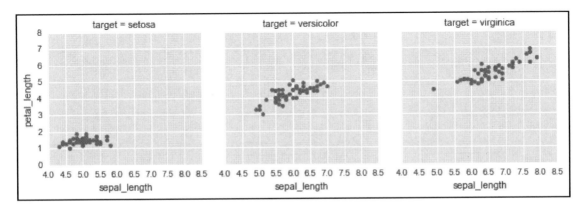

Similar comparisons can be made using distributions (sns.distplot) or regression slopes (`sns.regplot`):

```
In:
with sns.axes_style("darkgrid"):
chart = sns.FacetGrid(df_iris, col="target")
chart.map(sns.distplot, "sepal_length")
```

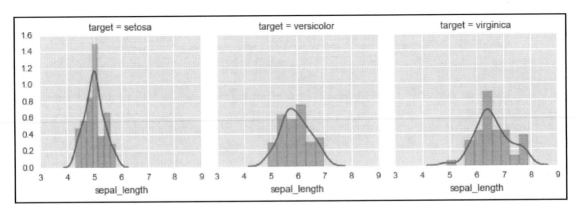

```
In:
with sns.axes_style("darkgrid"):
chart = sns.FacetGrid(df_boston, col="target_level")
chart.map(sns.regplot, "V4_NOX", "V7_DIS")
```

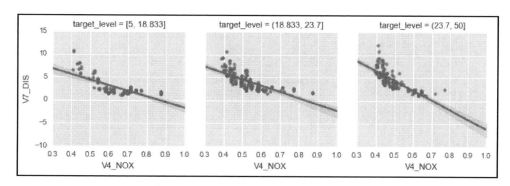

As for evaluating data distributions across classes, Seaborn offers an alternative tool, which is the violin plot (https://en.wikipedia.org/wiki/Violin_plot). A violin plot is simply a boxplot whose box is shaped based on density estimation, thus visually conveying information that is more intuitive:

```
In:
with sns.axes_style("whitegrid"):
    ax = sns.violinplot(x="target", y="sepal_length",
                        data=df_iris, palette="pastel")
    sns.despine(offset=10, trim=True)
```

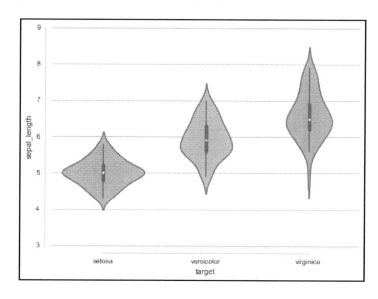

Finally, Seaborn offers a much better way of creating a matrix of scatterplots by using the pairplot command and allowing you to define group colors (parameter hue) and how to populate the diagonal row. This uses the `diag_kind` parameter, which can be a histogram (`'hist'`) or kernel density estimation (`'kde'`):

```
In:
with sns.axes_style("whitegrid"):
    chart = sns.pairplot(data=df_iris, hue="target", diag_kind="hist")
```

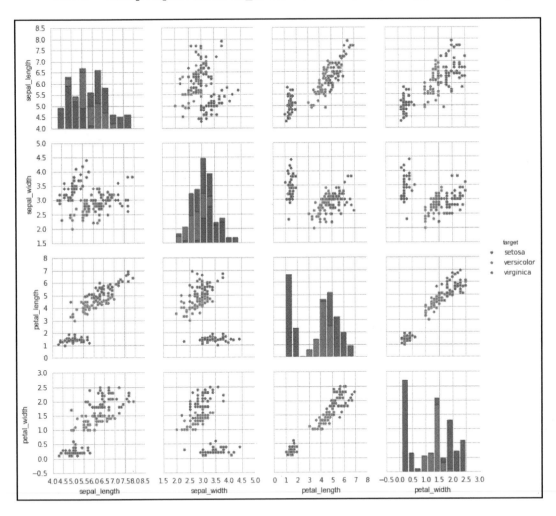

Interactive visualizations with Bokeh

The recent success of D3.js in visualization tasks in data science is due to its paradigm that leads to graphical computations happening in the browser, not on the server side. Visualizations can be delivered faster (no latency due to data going to a server and graphics getting back to the web browser) and in an interactive and personalized way.

Bokeh, from the Japanese "blurred" (a kind of photographic rendering that emphasizes the subject of the photo while blurring the background), is a Python package and part of the pydata stack that allows using web browser for presentations, mimicking the graphic style and interactivity of D3.js. It is a package that strives to make otherwise difficult representations an easy task, such as building dashboards, creating interactive plots, and representing large datasets.

We are just going to introduce it briefly, focusing on how to render matplotlib-based plots to be posted on the Web and leaving exploration of its most unique and advanced features to you. This is because Bokeh is such an incredible tool that it would need an entire chapter by itself to be fully explained.

You can find a complete tutorial explaining in detail all its features at: `http://nbviewer.ju pyter.org/github/bokeh/bokeh-notebooks/tree/master/tutorial/`.

Like other packages demonstrated in the book, Bokeh can be easily installed by both pip and conda:

```
pip install bokeh
conda install bokeh
```

In our examples, we will be using version 0.12.1, which is the current one at the time we wrote this chapter. This should handle all the prerequisites and put you immediately on track for testing how the package works using the following code:

```
In: import numpy as np
from bokeh.plotting import figure, output_file, show

x = np.linspace(0, 5, 50)
y_cos = np.cos(x)
output_file("cosine.html")
p = figure()
p.line(x, y_cos, line_width=2)
show(p)
```

The code will create a new html file (HTML5 since the package relies on the HTML5 Canvas library) to be found on the working directory and it will upload it on your browser (the visualization is not integrated into Jupyter because we stated that the output has to be a file using `output_file`). At this point, you can incorporate the output HTML into any website.

Another possibility for your chart to be on the Web is to have Bokeh read your code and serve the resulting chart as an as interactive web application. This has the advantage that you won't need to recreate the HTML output every time your data changes, because the Bokeh server will manage it for you. In order to achieve that, you need the Bokeh server command. All the essential documentation about its usage can be found here: `http://bokeh.pydata.org/en/latest/docs/user_guide/cli.html#module-bokeh.command.subcommands.serve`.

If you prefer to stay local, in order to have your output directly integrated on the Jupyter Notebook, you first have to reset the output (`reset_output`) and then direct it to the running notebook (`output_notebook`):

```
In: from bokeh.io import output_notebook, reset_output
reset_output()
output_notebook()
Out:
```

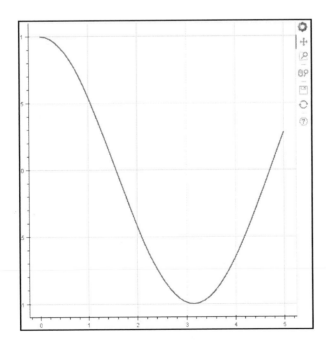

Notice the plot tools on the right of the plot, which will help you to drag, scroll, and enlarge the chart, making any chart elaborated by Bokeh extremely interactive. You can learn everything needed to configure how tools are displayed (the position of the toolbar, available tools, and so on) using the instructions at: `http://bokeh.pydata.org/en/latest/docs/user_guide/tools.html`.

Another advantage Bokeh gives is that it integrates with other visualization packages such as Matplotlib, Seaborn, and even ggplot. By using the `to_bokeh` method, any chart and plot from other packages can be easily ported into Bokeh. Moreover, Bokeh's commands can operate on pandas DataFrame, thus making its use easier during EDA and data manipulation. The Bokeh package itself can take advantage of many pandas functionalities, such as the conversion of dates.

In our example, we demonstrate how easily any of the previous charts we made with matplotlib can now be rendered with Bokeh:

```
In: from sklearn.datasets import make_blobs
import matplotlib.pyplot as plt
from bokeh import mpl
from bokeh.plotting import show

D = make_blobs(n_samples=100, n_features=2, centers=3, random_state=7)
coord, groups = D[0], D[1]

plt.plot(coord[groups==0,0], coord[groups==0,1], 'ys')
plt.plot(coord[groups==1,0], coord[groups==1,1], 'm*')
plt.plot(coord[groups==2,0], coord[groups==2,1], 'rD')
plt.grid()
plt.annotate('Squares', (-12,2.5))
plt.annotate('Stars', (0,6))
plt.annotate('Diamonds', (10,3))

show(mpl.to_bokeh())
```

Under the hood, the rendering from matplotlib is done by the mplexporter (`https://github.com/mpld3/mplexporter`) third-party package. Not all matplotlib features can be handled by mplexporter. Consequently some warnings may appear in the conversion, causing a graphical mismatch between the original chart and Bokeh's one. Yet, most of the charts will be rendered the same as the original ones.

Advanced data-learning representations

Some useful representations can be derived from the data science process. That is, the representation is not done directly from the data but it is achieved by using machine learning procedures, which inform us about how the algorithms operate and offer us a more precise overview of the role of each predictor in the predictions obtained. In particular, learning curves can provide a quick diagnosis to improve your models. It helps you figure out whether you need more observations or you need to enrich your variables.

Learning curves

A learning curve is a useful diagnostic graphic that depicts the behavior of your machine learning algorithm (your hypothesis) with respect to the available quantity of observations. The idea is to compare how the training performance (the error or accuracy of the in-sample cases) behaves with respect to cross-validation (usually tenfold) using different in-sample sizes.

As far as any training error is concerned, you should expect it to be high at the start and then decrease. However, depending on the bias and variance level of the hypothesis, you will notice different behaviors:

- A high-bias hypothesis tends to start with average error performances, decreases rapidly on being exposed to more complex data, and then remains at the same level of performance no matter how many cases you further add. Low-bias learners tend to generalize better in presence of many cases, but they are limited in their capability to approximate complex data structures, hence their limited performance.
- A high-variance hypothesis tends to start high in error performance and then slowly decreases as you add more cases. It tends to decrease slowly because it has a high capacity for recording the in-sample characteristics.

As for cross-validation, we can notice two behaviors:

- A high-bias hypothesis tends to start with low performance, but it grows very rapidly until it reaches almost the same performance as that of the training. Then, it stops growing.
- A high-variance hypothesis tends to start with very low performance. Then, steadily but slowly, it improves as more cases help it generalize. It hardly reads the in-sample performances, and there is always a gap between them.

Being able to estimate whether your machine learning solution is behaving as a high-bias or high-variance hypothesis immediately helps you in deciding how to improve your data science project. Scikit-learn makes it simpler to calculate all the statistics that are necessary for drawing the visualization thanks to the `learning_curve` class, though visualizing them properly requires a few further calculations and commands:

```
In: import numpy as np
from sklearn.learning_curve import learning_curve, validation_curve
from sklearn.datasets import load_digits
from sklearn.linear_model import SGDClassifier
digits = load_digits()
X, y = digits.data, digits.target
hypothesis = SGDClassifier(loss='log', shuffle=True, n_iter=5,
penalty='l2', alpha=0.0001, random_state=3)
train_size, train_scores, test_scores = learning_curve(hypothesis,
X, y, train_sizes=np.linspace(0.1,1.0,5), cv=10,
scoring='accuracy', exploit_incremental_learning=False,
n_jobs=-1)
mean_train   = np.mean(train_scores,axis=1)
upper_train = np.clip(mean_train + np.std(train_scores,axis=1),0,1)
lower_train = np.clip(mean_train - np.std(train_scores,axis=1),0,1)
mean_test    = np.mean(test_scores,axis=1)
upper_test = np.clip(mean_test + np.std(test_scores,axis=1),0,1)
lower_test = np.clip(mean_test - np.std(test_scores,axis=1),0,1)
plt.plot(train_size,mean_train,'ro-', label='Training')
plt.fill_between(train_size, upper_train, lower_train, alpha=0.1,
color='r')
plt.plot(train_size,mean_test,'bo-', label='Cross-validation')
plt.fill_between(train_size, upper_test, lower_test, alpha=0.1,
color='b')
plt.grid()
plt.xlabel('sample size') # adds label to x axis
plt.ylabel('accuracy') # adds label to y axis
plt.legend(loc='lower right', numpoints= 1)
plt.show()
```

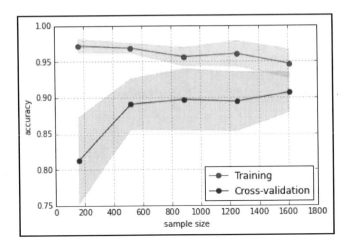

The `learning_curve` class requires the following as an input:

- A series of training sizes stored in a list
- An indication of the number of folds to use and the error measure
- Your machine learning algorithm to test (parameter estimator)
- The predictors (parameter X) and the target outcome (parameter y)

As a result, the class will produce three arrays—the first one containing the effective training sizes, the second presenting the training scores obtained at each cross-validation iteration, and the last one carrying the cross-validation scores.

By applying the mean and standard deviation for both training and cross-validation, it is possible to display in the graph both the curve trends and their variation. You can also provide information about the stability of the recorded performances.

Validation curves

As learning curves operate on different sample sizes, validation curves estimate the training and cross-validation performance with respect to the values that a hyper-parameter can take. As in learning curves, similar considerations can be applied, though this particular visualization will grant you further insight about the optimization behavior of your parameter, visually suggesting to you the part of the hyper-parameter space that you should concentrate your search on:

```
In: from sklearn.learning_curve import validation_curve
testing_range = np.logspace(-5,2,8)
hypothesis = SGDClassifier(loss='log', shuffle=True, n_iter=5,
```

```
penalty='l2', alpha=0.0001, random_state=3)
train_scores, test_scores = validation_curve(hypothesis, X, y,
param_name='alpha', param_range=testing_range, cv=10,
scoring='accuracy', n_jobs=-1)
mean_train  = np.mean(train_scores,axis=1)
upper_train = np.clip(mean_train + np.std(train_scores,axis=1),0,1)
lower_train = np.clip(mean_train - np.std(train_scores,axis=1),0,1)
mean_test   = np.mean(test_scores,axis=1)
upper_test = np.clip(mean_test + np.std(test_scores,axis=1),0,1)
lower_test = np.clip(mean_test - np.std(test_scores,axis=1),0,1)
plt.semilogx(testing_range,mean_train,'ro-', label='Training')
plt.fill_between(testing_range, upper_train, lower_train, alpha=0.1,
color='r')
plt.fill_between(testing_range, upper_train, lower_train, alpha=0.1,
color='r')
plt.semilogx(testing_range,mean_test,'bo-', label='Cross-
validation')
plt.fill_between(testing_range, upper_test, lower_test, alpha=0.1,
color='b')
plt.grid()
plt.xlabel('alpha parameter') # adds label to x axis
plt.ylabel('accuracy') # adds label to y axis
plt.ylim(0.8,1.0)
plt.legend(loc='lower left', numpoints= 1)
plt.show()
```

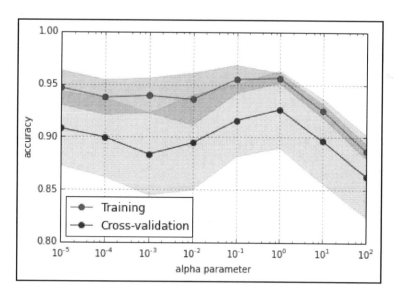

The syntax of the `validation_curve` class is similar to that of the previously seen `learning_curve` except for the `param_name` and `param_range` parameters, which should be provided respectively with the hyper-parameter and its range that has to be tested. As for the results, the training and test results are returned in arrays.

Feature importance for RandomForests

As discussed in the conclusion of `Chapter 3`, *The Data Pipeline*, selecting the right variables can improve your learning process by reducing noise, the variance of estimates, and the burden of too many computations. Ensemble methods, such as RandomForests in particular, can provide you with a different view of the role played by a variable when working together with other ones in your dataset. Here we show you how to extract the importance of RandomForests and ExtraTrees models. Importance is calculated in the fashion originally described in the book Classification and Regression Trees by Breiman, Friedman et al. in 1984. It was a true classic that laid solid foundations for classification trees. In the book, importance is described in terms of "gini importance" or "mean decrease impurity," which is the total decrement in node impurity due to a specific variable averaged over all trees of the ensemble. In other words, mean decreased impurity is the total error reduction of nodes split on that variable multiplied by the number of samples that were routed to each of the nodes.

Noticeably, accordingly to this importance calculation method, not only does error reduction depend on the error measure-Gini or Entropy for classification, and MSE for regression-but also splits at the head of the tree are deemed more important because they involve dealing with more examples.

In a few steps, we'll learn how to obtain such information and project it onto a clear visualization:

```
In: from sklearn.datasets import load_boston
boston = load_boston()
X, y = boston.data, boston.target
feature_names = np.array([' '.join([str(b), a]) for a,b in
zip(boston.feature_names,range(len(boston.feature_names)))])
from sklearn.ensemble import RandomForestRegressor
RF = RandomForestRegressor(n_estimators=100, random_state=101).fit(X,  y)
importance = np.mean([tree.feature_importances_ for tree in
RF.estimators_],axis=0)
std = np.std([tree.feature_importances_ for tree in
RF.estimators_],axis=0)
indices = np.argsort(importance)
range_ = range(len(importance))
plt.figure()
```

```
plt.title("Random Forest importance")
plt.barh(range_,importance[indices], color="r", xerr=std[indices],
alpha=0.4, align="center")
plt.yticks(range(len(importance)), feature_names[indices])
plt.ylim([-1, len(importance)])
plt.xlim([0.0, 0.65])
plt.show()
```

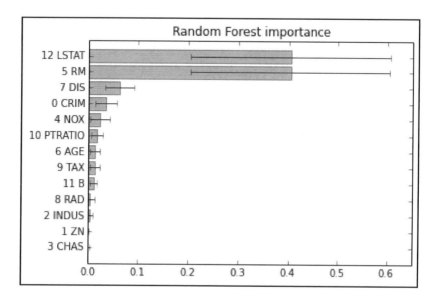

For each of the estimators (in our case, we have 100 models), the algorithm estimated a score to rank each variable's importance. The RandomForest model is made up of decision trees that can be made up of many branches, since the algorithm tries to obtain very small terminal leaves. One of its variables is deemed important if, after casually permuting its original values, the resulting predictions of the permuted model are very different in terms of accuracy as compared to the predictions of the original model.

The importance vectors are averaged over the number of estimators, and the standard deviation of the estimations is computed by a list comprehension (the assignment of variables importance and `std`). Now, sorted according to the importance score (the vector indices), the results are projected onto a bar graph with an error bar provided by the standard deviation.

In our LSTAT analysis, the percentage of lower status population in the area and RM, which is the average number of rooms per dwelling, are pointed out as the most decisive variables in our RandomForest model.

GBT partial dependence plots

An estimate of the importance of a feature is a piece of information that can help you operate on the best choices to determine the features to be used. Sometimes, you may need to understand better why a variable is important in predicting a certain outcome. Gradient Boosting Trees, by controlling the effect of all the other variables involved in the analysis, provide you with a clear point of view of the relationship of a variable with respect to the predicted results. Such information can provide you with more insights about causation dynamics than you may have obtained by using a very effective EDA:

```
In: from sklearn.ensemble.partial_dependence import
plot_partial_dependence
from sklearn.ensemble import GradientBoostingRegressor
GBM = GradientBoostingRegressor(n_estimators=100,  random_state=101).fit(X,
y)
features = [5,12,(5,12)]
fig, axis = plot_partial_dependence(GBM, X, features,
feature_names=feature_names)
```

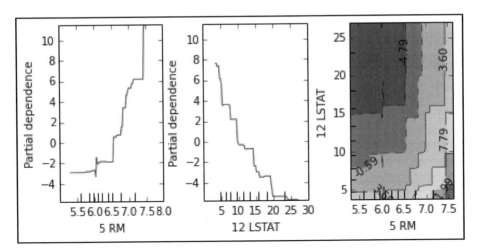

The `plot_partial_dependence` class will automatically provide you with the visualization after you provide an analysis plan on your part. You need to present a list of indexes of the features to be plotted singularly and the tuples of the indexes of those that you would like to plot on a heat map (the features are the axis, and the heat value corresponds to the outcome).

In the preceding example, both the average number of rooms and the percentage of lower status population have been represented, thus displaying an expected behavior. Interestingly, the heat map, which explains how they together contribute to the value of the outcome, reveals that they do not interact in any particular way (it is a single hill-climbing). However, it is also revealed that LSTAT is a strong delimiter of the resulting housing values when it is above 5.

Creating a prediction server for ML-AAS

Many times, during your working career as a data scientist, you'll find yourself having the need to have a predictor decoupled from the code you're currently working on. Examples are as follows:

- You're developing an App for your phone, and you want to save on memory
- You're coding in a non-Python programming language (Java/Scala/C/C++, …) and you need to call the predictor you've developed in Python
- You're operating on big data, and the model is trained in the same remote location where the data is stored

In all these cases, it would be nice to have a service over HTTP that does predictions-as-a-service, or generically, any machine-learning-algorithm-as-a-service (ML-AAS).

Bottle, a Python web framework, is the starting point for micro apps over HTTP. It is a very simple library for Python, providing the essentials objects and functions to create a web app. Also, it can be paired with all the other libraries available in Python. Before going to the prediction-as-a-service, let's see how a basic "Hello World" program is built with Bottle. Please note that the following listings are meant for Python REPL, as a script, and not for a Jupyter Notebook:

```
File: bottle1.py
from bottle import route, run, template
port = 9099
@route('/personal/<name>')
def homepage(name):
return template('Hi <b>{{name}}</b>!', name=name)
print("Try going to http://localhost:{}/personal/Tom".format(port))
print("Try going to http://localhost:{}/personal/Carl".format(port))
run(host='localhost', port=port)
```

Let's analyze the code line by line before executing it. We started importing the functions and the classes we need from the Bottle module. Then, we specify the port where the HTTP server will listen to. In the example, we selected port 9099; feel free to change it to another one, but first check whether any other service is using it (remember that HTTP is on top of TCP). The next step is the definition of the API endpoint. The "route" decorator applies the function defined below when an HTTP call to the path specified as argument is performed. Note that in the path, it says "name", and the same is the argument of the function below. That means "name" is a parameter of the call; you can select a whatsoever string in the HTTP call, and your selection will be passed to the function as the parameter name.

Then, inside the function home page, a template with an HTML code is returned. In a simple way, think that the template function creates the page you'll see from your browser.

 A template, is this example, is just a plain HTML page, but it can be more complex (it can actually be a template page with some blanks to fill in). A complete description of templates is out of the scope of this section, since we will be using the framework just for a simple, plain output. If you need additional information, surf the Bottle help pages.

Finally, after the print functions, comes the core `run` function. It's a blocking function, and will set up the web server on the host and port provided as arguments. When you run the code in the listing, once that function is executed, you can open your browser and point it to `http://localhost:9099/personal/Carl`. And you'll find the following text: **Hi Carl!**

Of course, changing the name in the HTTP call from `Carl` to `Tom` or any other name will result in a different page, containing the name specified in the call.

Note that, in this dummy example, we just defined the `/personal/<name>` route. Any other call will result in Error 404, unless defined in the code.

To turn it off, we need to press *Ctrl + C* in the command line (remember that the function run is blocking).

Let's now create a service that is more data science-oriented; we will create an HTML page with a form asking for the sepal length and width and the petal length and width to classify the iris sample. For this example, we will use the iris dataset to train our Scikit-learn classifier. Then for each prediction, we simply call the predict function on the classifier, sending back the prediction:

```
File: bottle2.py
from sklearn.datasets import load_iris
from sklearn.linear_model import LogisticRegression
from bottle import run, request, get, post
import numpy as np
port = 9099
@get('/predict')
def predict():
return '''
<form action="/prediction" method="post">
Sepal length [cm]: <input name="sl" type="text" /><br/>
Sepal width [cm]: <input name="sw" type="text" /><br/>
Petal length [cm]: <input name="pl" type="text" /><br/>
Petal width [cm]: <input name="pw" type="text" /><br/>
<input value="Predict" type="submit" />
</form>
'''

@post('/prediction')
def do_prediction():
try:
sample = [float(request.POST.get('sl')),
float(request.POST.get('sw')),
float(request.POST.get('pl')),
float(request.POST.get('pw'))]
pred = classifier.predict(np.matrix(sample))[0]
return "<p>The predictor says it's a
<b>{}</b></p>".format(iris['target_names'][pred])
except:
return "<p>Error, values should be all numbers</p>"
iris = load_iris()
classifier = LogisticRegression()
classifier.fit(iris.data, iris.target)
print("Try going to http://localhost:{}/predict".format(port))
run(host='localhost', port=port)
# Try insert the following values:
# [ 5.1, 3.5, 1.4, 0.2] -> setosa
# [ 7.0 3.2, 4.7, 1.4] -> versicolor
# [ 6.3, 3.3, 6.0, 2.5] -> virginica
```

After some imports, here we use the get decorator, specifying a route valid only for HTTP GET calls. The decorator, as well as the function below, has no parameters since all the features should be inserted into the HTML form, defined in the predict function. The form, when submitted, is passed to the `/prediction` page using an HTTP POST.

Now, we need to create a route for this call, and that's what we do in the `do_prediction` function. Its decorator is "post" (that is, opposite to "get"; it defines only POST routes) on the `/prediction` page. Data is parsed and transformed into a double (default parameters are strings), and then the feature vector is fed into the `classifier` global variable to obtain a prediction. This is returned using a simple template. The object request contains all the parameters passed to the service, including the entire variable we "POST-ed" to the route.

Finally, it seems we just need to define the global variable classifier, that is, a classifier trained on the iris dataset, and last we can call the run function. For this dummy example, we've used a Logistic regressor as a classifier and trained on the full iris dataset, leaving all the parameters as default. In a real case, here you would tune your classifier as best as possible.

When this code is run, if everything works well, you can point your browser to `http://localhost:9099/predict` and you'll see the form:

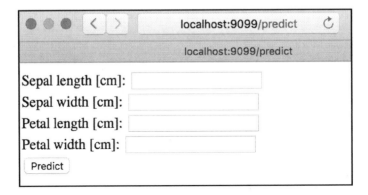

Inserting the values (5.1, 3.5, 1.4, 0.2) after clicking on the **Predict** button, you should be redirected to `http://localhost:9099/prediction`, where the string `The predictor says it's a setosa` should be displayed. Also note that if you insert invalid entries in the form (for example, leaving it empty or inserting a string instead of a number), you'll get an HTML page that says that there's an error.

We're half way in this section, and we've already seen how easy and quick it is to create an HTTP endpoint with Bottle. Now let's try to create a prediction-as-a-service that can be called in any program. We will submit the feature vector as a get call, and the returned prediction will be in JSON format. Here's the code for this solution:

```
File: bottle3.py
from bottle import run, request, get, response
import numpy as np
import json
port = 9099
@get('/prediction')
def do_prediction():
pred = {}
try:
sample = [float(request.GET.get('sl')),
float(request.GET.get('sw')),
float(request.GET.get('pl')),
float(request.GET.get('pw'))]
pred['predicted_label'] = iris['target_names']
[classifier.predict(np.matrix(sample))[0]]
pred['status'] = "OK"
except:
pred['status'] = "ERROR"
response.content_type = 'application/json'
return json.dumps(pred)
iris = load_iris()
classifier = LogisticRegression()
classifier.fit(iris.data, iris.target)
print("Try going to
http://localhost:{}/prediction?sl=5.1&sw=3.5&pl=1.4&pw=0.2".format(port))
print("Try going to
http://localhost:{}/prediction?sl=A&sw=B&pl=C&pw=D".format(port))
run(host='localhost', port=port)
```

The solution is pretty straightforward and easy; still, let's analyze it step by step. The entry point of the feature is defined by the `get` decorator on the path `/prediction`. In there, we will access the GET values to extract the predictions (note that if your classifier needs many features, it may be better to use a POPST call here). Exactly as in the previous example, the prediction is generated; finally the value is inserted in a Python dictionary, altogether with the value "OK" for the key "status". If any exception is raised in this function, there will be no prediction but an "ERROR" string in the "status" key. Then, we set the output application format to json, and we serialize the Python dictionary to a JSON string.

When it runs, we can use any way to access the URL `http://localhost:9099/prediction`, followed by the feature values, and we will get back the prediction as JSON. Note that we don't need a browser to interpret the returned HTTP response since it's a JSON. Therefore, we can call the endpoint from different applications (`wget`, `browser`, or `curl`) or any programming language (including Python itself). To see it working, start it and point your browser to (or request the URL in any way) `http://localhost:9099/prediction?sl=5.1&sw=3.5&pl=1.4&pw=0.2`. You'll get back the valid JSON: `{"predicted_label": "setosa", "status": "OK"}`. Also, if something goes wrong in the parsing of the parameters, you'll get this: JSON `{"status": "ERROR"}`. And that's your first ML-AAS!

Although simple and quick, Bottle has many other functions to be explored. It's not as complete as other frameworks, however. If your application needs some extraordinary functionality, check out the Flask or Django modules.

Summary

This chapter provided an overview of essential data science by providing examples of both basic and advanced graphical representations of data, machine learning processes, and results. We explored the pylab module from matplotlib, which gives the easiest and fastest access to the graphical capabilities of the package. We used pandas for EDA and tested the graphical utilities provided by Scikit-learn. All examples were like building blocks, and they are all easily customizable in order to provide you with a fast template for visualization.

In conclusion, we have completed our tour of a data science project, touching all the key points of a project, and presenting you with all the essential tools to operate your own projects using Python. As a learning tool, the book accompanied you through all the phases of data science, from data loading to machine learning and visualization, illustrating best practices and ways to avoid common pitfalls. As a reference, the book touched upon a variety of commands and packages, providing you with simple, clear instructions and examples that, if reused in your projects, can save you tons of time during your work.

From here on, Python will surely play a major role in your project developments, and we were glad to have accompanied you so far in your path towards mastering Python for data science.

Strengthen Your Python Foundations

The code examples that are provided along with the chapters don't require you to master Python. However, they will assume that you've previously obtained a working knowledge of at least the basics of Python scripting. They will also assume, in particular, that you know about data structures, such as lists and dictionaries, and you have an idea about how to make class objects work.

If you don't feel confident about the aforementioned subjects or have minimal knowledge of the Python language, we suggest that before you start reading this book, you should take an online tutorial, such as the Code Academy course at `http://www.codecademy.com/en/tracks/python` or Google's Python class at `https://developers.google.com/edu/python/`. Both the courses are free, and in a matter of a few hours of study, they should provide you with all the building blocks that will ensure that you enjoy this book to the fullest.

We have also prepared a few notes, which are arranged in this brief but challenging bonus chapter, in order to highlight the importance and strengthen your knowledge of certain aspects of the Python language.

In this bonus chapter, you will learn the following:

- What you should know about Python to be an effective data scientist
- The best resources to learn Python by watching videos
- The best resources to learn Python by directly writing and testing code
- The best resources to learn Python by reading

Your learning list

Here are the basic Python data structures that you need to learn to be as proficient as a data scientist. Leaving aside the real basics (numbers, arithmetic, strings, Booleans, variable assignments, and comparisons), the list is indeed short. We will briefly deal with it by touching upon only the recurrent structures in data science projects. Remember that the topics are quite challenging, but they are necessary if you want to write effective code:

- Lists
- Dictionaries
- Classes, objects, and Object-Oriented Programming (OOP)
- Exceptions
- Iterators and generators
- Conditionals
- Comprehensions
- Functions

Take it as a refresher or a learning list depending on your actual knowledge of the Python language. However, examine all the proposed examples because you will come across them again during the course of the book.

Lists

Lists are collections of elements. Elements can be integers, floats, strings, or generically, objects. Moreover, you can mix different types together. Besides, lists are more flexible than arrays since arrays allow only a single datatype.

To create a list, you can either use the square brackets or the `list()` constructor, as follows:

```
a_list = [1, 2.3, 'a', True]
an_empty_list = list()
```

The following are some handy methods that you can remember while working with lists:

- To access the *i*th element, use the [] notation:

  Remember that lists are indexed from 0 (zero); that is, the first element is in position 0.

```
a_list[1]
# prints 2.3
a_list[1] = 2.5
# a_list is now [1, 2.5, 'a', True]
```

- You can slice lists by pointing out a starting and ending point (the ending point is not included in the resulting slice), as follows:

```
a_list[1:3] # prints [2.3, 'a']
```

- You can slice with skips by using a colon-separated start:end:skip notation so that you can get an element for every skip value, as follows:

```
a_list[::2]
# returns only odd elements: [1, 'a']
a_list[::-1]
# returns the reverse of the list: [True, 'a', 2.3, 1]
```

- To append an element at the end of the list, you can use append():

```
a_list.append(5)
# a_list is now [1, 2.5, 'a', True, 5]
```

- To get the length of the list, use the len() function, as follows:

```
len(a_list)
# prints 5
```

- To delete an element, use the del statement followed by the element that you wish to remove:

```
dela_list[0]
# a_list is now [2.5, 'a', True, 5]
```

- To concatenate two lists, use +, as follows:

```
a_list += [1, 'b']
# a_list is now [2.5, 'a', True, 5, 1, 'b']
```

- You can unpack lists by assigning lists to a list (or simply a sequence) of variables instead of a single variable:

```
a,b,c,d,e,f = [2.5, 'a', True, 5, 1, 'b']
# a now is 2.5, b is 'a' and so on
```

Remember that lists are mutable data structures; you can always append, remove, and modify elements. Immutable lists are called tuples and are denoted with round parentheses, (and), instead of the square brackets as in the list, [and]:

```
tuple(a_list)
# prints (2.5, 'a', True, 5, 1, 'b')
```

Dictionaries

Dictionaries are tables that can find stuff very fast because each key is associated with a value. It is really like using the index of a book to jump immediately to the content you need. Keys and values can belong to different kinds of data types. The only requisite for keys is that they should be hashable (that's a fairly complex concept; simply keep the keys as simple as possible and, therefore, don't try to use a dictionary or a list as a key).

To create a dictionary, you can use curly brackets, as follows:

```
b_dict = {1: 1, '2': '2', 3.0: 3.0}
```

The following are some handy methods that you can remember while working with dictionaries:

- To access the value indexed by the k key, use the [] notation, as follows:

```
b_dict['2']
# prints '2'
b_dict['2'] = '2.0'
# b_dict is now {1: 1, '2': '2.0', 3.0: 3.0}
```

- To insert or replace a value for a key, use the [] notation again:

```
b_dict['a'] = 'a'
# b_dict is now {3.0: 3.0, 1: 1, '2': '2.0', 'a': 'a'}
```

- To get the number of elements in the dictionary, use the `len()` function, as follows:

```
len(b_dict)
# prints 4
```

- To delete an element, use the `del` statement followed by the element that you wish to remove:

```
delb_dict[3.0]
# b_dict is now {1: 1, '2': '2.0', 'a': 'a'}
```

Remember that dictionaries, like lists, are mutable data structures. Also remember that if you try to access an element whose key doesn't exist, a `KeyError` exception will be raised:

```
b_dict['a_key']
Traceback (most recent call last):
  File "<stdin>", line 1, in <module>
KeyError: 'a_key'
```

The obvious solution to this is to always check first whether an element is in the dictionary:

```
if  'a_key' in b_dict:
b_dict['a_key']
else:
print ("'a_key' is not present in the dictionary")
```

Otherwise, you can use the `.get` method. If the key is in the dictionary, it returns its value; otherwise, it returns `None`:

```
b_dict.get('a_key')
```

Finally, you can use a data structure from the `collections` module, called `defaultdict`, and it will never raise a `KeyError` because it is instantiated by a function taking no arguments and providing the default value for any nonexistent key it may want you to require:

```
from collections import defaultdict
c_dict = defaultdict(lambda: 'empty')
c_dict['a_key']
# requiring a nonexistent key will always return the string 'empty'
```

The default function to be used by `defaultdict` can be defined using a `def` or `lambda` command, as described in the following section.

Defining functions

Functions are ensembles of instructions that usually receive specific inputs from you and provide a set of specific outputs related to these inputs.

You can define them as one-liners, as follows:

```
def half(x) : return x/2.0
```

You can also define them as a set of many instructions in the following way:

```
import math
def sigmoid(x):
try:
return 1.0 / (1 + math.exp(-x))
except:
if x < 0:
return 0.0
else:
return 1.0
```

Finally, you can define on the fly an anonymous function by using a lambda function. Think about them as simple functions that you can define inline everywhere in the code, without using the "verbose" constructor for functions (the one starting with `def`). Just call `lambda` followed by its input parameters; then a colon will signal the beginning of the commands to be executed by the lambda function, which necessarily have to be on the same line. (No `return` command! The commands are what will be returned from the lambda function.)

You can use a lambda function as a parameter in another function, as seen previously for `defaultdict`, or you can use it in order to express a function in one line. This is the case in our example, where we define a function returning a lambda function incorporating the parameters of the first one:

```
defsum_a_const(c):
    return lambda x: x+c

sum_2 = sum_a_const(2)
sum_3 = sum_a_const(3)
print (sum_2(2))
print (sum_3(2))
# prints 4 and 5
```

To invoke a function, write the function name, followed by its parameters within the parenthesis:

```
half(10)
# prints 5.0
sigmoid(0)
# prints 0.5
```

By using functions, you ensemble repetitive procedures by formalizing their inputs and outputs without letting their calculation interfere in any way with the execution of the main program. In fact, unless you declare that a variable is a global one, all the variables you used inside your function will be disposed, and your main program will receive only what has been returned by the `return` command.

By the way, please be aware that if you pass a list to a function-only list, which won't happen with variables—this will be modified, even if not returned, unless you copy it. In order to make a duplicate of a list, you can use the `copy` or `deep copy` functions (to be imported from the copy package) or simply the `operator [:] applied to your list.`

Why does this happen? Because lists are in particular data structures that are referenced by an address and not by the entire object. So, when you pass a list to a function, you are just passing an address to the memory of your computer, and the function will operate on that address by modifying your actual list:

```
a_list = [1,2,3,4,5]
def modifier(L):
L[0] = 0
defunmodifier(L):
    M = L[:]
M[0] = 1
unmodifier(a_list)
print (a_list) # you still have the original list, [1, 2, 3, 4, 5]
modifier(a_list)
print (a_list) # your list have been modified: [0, 2, 3, 4, 5]
```

Classes, objects, and OOP

Classes are collections of methods and attributes. Briefly, attributes are variables of the object (for example, each instance of the Employee class has its own `name`, `age`, `salary`, and `benefits`; all of them are attributes). Methods are simply functions that modify attributes (for example, to set the employee name, to set his/her age, and also to read this info from a database or from a CSV list). To create a class, use the `class` keyword. In the following example, we will create a class for an incrementer. The purpose of this object is to keep track of the value of an integer and eventually increase it by 1:

```
class Incrementer(object):
def __init__(self):
print ("Hello world, I'm the constructor")
        self._i = 0
```

Everything within the `def` indentation is a class method. In this case, the method named `__init__` sets the `i` internal variable to zero (it looks exactly like a function described in the previous chapter). Look carefully at the method's definition. Its argument is `self` (this is the object itself), and every internal variable access is made through `self`. Moreover, `__init__` is not just a method; it's the constructor (it's called when the object is created). In fact, when we build an `Incrementer` object, this method is automatically called, as follows:

```
i = Incrementer()
# prints "Hello world, I'm the constructor"
```

Now, let's create the `increment()` method, which increments the `i` internal counter and returns the status. Within the class definition, include the method:

```
def increment(self):
        self._i += 1
    return self._i
```

Then, run the following code:

```
i = Incrementer()
print (i.increment())
print (i.increment())
print (i.increment())
```

The preceding code results in the following output:

```
Hello world, I'm the constructor
1
2
3
```

Finally, let's see how to create methods that accept parameters. We will now create the `set_counter` method, which sets the `_i` internal variable.

Within the class definition, add the following code:

```
defset_counter(self, counter):
        self._i = counter
```

Then, run the following code:

```
i = Incrementer()
i.set_counter(10)
print (i.increment())
print (i._i)
```

The preceding code gives this output:

```
Hello world, I'm the constructor
11
11
```

 Note the last line of the preceding code, where you access the internal variable. Remember that in Python, all the internal attributes of the objects are public by default, and they can be read, written, and changed externally.

Exceptions

Exceptions and errors are strongly correlated, but they are different things. An exception, for example, can be gracefully handled. Here are some examples of exceptions:

```
0/0
Traceback (most recent call last):
  File "<stdin>", line 1, in <module>
ZeroDivisionError: integer division or modulo by zero

len(1, 2)
Traceback (most recent call last):
  File "<stdin>", line 1, in <module>
TypeError: len() takes exactly one argument (2 given)

pi * 2
Traceback (most recent call last):
  File "<stdin>", line 1, in <module>
NameError: name 'pi' is not defined
```

In this example, three different exceptions have been raised (see the last line of each block). To handle exceptions, you can use a try/except block in the following way:

```
try:
    a = 10/0
exceptZeroDivisionError:
    a = 0
```

You can use more than one `except` clause to handle more than one exception. You can eventually use a final "all-the-other" exception case handle. In this case, the structure is as follows:

```
try:
<code which can raise more than one exception>
exceptKeyError:
print ("There is a KeyError error in the code")
except (TypeError, ZeroDivisionError):
print ("There is a TypeError or a ZeroDivisionError error in the code")
except:
print ("There is another error in the code")
```

Finally, it is important to mention that there is the final clause, `finally`, that will be executed in all circumstances. It's very handy if you want to clean up the code (closing files, de-allocating resources, and so on). These are the things that should be done independently, regardless of whether an error has occurred or not. In this case, the code assumes the following shape:

```
try:
<code that can raise exceptions>
except:
<eventually more handlers for different exceptions>
finally:
<clean-up code>
```

Iterators and generators

Looping through a list or a dictionary is very simple. Note that with dictionaries, the iteration is key-based, which is demonstrated in the following example:

```
for entry in ['alpha', 'bravo', 'charlie', 'delta']:
  print (entry)
# prints the content of the list, one entry for line

a_dict = {1: 'alpha', 2: 'bravo', 3: 'charlie', 4: 'delta'}
for key in a_dict:
```

```
    print (key, a_dict[key])

# Prints:
# 1 alpha
# 2 bravo
# 3 charlie
# 4 delta
```

On the other hand, if you need to iterate through a sequence and generate objects on the fly, you can use a generator. A great advantage of doing this is that you don't have to create and store the complete sequence at the beginning. Instead, you build every object every time the generator is called. As a simple example, let's create a generator for a number sequence without storing the complete list in advance:

```
def incrementer():
  i = 0
  whilei<5:
    yield i
    i +=1

for i in incrementer():
print (i)

# Prints:
# 0
# 1
# 2
# 3
# 4
```

Conditionals

Conditionals are often used in data science since you can branch the program. The most frequently used one is the if statement. It works more or less the same as in other programming languages. Here's an example of it:

```
def is_positive(val):
  ifval< 0:
    print ("It is negative")
elif val> 0:
  print ("It is positive")
else:
  print ("It is exactly zero!")


is_positive(-1)
```

```
is_positive(1.5)
is_positive(0)


# Prints:
# It is negative
# It is positive
# It is exactly zero!
```

The first condition is checked with `if`. If there are any other conditions, they are defined with `elif` (this stands for else-if). Finally, the default behavior is handled by `else`.

 Note that `elif` and `else` are not essentials.

Comprehensions for lists and dictionaries

Comprehensions, lists, and dictionaries are built as one-liners with the use of an iterator and a conditional when necessary:

```
a_list = [1,2,3,4,5]
another_list = ['a','b','c','d','e']
a_power_list = [value**2 for value in a_list]
# the resulting list is [1, 4, 9, 16, 25]
filter_even_numbers = [value**2 for value in a_list if value % 2  == 0]
# the resulting list is [4, 16]
a_dictionary = {key:value for value, key in zip(a_list,  another_list)}
# zip is a function that takes as input multiple lists of the same  length
and iterates through each element having the same index at  the same time,
so you can match the first elements of every lists  together, and so on.
# the resulting dictionary is {'a': 1, 'c': 3, 'b': 2, 'e': 5,  'd': 4}
```

Comprehensions are a fast way to filter and transform data that is present in any iterator.

Learn by watching, reading, and doing

What if the refresher courses and our learning list are not enough and you need more support to strengthen your knowledge of Python? We will recommend further resources that are available free on the Web. By watching tutorial videos, you can try out complex and different examples and challenge yourself in a difficult task that requires you to interact with other data scientists and Python experts.

MOOCs

MOOCs have become increasingly popular in recent years, offering free on their online platforms some of the best courses from the best universities and experts from around the world. You will find Python courses on Coursera (`https://www.coursera.org/`), Edx (`https://www.edx.org/`), and Udacity (`https://www.udacity.com`). Another great source is the MIT open course ware, which is easily accessible (`https://ocw.mit.edu/courses/electrical-engineering-and-computer-science/6-00sc-introduction-to-computer-science-and-programming-spring-2011/`). When you consult each of these sites, you may find different active courses on Python. We recommend a free, always available, and *do it at your own pace* course by Peter Norvig, the Director of Research at Google Inc. This course aims to take your knowledge of Python to a higher level of proficiency.

PyCon and PyData

The **Python Conference** (**PyCon**) is an annual convention organized at various locations around the world with the purpose of promoting the usage and diffusion of the Python language. During such conventions, tutorials, hands-on demonstrations, and training sessions are commonly held. You can check out `http://www.pycon.org/` to find out where and when the next PyCon will be held near you. If you cannot attend, you can still perform a search on `https://www.youtube.com/` because most of the interesting sessions are recorded and uploaded there. Attending and watching the real demonstration is a different thing anyway, so we warmly suggest you attend such conventions because they are really worth it. Similarly, PyData, a community of Python developers and users devoted to data analysis, hold many events around the world. You can check out `http://pydata.org/events.html` for upcoming events (to go to and attend) and check whether any past event may have interested you. As with PyCon, presentations are often available on YouTube, on dedicated channels such as PyDataTV.

Interactive Jupyter

Sometimes, you need some written explanations and the opportunity to test some sample code by yourself. Jupyter, an open tool like Python itself, offers you all of this via its notebooks—interactive web pages where you will find both explanations and example code that can be tested directly. We devote explanations about Jupyter and its kernels throughout the book because it is a real data science workhorse. It allows you easily to run Python scripts and evaluate their effects on the data that you are working on.

The GitHub location of the IPython kernel (the Python kernel of Jupyter, since Jupyter can run many different programming languages) offers a complete list of example notebooks. You can check it out at: `https://github.com/ipython/ipython/wiki/A-gallery-of-int eresting-IPython-Notebooks`. In particular, a section of the list is about *General Python Programming*, whereas another one is about *Statistics, Machine Learning, and Data Science*, where you will find quite a lot of examples of Python scripts that you can take inspiration from in your learning.

Don't be shy, take a real challenge

If you want to do something that can take your Python coding ability to a different level, we suggest you go and take a challenge on Kaggle. Kaggle (`http://www.kaggle.com/`) is a platform for predictive modeling and analytic competitions, which applies the idea of competitive programming (participants try to program according to the provided specifications) in data science by proposing challenging data problems to participants and asking them to provide possible solutions that are evaluated on a test set. The results of the test set are partly public, partly private. The most interesting part for a Python learner is the opportunity to take part in a real problem with no obvious solution, which requires you to code something to propose possible solutions to the problem, even something simple or naive (which we warmly suggest you start with first before getting involved in complex solutions). By doing so, the learner will come across interesting tutorials, beat-the-benchmark codes, helpful communities of data scientists, and some very smart solutions proposed by other data scientists or Kaggle itself in its blog, *no free hunch* (`http://blog.kag gle.com/`).

You may wonder how to find the right challenge for yourself. Just have a look at the present and past competitions at `https://www.kaggle.com/competitions` and look for every competition that has knowledge as a reward. You will be surprised to find an ideal stage for learning about how other data scientists code in Python, and you can immediately apply what you learn from this book.

Index

A

AdaBoost 227
Additive White Gaussian Noise (AWGN) 133
Anaconda 17
Application Programming Interface (API)
  URL 64
Arbitrary Waveform Generator (AWG) 141
area under a curve (AUC) 165
Artificial Intelligence (AI) 240

B

Bag Of Words (BoW) 263
bar graphs 298
Beautiful Soup
  about 27
  URL 27
  web, scraping 96, 97, 98, 99
big data
  dealing 232
  examples, creating 232
  Principal Component Analysis (PCA) 140
  scalability, with volume 233
  Stochastic Gradient Descent (SGD), overview
   239, 240
  variety, dealing with 237, 238, 239
  velocity, maintaining 235
binary classification 165
Bokeh
  interactive visualizations 325, 326, 327
  reference link 325, 326, 327
boxplots 304, 305, 306, 307
broadcasting 114

C

categorical data
  working 87, 88, 89, 90

centrality
  about 277
  betweenness centrality 277
  closeness centrality 278
  degree centrality 278
  eigenvector centrality 279
  harmonic centrality 279
classes 350, 351
Code Academy
  URL 7, 343
code
  using 51, 52
collection of edges 272
Color Brewer tool
  URL 317
conda
  leveraging, for package installation 17, 18
  URL 17, 18
  used, for managing environments 22, 23
conditionals 353
covariance matrix 133, 135
cross-validation
  about 172, 173, 174, 175
  bootstrapping 177, 178, 179
  iterators, using 175, 176, 177
  sampling 177, 178, 179
curve
  plotting 291, 292, 293
custom scoring function
  building 183, 184, 185
custom transformation functions
  building 199, 200

D

data operations
  custom transformation functions, building 199,
  200

77971196R00211

Made in the USA
San Bernardino, CA
31 May 2018